Microeconomics

FOR

DUMMIES®

A Wiley Brand

C000260895

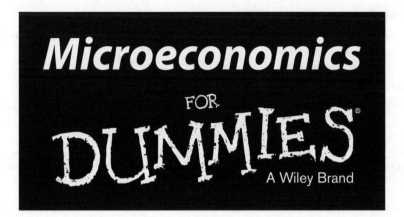

Microeconomics

FOR

DUMMIES®

A Wiley Brand

by Peter Antonioni and
Manzur Rashid

FOR

DUMMIES®

A Wiley Brand

Microeconomics For Dummies®

Published by: **John Wiley & Sons, Ltd.,** The Atrium, Southern Gate, Chichester, www.wiley.com

This edition first published 2014

© 2016 John Wiley & Sons, Ltd, Chichester, West Sussex.

Registered office

John Wiley & Sons Ltd, The Atrium, Southern Gate, Chichester, West Sussex, PO19 8SQ, United Kingdom

For details of our global editorial offices, for customer services and for information about how to apply for permission to reuse the copyright material in this book please see our website at www.wiley.com.

All rights reserved. No part of this publication may be reproduced, stored in a retrieval system, or transmitted, in any form or by any means, electronic, mechanical, photocopying, recording or otherwise, except as permitted by the UK Copyright, Designs and Patents Act 1988, without the prior permission of the publisher.

Wiley publishes in a variety of print and electronic formats and by print-on-demand. Some material included with standard print versions of this book may not be included in e-books or in print-on-demand. If this book refers to media such as a CD or DVD that is not included in the version you purchased, you may download this material at `www.dummies.com`. For more information about Wiley products, visit `www.wiley.com`.

Designations used by companies to distinguish their products are often claimed as trademarks. All brand names and product names used in this book are trade names, service marks, trademarks or registered trademarks of their respective owners. The publisher is not associated with any product or vendor mentioned in this book.

LIMIT OF LIABILITY/DISCLAIMER OF WARRANTY: WHILE THE PUBLISHER AND AUTHOR HAVE USED THEIR BEST EFFORTS IN PREPARING THIS BOOK, THEY MAKE NO REPRESENTATIONS OR WARRANTIES WITH THE RESPECT TO THE ACCURACY OR COMPLETENESS OF THE CONTENTS OF THIS BOOK AND SPECIFICALLY DISCLAIM ANY IMPLIED WARRANTIES OF MERCHANTABILITY OR FITNESS FOR A PARTICULAR PURPOSE. IT IS SOLD ON THE UNDERSTANDING THAT THE PUBLISHER IS NOT ENGAGED IN RENDERING PROFESSIONAL SERVICES AND NEITHER THE PUBLISHER NOR THE AUTHOR SHALL BE LIABLE FOR DAMAGES ARISING HEREFROM. IF PROFESSIONAL ADVICE OR OTHER EXPERT ASSISTANCE IS REQUIRED, THE SERVICES OF A COMPETENT PROFESSIONAL SHOULD BE SOUGHT.

For general information on our other products and services, please contact our Customer Care Department within the U.S. at 877-762-2974, outside the U.S. at (001) 317-572-3993, or fax 317-572-4002. For technical support, please visit www.wiley.com/techsupport.

For technical support, please visit www.wiley.com/techsupport.

A catalogue record for this book is available from the British Library.

ISBN 978-1-119-02669-3 (paperback); ISBN 978-1-119-02670-9 (ebk); ISBN 978-1-119-02671-6 (ebk)

Printed in Great Britain by TJ International, Padstow, Cornwall

10 9 8 7 6 5 4 3 2 1

A Wiley Brand

Contents at a Glance

Table of Contents

Introduction

Economics is about many things. On one level, it's concerned with humanity's struggle to cope with scarcity and how it leads people to make choices about the things that should have priority. On another level, it's about the human quest for happiness in an uncertain world, and the ways people have found to achieve it. On yet another level, it's interested in how societies organise themselves from the bottom up, using markets as a way of trading with each other. But however you look at it, economics is a huge subject!

Microeconomics looks at economics on the smallest scales – individuals, consumers, firms – and uses that picture to build up an understanding of how more complicated parts of the world – markets, industries – work. Microeconomics has become a very big subject too, taking in everything from what kinds of decisions people make to the right way to measure and analyse those decisions. It's the part of economics that's like looking through a microscope as small creatures go about their business.

So that's what microeconomists do. The microscope, though, is a bit unusual. It's not made of glass but of tools, called models, which are ways of representing the world that you can use to examine real life. They're not real life itself – making a model of real life that was accurate in every way would be like the perfect global map in a Lewis Carroll story that ended up being the size of the entire world! Instead, models are guides to help you when you need to know what's going on in a particular situation.

Maybe you're thinking about starting a business – microeconomics can help with everything from working out how much to pay staff to knowing which markets to avoid. Maybe you're wondering whether a company is a good place to invest – microeconomics can help you figure out whether the market it's in would let the firm make profits. Maybe you want to figure out how to get the best price for something you want to sell – microeconomics can help you work out how to auction it to get the highest price. In all these places in life, microeconomics can help you figure out an answer.

With all that, please come and join us as we tell you more of what this book is all about!

About This Book

This book takes you through the most common tools and models that micro-economists use to make sense of a complicated world. The aspects that we cover include the following:

- What utility is and why microeconomists assume people maximise it.
- What a firm is and what it does.
- What happens when firms and consumers interact in a market.
- Why competition is better than monopoly.
- How to understand competition between firms, and how the results depend on what type of competition is going on.
- What happens when some people in a marketplace know more than others.
- How you can generalise – to some extent – the results from one market to all markets, and how that informs decisions you may make about distributing resources.
- How you can figure out which options a firm will choose to take when it has competitors who also want to do the best for themselves.
- How and why markets fail, and some of the things you can do about it.

Foolish Assumptions

Economists often make assumptions – they have to make models when they don't know exactly how things work in a specific case. Sometimes those assumptions can be foolish – something we learnt from Samuel L. Jackson in *The Long Kiss Goodnight* and Eric Bogosian in *Under Siege 2: Dark Territory*! In writing this book, we make some foolish assumptions about you:

- You're interested in putting together a picture of why the world is as it is.
- You're smart and you don't just accept a glib and easy answer – like us!
- You're interested in learning more about economics and are looking for a good place to start – maybe you're considering studying more at school or university, or adding to your impressive portfolio of professional skills.

✔ You're a citizen bemused by discussion of business news, and want to know how anyone arrives at the opinions they do.

✔ You're not frightened about using the odd number or bit of simple maths – we try to do nearly everything in words, but economics deals with money and money comes in numbers and that's not something we can do anything about!

✔ You're sure, from the book's branding and its fun, accessible style and easy-to-read layout, that you'll gain more utility from reading it than from other activities, such as archaeology or knitting!

Some of or all these assumptions may turn out to be true. Whichever are, we hope that this book chimes with your desire to understand the wild world of microeconomics!

Icons Used in This book

To help you get the most out of this book, we use a few icons to flag up particularly noteworthy items.

This icon highlights handy hints for smoothing out your microeconomics journey.

Some of the ideas in this book are so important for understanding microeconomics that they need special emphasis – often because they're easy to get wrong! When you see this icon, you know that the associated text is something economists really want you to understand!

The world is full of pitfalls for the unwary. Here we stress areas for which you need to watch out.

Economists use technical terms to speak to each other – it's just shorthand usually, so that no one needs to go through pages and pages of the same things. When you see this icon, you know that you're being let into the clubhouse – economics is an inclusive science! – and picking up a piece of lingo that economists use to cut long stories short!

Theories are great, but ultimately economics is about the real world, and the best way to see what microeconomics can do is to see it in action. This icon tells you that you're getting something from real-life practice to help you get the idea!

Beyond the Book

But wait! There's more! We've not only put together a book that takes in a journey from simple microeconomics to complex models of competition, but also compiled some online bonus bits (at www.wiley.com/extras/microeconomics) to help you take things further:

- ✔ An online Part of Tens with suggestions for places to take your understanding of microeconomics to the next level – from how to deal with government to how economists test their models.

- ✔ Four online articles with further looks at the bits and pieces of microeconomics – from what 'economically rational' means to how you deal with the really long term.

- ✔ A handy e-cheat sheet to keep with you – at least mentally! – at all times.

Where to Go from Here

The great thing about a factual book like this one is that you don't have to worry about spoilers and can dive straight in anywhere you choose! If you've just seen the film *Dr. Strangelove* and you want to jump further into the wacky world of game theory in Part V, be our guest! If you want to think about why someone wants to break up a monopoly, move straight to Chapter 13 without passing Go! To see how economists think about pollution, check out Chapter 14!

Economists are fine with choice – trust us, we make a living *because* people are able to choose! However, if your choice is to start at the beginning, you also get to see how the whole subject unfolds, from simple ideas to more complex levels.

Of course the two approaches aren't mutually exclusive, and no reason exists why you can't do both – although obviously at different times!

With that, we wish you *bon appétit*!

Part I

Getting Started with Microeconomics

getting started

with

microeconomics

web extras

For Dummies can help to get you started with lots of subjects. Visit www.dummies.com to discover more and do more with *For Dummies* books.

In this part . . .

- ✔ See how microeconomics looks at firms and individuals.
- ✔ Discover how microeconomics builds on people's choices.
- ✔ Understand how consumers choose.
- ✔ Look at the ways firms make their decisions.

Chapter 1

Discovering Why Microeconomics Is a Big Deal

As we're sure you know, *micro* as a prefix often indicates something very small, such as a microchip (a tiny French fry) or a microbrain (your arch enemy's intellect). Micro can also mean something that isn't small itself but is used to examine small things, such as a microscope (necessary to see your nemesis's minuscule brain).

Well, *microeconomics* is the area of economics that studies the decisions of consumers and producers and how they come together to make markets. It asks how people decide to do what they do and what happens when interests conflict. It also considers how people can improve markets through their actions, the effects of laws and other outside interventions. However you look at it, and despite the name, microeconomics is a huge subject!

Traditionally, people contrasted microeconomics with macroeconomics – the study of national economies and big phenomena such as growth, debt or investments. But over the years, the scope of microeconomics has grown; today economists analyse some parts of what used to be macroeconomics – for instance, negotiations on loans – using microeconomic tools.

Microeconomists employ those tools to look at things that form from the bottom up, because markets build on the actions of individual firms and consumers. This approach involves starting with an account of how firms and consumers make decisions and building on that to investigate more complex things that 'emerge' from those decisions – such as how a market is structured.

In general, microeconomics works by building models of these situations. *Models* are mathematical – or graphical – pictures of how the world works given some basic assumptions. Models aren't reality; they're a description of something that resembles it. Like an architect's model of a house, they don't have to stand up to reality; they just have to provide a feeling for what the world looks like. Microeconomists use additional data to refine the models until they provide a more accurate picture. They also test models against real data to see how well the models work – the answer is usually 'variably'!

In this chapter we introduce you to microeconomics and its core areas of interest, and we touch on the fact that markets don't always work.

Peering into the Economics of Smaller Units

Microeconomics is fundamentally about what happens when individuals and firms make decisions. The idea is to think through those decisions and explore their consequences.

What happens – for example – when prices, say of ice cream, go up? Well, on the one hand, people are likely to buy less ice cream. On the other hand, firms may want to make more of it so that they can get more revenue. The result is a lot of unsold ice cream! Then people want to get rid of those stocks to avoid holding onto them, and they probably do that by cutting the price.

When does that process stop? At the limit, the only logical place to stop cutting the price is when exactly as much is sold as is made. This point is an *equilibrium* in the market for ice cream – a place where supply and demand are equal. We discuss equilibria more fully in Chapter 9.

When people talk about *market forces,* they're talking about the sum of all these decisions. No vast impersonal power called 'market forces' exists, just a lot of smaller entities – consumers and firms – making a lot of simple decisions based on signals that come from prices. That's really all market forces means.

The way markets work seems so impersonal because every one of the smallest units – small firms and individuals– makes up just a tiny fraction of all the decisions taken. Even the biggest companies or most powerful governments have limitations on their ability to influence the world. Microeconomists take this fact for granted and explore cases where it looks like they're less limited as exceptions, not the rule!

All these smaller units do the best they can, given that ultimately they're acting with imperfect knowledge of a complicated world. People and firms can't know *exactly* how much they'll be earning next year or exactly how much they'll sell. They just look for ways of making decisions that give them the best chance of doing the best that they can – which is about all anyone can ask for in an uncertain world!

Making Decisions, Decisions and More Decisions!

One word that's central to microeconomics is 'decision'. Microeconomics is ultimately about making decisions – whether to buy a house, how much ice cream to make, at what price to sell a bicycle, whether to offer a product to this or that market and so on.

This is one reason why economists centre their models on choice. After all, when you don't have options to choose from, you can't take a decision! Deciding to make something or to buy something is the starting point for microeconomics.

To a microeconomist, decisions aren't right or wrong; instead they're one of the following:

- **Optimal:** Getting the best of what you want, given what's available (check out Chapter 6).
- **Sub-optimal:** Getting less than the best.

Of course, a model of decisions needs two sides:

- **Consumers:** Base their decisions on the value from choosing one option as opposed to another.
- **Firms:** Base their decisions on a measure of benefit – revenue – against costs (see Chapter 7).

This book presents a few ways that microeconomists look at these decisions. In Chapters 2–8, we use a framework for making the best decision given some kind of constraint – budget, time or whatever else constrains you – to show you how microeconomists look at individuals and firms separately. In Chapters 9–15, the famous supply and demand model shows you how different types of market lead to different results. And in Chapters 16–19, we introduce you to the set of techniques known collectively as game theory, which look at how individuals or firms (or even other entities, such as governments) interact with each other.

Addressing how individuals and firms make decisions

Economists look at decisions in a slightly different way from how you might expect. They don't have a model of all the things that you as a consumer use to inform your decisions. They don't know, for a start, who you are, or what all your values are. They make no assumptions about gender, ethnicity, sexuality or anything else (though applied economists may test what they know about one population's decisions against a more general model). They just know that you need to make choices, and explore how you may do so.

Starting simply

Economists make the least possible number of assumptions about the decision-making process and ask what you'd do if you only wanted the best possible outcome. Here are the two basic assumptions:

- ✔ **The consumer is utility-maximising:** She seeks to maximise her *utility* – that is, the value of her choice (see Chapters 2 and 4 for more details).

- ✔ **The firm is profit-maximising:** It wants to maximise its profit – see Chapters 3 and 8.

These choices don't necessarily involve selfishness – a utility-maximising consumer can get benefit from helping other people and a profit-maximising firm may want to redistribute surplus profits to charitable causes.

Growing more complex

To begin with, these models are quite simple. If Billy Bob has £10 in his pocket and he wants to decide between having a burrito or a pizza, he'll get the meal that gives him most utility given that it costs less than £10. Simple!

But later on, the models start to incorporate all kinds of other things, such as budget constraints (which we discuss in Chapter 5): if Billy Bob's income goes up, will he buy more or less pizza? Or what about the utility gained by other people: if Billy Bob's friends won't eat pizza with him (perhaps he chews with his mouth open and makes an unappetising noise), he may get less utility from the pizza. Eventually, even with simple assumptions, models can end up incorporating some pretty complicated reasoning!

When you look at this example from the perspective of the pizza restaurant, things also start off simple: the restaurant just wants to make as much profit as possible, working to reduce its costs to do so. But what if you build in competitors? What about if the shareholders of the pizza company – the firm has grown, adding layer on tasty layer! – have different interests from the managers? What if the managers don't just want to get costs down, but to keep competitors out? Again, the key is to start from the fewest justifiable assumptions and then build up as you get more familiar with models.

Even at the simplest level, models tell you plenty about reality. They can give you an account of how people and companies react to prices, and how this reaction changes as industries get more competitive or as companies get bigger.

Seeing how decisions come together to make markets

Markets are places – real or virtual – where consumers and producers come together to trade. In theory, the trades make both sides better off, though not necessarily to the same extent.

Markets co-ordinate people's desires for stuff with producers' ability to make stuff, but importantly with one being in charge of the process! The only thing you need is that both sides respond to a price signal. That's it!

Microeconomists say that markets are *equilibrium-seeking,* which means that trading in a market ultimately leads to a point where as much is supplied as consumers demand (and no more or less). The concept of equilibrium is much used in microeconomics, especially in the supply and demand model that we introduce in Chapter 9. This model looks at 'partial equilibrium' or the equilibrium in one given market (for example, the market for tinned tuna, or the market for books). It's also used for a couple of special types of equilibrium:

- ✔ **Nash equilibrium:** A point where two people or entities are competing for something and arrive – separately – at a point where no one has an incentive to change their behaviour. (We cover this situation in Chapters 16–19.)
- ✔ **General equilibrium:** An equilibrium state that exists across a whole economy given certain conditions. This is used for the analysis of welfare, and we write about it in Chapter 12.

Of course reality gets very complicated and usually someone – often government, but sometimes private monopolists or property owners – wants to control the price, which is often not desirable. Take a rent control, for instance. Introduce too low a maximum rent and more people want to rent than people who're willing to put their house up to rent. As a result, setting a rent control at a very low level just creates homelessness – more people trying to rent, but landlords withdrawing their properties from the market because the price is too low for them to bother.

What about if we set the rents at too high a price? Well, if the maximum rent is above the equilibrium in the market, it has no effect because landlords are more willing to rent at that price and so more enter the market. But fewer renters are willing to rent at that price, and so the result is an excess supply of rentable flats. As a result some landlords drop out – those that need the highest level of rent to make a profit – and the price falls until it reaches the market equilibrium again!

Controlling prices can have many other consequences too. The price signal isn't just an absolute number – say a price of £5 – it's also a *relative* measure: for example, this car costs more in other things you can do with your money than this sofa. The model of a consumer eventually tells you that the relative price encapsulates consumer preferences. When you affect the relative price, you affect choices *everywhere*. That's one reason why economists prefer almost any solution to one that affects relative prices!

Markets are themselves complex things in reality and vary widely from type to type. For example, financial markets are different in their scope, participants and trading outcomes to labour – jobs – markets. Microeconomists look at all these types of market starting with the simplest model, and then as they get more data on how they differ, they start to incorporate that into the models.

The great economist Alfred Marshall was the first to make a key point, though: a big difference exists between the practical results of *markets* in reality and the simulation that economists use – which he called *The Market*. When you encounter a type of market you don't understand, starting to analyse it by using the simulation is a decent idea. If you know more about the market, however, relying on a simple simulation may not work as well!

Understanding the Problems of Competition and Co-operation

Society reaps the benefit of all the things that innovation and production make through two different forces: competition and co-operation.

Many firms following their own interests leads to competition (we discuss perfect competition, which consumers usually love, in Chapter 10 and imperfect competition in Chapter 11). In almost all circumstances competition is a pretty good thing, because it leads to lower costs or more innovation. For example, if only one store operates in your area, it may be able to get away with selling milk for £2 a pint. But with other stores, the competition leads to the price falling.

Businesses are competitive in some ways, but they're also co-operative exercises where people have to work together to achieve common goals. Microeconomics studies co-operation as often as it studies competition, but it starts with competitive models to build the foundations. It moves on from that focus, though, looking at what type of circumstances lead people to choose to co-operate, and where the pitfalls of those situations can lie.

Even businesses that are competitors in one area sometimes form alliances in others – Apple's relationship with Motorola in the early 2000s being just one example.

Microeconomists are often accused of overselling the benefits of competition, but they also point out that co-operation can be perilous too. When a group of firms with large shares of a relevant market work together, the result is often harmful to the public, as Adam Smith pointed out. Working together in that way is illegal, not surprisingly! Similarly, a trade union where a lot of people work together to get the best bargain with their industry can have negative effects on anyone not a member of that union. Microeconomists go on to investigate all these possibilities.

Realising why authorities regulate competition

At some point, the businesses operating in every market in the world have to deal with the legal structures under which they operate. In general, a lot of basic conduct rules underpin every – legal – market – from ensuring that your product is what you say it is to not exploiting market dominance. If the essential point of microeconomics is that organisation happens with no one in charge, why is this even an issue?

Well, markets in reality aren't perfect! Sometimes they impose costs upon people who aren't involved in that particular market. Sometimes setting a floor under the conduct of a given market leads to better behaviour! But perhaps the most interesting reason for regulation is because of what happens when a competitor gets too successful.

When that happens, the firm makes larger profits, which is good for shareholders. But suppose that conditions also mean that no firm can set up as a rival – maybe the costs involved in being in that market are too high or the successful competitor holds the entire supply of a key resource.

In general, the idea is that you don't want someone to get permanent advantage in a way that leads to too many losses for everyone else. At this point, competition law steps in and places restrictions on what a company can and can't do (see the next section), because the costs of runaway success can be very large indeed!

Considering Competition Law

Competition Law (called *antitrust law* in the US) is at the very top of things that a society can do to make sure that markets don't hurt the public good. The purpose is to ensure that if a market isn't competitive at least the costs can be minimised. Competition law is the last line of defence against the worst kinds of behaviour, preventing the biggest firms from prejudicing competition.

The idea is that, although competition is good, stopping the biggest firms from subverting competition requires eternal vigilance. In practice, it means that part of the legal system switches from treating everyone equally to treating those companies with the biggest market shares differently from smaller ones.

Many rules are in place to stop large firms from subverting competition:

- ✓ **Limit pricing:** Makes it illegal for a large player to drop its prices below cost to deter potential rivals.

- ✓ **Merger rules:** Prevents a large player from buying out its competitors and ensuring that competition is achieved where possible.

- ✓ **Behavioural remedies:** Stops the largest competitor from owning a key resource. For instance, if you own a port, you aren't allowed to offer your own ships preferential prices to dock.

In all these cases, companies are treated differently because everyone recognises that if competition fails, everyone loses out in the long run – getting poorer quality goods at higher prices.

Microeconomists examine all these cases with models that compare competitive outcomes to those achieved by non-competitive organisations. In most situations, the intuition microeconomists form is that competition is good. But not always! In some cases, competitive markets just don't produce a good and in others the diversity of products isn't as good in a competitive market, and so economists – as a whole – aren't ideologues about this idea!

Investigating Why Markets Can Fail

If you look around the world, you find almost no examples of countries where absolutely everything gets produced through markets alone. Almost everywhere, markets co-exist with other systems: sometimes the government, sometimes philanthropy, sometimes even the 'command and control' structure of a military.

The ultimate reason for this situation is that markets, like anything else, sometimes fail: for example, where monopolies exist (see Chapter 13) or where adverse selection problems – Chapter 15 has the details – result in people who need health insurance not getting it. Or where you sell your land to a company with a polluting factory, making you and the company happier but certainly not all the residents living around you, who have to put up with the factory belching fumes (see Chapter 14)!

Economists tend to take a practical attitude to markets, perhaps more so than the general public suspects. Economists certainly don't assume that markets can inevitably produce everything that everyone wants with no drawbacks. They believe that in some cases genuine price signals would help improve matters, and tend to believe that choice is valuable in and of itself, but that doesn't mean that economists want to introduce markets in absolutely everything.

Most economists believe that markets sometimes need a helping hand, especially in two situations – when they don't produce what people want and when they cost too much doing it. This is because markets have trouble pricing goods when all the costs of making those goods are upfront and not related to consumption of those goods. You can read more about these situations, along with the instance of markets producing what people don't want, in Chapter 14.

Chapter 2

Considering Consumer Choice: Why Economists Find You Fascinating!

onsumer choice is the backbone of most Western economies. You can choose to buy from among more items now than at any time in the past, and people are certainly taking advantage of the opportunity. Today in the UK, consumers undertake approximately 60–70 per cent of total national spending depending on how you measure it: that is, their spending is £278,000 million! Much the same holds for most developed economies. When you look at consumer spending that way, you can see why economists want to understand the consumer as fully as possible!

But consumers' actions and choices aren't easy to comprehend. People have individual preferences, ideas, backgrounds, histories, identities and all manner of complicated determinants that make understanding them, if you don't know them personally, a lot more difficult than you may think. This is a problem, especially if what you really want to understand isn't so much the consumer in person, but the way markets, where the consumer is the buyer, behave.

As a result, economists have developed their tools so that an analysis of markets can make sense, even when they know very little about the individual consumer. These tools don't attempt to understand people in all their complexities, but instead represent what they may do in an abstract sense. The economic model of a consumer that we describe in this chapter may seem a very simplistic view of a person, but it's a view that's adapted for a specific way of looking at a specific type of interaction.

Ultimately, microeconomists want to lay out a set of conditions that explain how consumers come to their decisions in a way that makes sense – we describe what we specifically mean by 'makes sense' in this chapter – and how that then affects their behaviour in the marketplace. In this chapter we show you how to set the foundations of the microeconomist's view of consumers – how they behave and why – which you can use when building more complicated models (such as the ones in Chapters 4–6).

Studying Utility: Why People Choose What They Choose

Many views exist about why people choose what they do, with say psychologists and sociologists approaching the question in their own ways. In turn, microeconomists focus on one explanation for people making a given choice over another one: that the choice delivers more utility.

Introducing the idea of utility

Utility is a tricky term to pin down (see the nearby sidebar 'The complex history of utility' for a discussion of some of the difficult elements involved). Economists focus on *utility* as simply the value of someone's choice, whether that comes from them trying to increase their happiness (or not) and whatever their motivation. To economists, the simple value is that for a person to make a choice, say, of whether to select tea over coffee, he must have gained a greater amount of utility as a result of that choice.

Contrasting two ways of approaching utility: Cardinal and ordinal

You can look at utility in two, general ways:

- ✔ **Cardinal utility:** The less often used of the two options, cardinal utility *measures* the utility and so requires a unique level of utility associated with each choice in the bundle of goods (called the *consumption bundle*). Often, that utility is measured in an invented unit called *utils*.

- ✔ **Ordinal utility:** Measuring utility exactly isn't always the method chosen. Ordinal utility models preserve only the *ranking* information from the ordering of choices, so that they tell you the order in which things are preferred. To see how this approach can affect the way an economist chooses to use utility in models, we walk you through an example.

The complex history of utility

No single concrete thing called *utility* exists, and the meaning of the term changed over time, before economists settled on using the modern definition in the way it is now. Plus, utility generally doesn't get measured directly in any particular set of units, but is *revealed* when someone makes a choice between options. Despite the complexities, utility is at the basis of microeconomic analysis, and for some good reasons.

Philosophers in the 18th century were the first to use the term utility. These philosophers were concerned with understanding the nature of something else that can't usually be measured, *good,* in the sense of moral goodness! One group, often associated with the English reformer and thinker Jeremy Bentham, proposed an answer based on the consequences of actions – good actions tend to promote good consequences and bad ones bad consequences. This philosophy is called *utilitarianism,* and in its early versions, as laid out by Bentham, it attempted to refine the concept so that a formula could be used to determine how much of a good thing any given item was, from a cup of tea to a decision on making something. Later John Stuart Mill identified utility with happiness, and went on to argue that the ultimate guiding principle of goodness was whether it produces a greater happiness for a greater number.

Thinking about utility as aligned with happiness is a decent start, but other thinkers produced some objections that modern economics has accepted. The first objection comes from GE Moore, who pointed out that 'happiness' and 'good' have a more complex relationship than Mill would've liked. The second is that even if you take the moral position out of the equation, it's not hard to think about situations where someone may make a choice that yields less 'happiness'. A favourite example of ours is Mrs Doyle in TV's *Father Ted* who rejects a tea-making machine that 'takes the misery out of making tea'. ' Maybe I like the misery,' she tells the salesman.

Consider the example of a consumer to illustrate the two options in practice. Allan has three possible goods (tea, coffee and cocoa) and has measured (in some bizarre way) the utility he receives from consuming a unit of the three delicious hot beverages available (see Table 2-1). For a system of cardinal utility, you need to be able to ascribe a level of utility to each unit consumed, just as Allan does.

Table 2-1	Example of Cardinal Utility
Good	*Utility from Consuming the Good*
Tea	10
Coffee	7
Cocoa	5

As the table shows, Allan prefers tea to coffee and coffee to cocoa. Therefore, you can re-write the table so that Allan's preferences are expressed as ranks to provide the ordinal utility (see Table 2-2).

Table 2-2	Example of Ordinal Utility	
Good	*Utility from Consuming the Good*	*Rank of Choice*
Tea	10	1
Coffee	7	2
Cocoa	5	3

As you can see, the ordinal utility preferences preserve the ranking of the preferences without using a particular value for utility. Crucially, therefore, you can easily transfer any representation of utility that's cardinal into an ordinal representation – just by writing down the numbers in order. But you need to know something more exact about what a person values than economists usually know about a person, and so by the principle of fewest assumptions, you encounter ordinal utility more often than cardinal.

Modelling Consumer Behaviour: Economic Agents

Economists call a person who does something an *agent* (the actions don't need to be secret to gain the name!). Economists begin their understanding of how an agent acts by building a generalised picture of him, often called *Homo economicus,* meaning 'the economic person'. Instead of being a particular person, the agent is an abstract representation based on making the fewest possible reasonable assumptions about what a person may do.

Making assumptions is necessary as a first stage of modelling anything. A model doesn't attempt to replicate everything in the world, but represents a simplified view of the world so that you can draw enough conclusions to suit your purposes. As a result, modelling begins by making some restrictions and looks at the small picture where those restrictions are binding (some of them can be relaxed later, after you develop an intuitive feeling for what's going on in the model, and some of them hold throughout most models).

The restrictions that economists place on a completely generic and abstract person are often something that non-economists find funny. However, the reasons for doing so make sense when you're trying to create a model. In essence, what they demand isn't that the representative agent is a type of psychological make-up, but is mathematically consistent enough to come up with a model that won't be internally contradictory.

Acting rationally in economic terms: A mathematical tool

Economists demand that a model begins with *rational* agents – in the sense of them being mathematically consistent – and they make the fewest assumptions about what makes sense for people to adopt as possible. Because economists don't know very much about the people they're modelling – 7 billion people live on the Earth, after all – starting with what you think is common to them all makes sense.

We describe the assumptions here so that you can see what lies behind all the models that economists build from those foundations:

- ✔ **(Local) Non-satiation:** In general a person prefers more of something to less of it. The local aspect acknowledges that at times, for instance after the tenth slice of chocolate cake, people don't prefer more to less (something we discuss more in Chapter 4); but up to that point they generally do.

- ✔ **Completeness:** You can take a list of the possible choices or actions that can be made in a situation and rank them from best to worst, even if some of them may be choices of equal rank. This means that you can construct a *utility function* (a mathematical representation of the consumer's preferences) that incorporates all those choices.

- ✔ **Transitivity:** If an agent prefers one thing to another, and the other thing to a third thing, it must follow that a person prefers the first thing to the third. So if you prefer tea to coffee and coffee to cocoa, you prefer tea to cocoa. Again, if preferences aren't transitive, the utility function would be inconsistent and you wouldn't be able to use it to build models.

- ✔ **Reflexivity:** Any bundle of goods is at least as good as itself, so that the utility associated with a bundle isn't surpassed when the same bundle is offered in a different way.

When these conditions are satisfied, economists say that a person's preferences are *well-behaved*. This term means that it satisfies all the mathematical conditions that ensure consistent behaviour and therefore it's a suitable tool for modelling choices in the context of a market. More exactly, it means that you can construct a utility function.

Addressing an objection to the representative economic agent

A criticism sometimes levelled at the economists' view of a representative 'person' is that the construction describes a psychopath, in the sense that representative consumers follow their own interests and make a rational choice between options that allows them to maximise their own utility.

We aren't psychiatrists and so can't give a medical view on whether this description satisfies the conditions for diagnosing a psychopath, but we do want to point out a couple of flaws in this view of what economists think of as a representative agent:

- ✔ **This criticism contains what we can call a 'framing' problem.** Suppose we're talking about a person who has ten free hours a week and wants to get the best allocation between the time available to spend on two charitable activities. Microeconomists see no difference between the model used to look at this choice and choosing between a Ferrari and a Lamborghini. But *framing* the example of the choice in these two different ways tends to affect the way you perceive the choice: the second person does on the face of it seem a more selfish individual. When you don't know why an economist chooses to look at things from a non-moral perspective, you may believe that the economist's representative agent is selfish. Economists, though, are just more interested in the process of choosing than in the reasons why a person chooses one thing or another.

- ✔ **Economists make no argument about people's motivations beyond that they like doing certain things.** They do so because people are very different in how they approach things and an economist needs a theory that accommodates all those different motivations. The way economists choose to do this is to entirely remove them from the model. Economics doesn't even require that people follow this method as a way of choosing, just that they at least act *as if* they do. It doesn't matter that you actually go through a process of consciously deciding preferences, ranking them and working out what gets you most utility, as long as the result is more or less the same as the way economists model the choice.

We don't mean to imply that the model we describe has no issues – in fact, in the later section 'Noting issues with the preference model' we introduce a few points of criticism – we only mean that the psychopath objection isn't really one of them!

Pursuing Preferences and Investigating Indifferences

Microeconomists want to look at the different ways in which a consumer may prefer one bundle of goods to another. This requires them to examine people's preferences.

Mathematically, economists use three different ways of expressing a relation between two consumption bundles:

- **Strong preference:** A consumer gets more utility from a good that's strongly preferred to another (for a definition of utility, flip to the earlier section 'Studying Utility: Why People Choose What They Choose').

- **Weak preference:** A consumer gets at least as much utility from one good as another.

- **Indifference:** A consumer gets exactly as much utility from any one option as from another; that is, the consumption bundles yield exactly the same level of utility.

To illustrate how economists use these relations, we consider Allan's preferences in hot beverages. Whether you look at the cardinal or the ordinal model, Allan prefers tea to coffee (see the earlier section 'Contrasting two ways of approaching utility: Cardinal and ordinal'). In fact, Allan gets more utility from tea than from coffee, and so for this case Allan strongly prefers tea to coffee. Economists express this preference as follows:

$$Tea \succ Coffee$$

If he were to get at least as much utility from tea, and possibly more, as from coffee, you'd say that the preference was 'weak' and write:

$$Tea \succeq Coffee$$

If he were indifferent between the two, you'd write:

$$Tea \sim Coffee$$

The key point is that you can use these relations to picture choice and utility for Allan. Economists use a tool called an indifference curve to describe the choices. In this section we use it to look at how to represent some different situations in terms of choice.

Becoming bothered with indifference curves

Indifference curves are a popular tool among economists for analysing why consumers choose one option over another (we use them in Chapters 4–6 to look at how consumers choose given a budget constraint). Here we explain the concept briefly and describe what they can tell you.

An *indifference curve* plots all the points for which a consumer gets the same level of utility: that is, all the possible consumption bundles between which a consumer with well-behaved preferences is indifferent. Any given indifference curve yields the same amount of utility along the curve. In order to move up to a higher level of utility you have to be on a different – higher – indifference curve.

We plot a simple indifference curve in Figure 2-1: here are a few things you're looking at. We imagine that over a week, Allan allocates his consumption to tea and coffee, so that each point on the line of the indifference curve is a combination of a week's tea and coffee usage that yields Allan exactly the same utility.

Figure 2-1:
Allan's
indifference
curve. All
points on
the curve
yield the
same
amount
of utility,
but the
combina-
tions of tea
and coffee
must yield
a constant
level of
utility along
the curve.

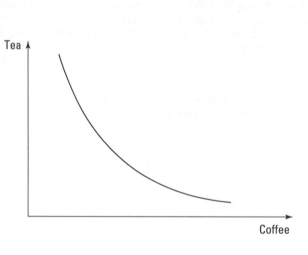

Figure 2-1 shows that if he wants to maintain the same utility while increasing his consumption of tea, he can only do so by reducing his consumption of coffee: an indifference curve tells you that the total utility from achieving coffee *and* tea must be a constant, so if tea goes up, coffee must come down! The slope of the indifference curve at any given point on the line expresses this as the economic concept of the *marginal rate of substitution* (MRS).

We draw the MRS in Figure 2-2 and annotate the original indifference curve to show how you depict it on a graph. Mathematically, the slope of the indifference curve at any given point is the MRS of Good 1 for Good 2 at that point, or in numbers:

$$MRS = (\Delta \ Good \ 2)/(\Delta \ Good \ 1)$$

Indifference curves have to slope downwards and can't cross, because the distance from the origin is reflective of the degree of utility gained by consuming a bundle on the indifference curve. Thus if the indifference curve sloped upwards, the consumer would be indifferent between consuming a lower level of utility and a higher one. To an economist this is absurd, and so a restriction gets placed on the curves so that they don't. (One exception, however, is when one of the goods is *a bad*, which is a good that gives disutility when consumed, for example broccoli – like George Bush senior, we have well-behaved preferences concerning vegetables!)

Figure 2-3 shows two indifference curves, which theoretically show the same level of utility along each curve. Bundles X and Y are along the same curve, correctly. However, look at Bundle Z: it delivers a higher level of utility than Bundle Y and therefore can't lie on the same line as Bundles X and Y. And yet, because the two curves cross, where they cross they *must* yield the same level of utility as each other. Thus, Bundle Z can't be on the same indifference curve as both X and Y, and therefore can't be on a curve that crosses I_1.

Bowing to convex curves

Indifference curves tend to be *convex*, which means they have the scooped bow shape we show in Figures 2-1 to 2-3, where the marginal rate of substitution is negative along the entire curve. At any given point, getting more of Good 2 requires a greater sacrifice of Good 1 and the more of Good 2 you desire, the more of Good 1 you have to give up.

Figure 2-2:
The marginal rate of substitution. The tangent is a straight line with the same slope as the indifference curve for the number of cups of tea and coffee you're evaluating. Both the tangent and the indifference curve have the same slope — which equals the marginal rate of substitution of tea for coffee.

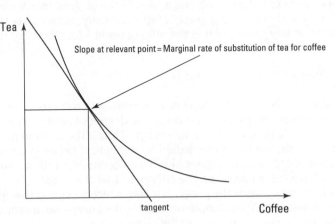

Slope at relevant point = Marginal rate of substitution of tea for coffee

Figure 2-3:
Indifference curves can't cross.

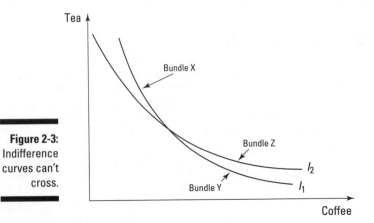

Two limiting cases apply (see Figure 2-4):

✔ **Perfect substitutes:** Any consumption bundle along the line is equivalent to any other, and giving up Good 1 just means getting a corresponding amount of Good 2. Consider yellow and white tennis balls as an example. For these two goods, the indifference curves are straight lines.

✔ **Perfect complements:** These must be consumed in fixed amounts of each, but only one unique way of allocating your spending exists between bundles. So only one point on the curve is useful and the curve has an 'L' shape, reflecting the fact that when a consumer is away from the ideal combination, adding more of Good 1 or of Good 2 is of no use on its own.

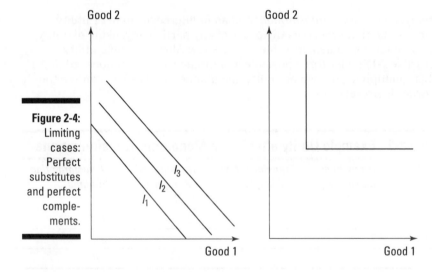

Figure 2-4: Limiting cases: Perfect substitutes and perfect complements.

Mostly, though, unless disutility is involved, as may be in the case of goods that economists call *bads,* indifference curves are convex. In fact, in some cases they can be *strictly convex,* which means that the weighted average of a bundle of goods is preferred to an extreme bundle where only one of the two goods is consumed.

If utility functions don't at least have the feature of being convex, drawing implications is difficult for the functioning of a market (the way we do in Chapter 9), and so this general restriction on 'goods' gets imposed to prevent badly behaved results later.

Staying interesting with monotonicity

When you're sitting in of an evening reading economic papers, you often see utility functions described as *monotonic* (note, not monotonous!).

Monotonicity is a key feature of well-behaved indifference curves, and means that if you were to increase a person's capability to consume both goods at the same time, the new bundle must be preferred to the old. This means that if hot-beverage consumer Allan (from the earlier section 'Contrasting two ways of approaching utility: Cardinal and ordinal') has the wherewithal to buy more tea and more coffee (for instance, if random circumstances make his income go up or both goods cheaper), he must prefer this bundle to his old bundle.

Relatedly, a *monotonic transformation* of an indifference curve or utility function is one that preserves the order of any particular ranking of utility of any bundles consumed. In Table 2-3 we show Allan's original utility (from Table 2-1) under three possible monotonic transformations, adding a number, multiplying by two or cubing the number, and as you can see the rank order is preserved.

Table 2-3	Example Utility after Three Monotonic Transformations			
Good	*Utility from Consuming the Good*	*Transformation (Adding 1)*	*Transformation (Multiplying by 2)*	*Transformation (Cubing)*
Tea	10	11	20	1,000
Coffee	7	8	14	343
Cocoa	5	6	10	125

Together, convexity and monotonicity mean two things:

- ✔ Indifference curves can't slope upwards, for the reasons we indicate in the earlier section 'Becoming bothered with indifference curves'.
- ✔ When you move out to higher levels of utility, the rank order of the bundle of goods is preserved. We ask you to accept this for a moment, but we make use of it in Chapters 4–6.

Noting issues with the preference model

We want to examine briefly a couple of issues that people have raised with the model of consumer preferences. For now, please note them, and even if you fully accept them, keep in mind that using the preference model is still useful as a yardstick to compare with other versions – it may after all be worth knowing *how* models differ and *from what* it is they differ.

✔ **Lack of rationality:** Experiments tend to confirm that an individual's weighting of utility isn't rational (as we describe 'rational' in the earlier section 'Acting rationally in economic terms: A mathematical tool'). For instance, take an offer of ≨10 now versus entry in a lottery where you have a 1 in 10 chance of earning ≨100. The expected gain from both offers is ≨10 – the first offer gives ≨10 with a probability of 1, whereas the expected outcome of the second is 0.1 (that is, 1 in 10) times 100, which equals, yes that's right, ≨10. If someone is strictly rational as the model suggests, that person will be indifferent between the two offers. But relatively few people would accept that the offer of ≨10 with certainty is the same as the option of ≨100. So people must, in general, be not quite rational.

A number of similar experiments show some quite consistent biases. One, for instance, is that people tend to value losses more negatively than they value gains positively, which means that they tend to do irrational things such as throwing money at a losing position rather than doing as rationality suggests and closing down their trading book and walking away.

✔ **Bounded rationality:** People can be 'bounded' by a number of constraints in their lives, which means that they can't possibly optimise their utility. Instead, they go for 'good enough' given the time taken to make a decision or the resources or ability to think that they possess. Bounded rationality is becoming more widely used in economics, particularly in complex systems models. The key implication of the bounded rationality approach is that the inference economists make from applying utility and preference theory to markets isn't always correct. We talk more about constraints in Chapter 5.

By contrast, the *behavioural economics* approach seeks to map and explore the differences between the results the utility and preference models predict and what happens in reality. It does so by using lab experiments and real-world data and testing how preferences really work in people. Some results already show the existence of persistent biases in people's reasoning. The example where people value their losses more than their potential gains is one such bias.

Both these approaches – the behavioural and the bounded rationality approach – make some specific challenges to the model that we present. The key one is that people may not have such well-behaved preferences as economists like to ascribe to them, and therefore the results of such preferences may be less robust than economists would like them to be.

Getting the 'standard' utility model under your belt is a good idea, however, before jumping in to questioning to the results. Even if consumers don't reason like that, they may behave *as if* they do, and even if they don't behave exactly like that, you're best exploring how they might before making changes to the model. Either way, a microeconomics course probably won't feature much of these approaches at first, but will introduce them in later modules.

Chapter 3

Looking at Firm Behaviour: What They Are and What They Do

*O*ne of the key pieces of knowledge for understanding the way a market economy organises production is the concept in microeconomics of *a firm:* something that produces things. This description is very general, necessarily, because in the real world many different types of organisation can be called a firm. For simplicity, we start from an assumption that all these firms are the same type of entity – even if we give them many different names in reality – sharing similar essential features.

In this chapter, we expand on this general description and then firm up (sorry!) a few of the concepts that underlie the arrangement of production that firms do. We look at some of the different structures of firms and into some of the critical problems associated with organisation. After reading this chapter you'll have a firm (oh no, not again!) grasp of how firms form the backbone of production in an economy.

Delving into Firms and What They Do

The best approach to start thinking about the firm is in a simple way, by considering the smallest possible unit of production: a single-person-operated firm such as a market stall (in British Law called a *sole trader*). We also introduce you briefly to the other types of firms in this section.

Looking at this sole-trader firm, an economist would want to make some general statements about what it does, and why it does it like that. Therefore, microeconomists abstract away any particular features (such as what industry or market it's in, or any special features about its operation that aren't generalisable across industries or markets) unless they're absolutely necessary. The simplest way to do so is to turn to the foundation of business and accounting, and make some general statements about the costs and benefits that accrue. To find out why economists think of firms this way, check out the later section 'Considering How Economists View Firms: The Black Box'.

Recognising the importance of profit

At its simplest, a firm takes something in, transforms it in some way and places it on the market hoping that the difference between what it receives *(revenues)* is bigger than the costs of taking that thing in and transforming it *(costs)*. That difference is called *profit* (or if you're unfortunate in running your firm, *loss,* which economists write as a negative profit). The Greek symbol, Π, denotes profit so that you can write the following simple equation:

$$\Pi = TR - TC$$

The equation says that the total profit the firm makes is the difference between all revenues that the firm takes in and all costs that the firm pays to conduct its activities.

At this stage, you haven't done anything to break down those costs into particular activities (we do so in Chapter 7) and so for the moment we suggest that the market trader's costs include not only the cost of goods bought in and the cost of labour, but also the fixed costs of operating, that is, the rent due on the stall irrespective of how many things are sold individually.

At heart, economists treat every firm in this way. Ultimately, you don't have to be a red in tooth and claw free-market supporter to point out that a business that doesn't make profits is most unlikely to stay a business for very long! Of course, not all firms want to do the same things in the same ways – comparing the *activities* of a transnational corporation to a market trader would be a little facile – but for all firms, whatever their motives, profit is the indicator of revenues being in excess of costs and a 'rational' firm (in economic terms) seeks to maximise it.

We write more about profit, revenue and costs in Chapter 7, but we just want to make one very important point about profits here: they accrue after all relevant costs have been paid. This approach is slightly different from an accountant's point of view, where several different figures can be relevant as an indicator of profit (and it depends on the accounting terms the accountant chooses). These figures can be called *income*, *earnings* or *net* or *gross profit*

for various types of firm depending on which part of the firm's accounts you're looking at.

An economist is more interested in what happens when a consumer (economists begin from the assumption that the consumer wants to maximise utility as in Chapters 4–6) shops with a profit-maximising company (which we discuss in Chapters 9–13). As a result, economists take a more general view on profit than accountants, and it tends more usually to be taken as one figure.

Discovering types of firms

Many firms are of course significantly more complex than the simple person trading alone of the preceding section.

Companies Law defines many such vehicles, including:

- ✔ **Partnership:** The owners are permitted to share in any profits generated by the business but are equally liable for all its losses.

- ✔ **Limited company:** An entity that the law defines as owning its own profits (which may then be redistributed to those who own the company – *shareholders*). In a limited company, shareholders are only liable for losses up to the stake they hold in the company.

- ✔ **Co-operative:** Owned and operated by its members. Typically, it redistributes profits to those members.

Each of these types of firm has legal advantages in certain situations and drawbacks in other situations. For instance, the limited liability company has advantages in its ability to raise capital but disadvantages in terms of the ability of owners to observe and control the activities of managers. For much more on companies, flip to the later section 'From Firm to Company: Why People Form Limited Liability Companies'.

Considering How Economists View Firms: The Black Box

Economists are often accused of treating firms too simply. By disregarding differences in product, technology or place (as we touch on in the earlier section 'Recognising the importance of profit') and treating firms simply as a black box, which mysteriously takes inputs in and creates outputs from them, aren't they arriving at a misleading picture that makes firms interchangeable and ignores important differences between them?

We've faced this accusation many times and so in this section we describe why economists view firms as they do.

Seeing why economists think as they do

Economists are interested in what a modelled firm *would do,* first and foremost. When they understand that, they can start to look at how the model differs across different industries or markets.

The economist looking at a firm makes simplifications for two reasons:

- ✔ You can't model anything without placing some restrictions on your model. If you rule nothing out, you rule anything in and before you know it you've re-enacted the Lewis Carroll story about the map so accurate that it has to be as big as the kingdom it maps!

- ✔ You want to use a specification in order to compare common features of firms, without focusing on all those details, so that you can zero in on the ones that are most important to building a model of a market.

Peering inside the Black Box: Technologies

The preceding section's rationale doesn't mean that economists take the nature of changing inputs into outputs for granted. Since Adam Smith, they've been describing in various ways the methods a firm can use to transform inputs into outputs: called *technologies.*

A *technology* is a description of the way a firm combines inputs into outputs (see Figure 3-1). Economists aren't particularly fussy about what makes a technology, and so instead of taking a narrow definition or restricting the meaning of technology to a particular kind of machine, they take a wider view and say that any method of turning inputs into outputs is sufficient. Whether it involves buying in wood and carpenters and turning them into furniture, or simply employing people to help clients understand markets, doesn't matter: they're both descriptions of a technology.

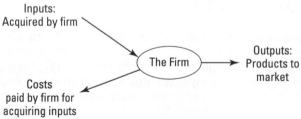

Figure 3-1: The micro-economist's view of what the firm does.

The inputs that go into a technology are the factors of production:

- Land
- Labour
- Capital

We take a closer look at each factor in turn.

Land: They ain't making any more of it

Land is without doubt an important factor of production, but it tends to be studied apart from other inputs. Land costs can be significant and important to the firm, taking up the greater fraction of operating costs for businesses in some places. Land costs can be made worse by restrictions on bringing new land into use or preventing new uses for old land, for instance in turning former agricultural land into housing.

But when economists consider the inputs for a firm, land is generally held constant and looked at in specific contexts rather than considered as part of a technology.

Labour: Getting the job done

The human element of production is labour, usually denoted L in the maths. The firm hires labour by paying wages, w, to the workers who do that work. Thus the total a firm pays out in labour costs is w times L or wL.

To begin with, economists assume that workers are indistinguishable and undifferentiated and each individual makes the same contribution to output. This is only where they begin, though, because later, when you've got the hang of the general picture, you can use a variety of more advanced tools to look at various kinds of difference between or among workers and how they affect output or costs. But for the moment, assume that workers are neither harder working nor shirkers.

Capital: Tangible and intangible

Labour is important, but workers can't create an output on their own without at least some equipment – carpenters need woodworking tools and authors need nice flashy laptops. Therefore, labour has to be combined with the other factor of production: capital.

Two types of capital exist:

- **Tangible:** Includes physical capital such as machines and plant equipment.
- **Intangible:** Includes brand value, and knowledge and skills embodied in the firm. (Skills are sometimes called *human capital* for this reason.)

In each case, the capital plus labour together makes the *output,* and so capital is generally held to be useless on its own. The cost of capital is *r.* This isn't quite the same as the interest rate, because it has to cover the *opportunity cost* of doing something else with your money. If *r* goes up then investment by firms falls because:

✓ If the firm has to borrow money to increase its use of capital at a higher cost of borrowing, the firm has to borrow more money to invest in the capital it wants.

✓ If the firm is investing its own money then a higher cost of capital implies that the opportunity cost of investing is higher and that a firm wants higher returns to capital to compare with other opportunities. Therefore, the firm is likely to use less capital.

You can use a number of techniques to evaluate the costs of using and deploying capital, most of which are based on the techniques of discounting so that future and present costs and benefits can be compared (we don't have space to go further into discounting in this book).

Minimising costs

A firm with a given technology makes a choice as to how much of each of the factors of production to use to make how much output – and pays a cost for doing so. The question for the firm is how to use its technology and choose its inputs in order to make its profits as large as possible. The way it does so is to choose its inputs in order to make the costs as small as possible (see Figure 3-2).

Talent: The alchemy of factors

Some economists like to think of entrepreneurship and talent as a factor of production. *Talent* differs from the other factors of production (land, labour and capital) by being concerned more with seeing the opportunity to create a firm or a product or somehow find a way of creating value for someone.

A firm may need to buy in talent at great expense, particularly if it's rare. But talent can also be a collective phenomenon, something that comes from a great number of people working together or embodied in one entrepreneur who has the gift of this insight. As a result, research into entrepreneurship tends to be an enterprise of its own, using substantially different sets of tools to those in this book.

Figure 3-2:
An example
of how an
economist
looks at a
technol-
ogy – the
technology
here is a
specific
form known
as a Cobb-
Douglas
production
function.

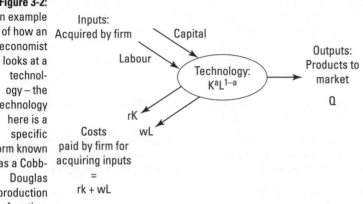

If you're wondering why economists think this way, consider profit maximisation (something we discuss in detail in Chapter 8). In the following equation (which we introduce in the earlier 'Recognising the importance of profit' section), profit equals the difference between total revenue and total cost:

$$\Pi = TR - TC$$

When a firm makes something, it can determine what to make and how much to make, but doesn't have any control over what consumers choose to buy. Therefore, it makes sense that economists model the things that the firm does control – its own costs – and so they assume that profit maximisation is the same thing as cost minimisation. (In Chapter 4, we look inside the costs of production at how a firm actually makes its decisions.)

Maximising profits

When discussing a firm, economists generally assume that it wants to maximise profits: in other words, that the difference between total revenue and total costs is positive and as large as possible. Economists don't think that anything is immoral about profit maximisation; they do believe that it's a goal that helps a firm be efficient and that firms which don't make profits tend not to operate as firms for very long!

Of course, some nuances apply to this view of profit. For one, the existence of profits in the economist's sense says nothing about how those profits may be distributed. For example, a limited liability company may want to retain some for future investment and return some to shareholders as dividends. But although a nonprofit company still intends to make a *surplus* (as it would be called in the accounts, reflecting the different *legal* as opposed to *economic* definition of the company), it does different things with that surplus, which may include distribution to workers or to chosen worthy causes.

But beyond this consideration, other reasons may exist why a firm may not be acting as a profit maximiser:

✔ Tax systems where company taxes fall on profits can provide an incentive to declare lower levels of profit.

✔ Managers may have different incentives to shareholders and prefer to generate higher salaries for themselves than higher profits for the company (managers' wages here would be a cost to the company).

✔ A company may prefer to evaluate its performance using some other measure, at least in the short run. Some examples include companies in industries whose product is information, where interim measures commonly used include market share or number of users.

Is this a problem for microeconomists? Not necessarily. In most situations they want to make a simplification that helps them understand the world instead of covering every possible case. So, when considering different types of market, the benchmark of the profit-maximising firm helps economists consider how they may be similar or different.

Economists also want to compare their models to real-world situations to see how they approach theoretical (not real) conditions. In order to do that, they can start from a simple assumption and then, as things become more complicated, refine it in the light of real-world events.

From Firm to Company: Why People Form Limited Liability Companies

A good many economic activities require rather more than simply buying something and selling it on. These stages of creating the product involve more complex forms of organisation than the sole trader.

Consider, for example, the set of production processes involved in making the computers we're using to write this book. Instead of a simple set of activities, they require a complex set: dealing with contractors; managing international product development; creating the complementary products (software or operating system, for instance); and managing the people and processes involved. As a result, a structure that places all these activities into one entity can bring a number of advantages.

Also, the limited liability company is only one potential structure among many in which people could do this. Over human history, people have used a number of other structures to arrange production: armies, hierarchies – literally a rule of priests – and various kinds of state actors have all been involved in the production process. Some key advantages, however, apply to arranging production in a limited liability company (which we introduce in the earlier section 'Discovering types of firms'):

- ✔ Shareholders are liable only for losses up to the extent of their own stakes. By having many shareholders, the limited liability company structure allows the spreading of risk among shareholders, which in turn means that more capital is available if companies need to raise some.

- ✔ A pool of capital sources for a company to draw upon helps to cover it if an individual shareholder decides not to continue investing.

Although reasonably compelling reasons exist for some types of investor to favour the limited liability company structure, pooling activities into a single entity also provides an additional advantage. The eminent economist Ronald Coase first pointed out in the 1960s that in reality using the market might not be free and costless, especially if you have to search for different people to do business with (in itself, a cost).

Putting all these costs in one place has the advantage of ensuring that you incur them once only. Check out the nearby sidebar 'Putting all your bows in one basket' for an example.

A limited liability company structure has one key implication: owners aren't necessarily the same people as managers.

Putting all your bows in one basket

In the Middle Ages, demarcation of jobs by guilds was a fact of life. However, these guilds often had very narrow boundaries. Buying a bow and arrow – and bear in mind all English adult males were required to practise archery – involved a visit to a bowyer to make the bow, a stringer to string it and a fletcher to make the arrows. If you had to search for all these suppliers in town in turn, you'd encounter three sets of *transactions costs*, that is, the costs of using the market itself.

But if someone merged all those activities into one company, Ye Olde Archery Supplies Store ('we bow to all our customers' needs'!), you'd incur those costs just once. Thus a structure that permits this consolidation of costs is preferable to one which doesn't, on the grounds of efficiency if nothing else. Thus, transactions costs lead to people finding a way to minimise those costs by putting them in one consolidated place.

Instead, economists describe owners (that is, shareholders) as *principals,* and the managers as their *agents.* This distinction is important when you start to think about firms in the real world and discuss how they behave in a marketplace.

Why would anyone want to separate ownership from management? Aside from the advantages of diffusing ownership in a limited liability company (which includes greater sources of capital for a company and some protection against losses for an owner), a shareholder may have shares in many different companies. Could such a shareholder be able to manage all those companies full time? Not unless the person was some type of shareholding superhero. So in each venture, companies need to appoint professional managers.

But this arrangement doesn't work perfectly, in all situations. The *principal–agent problem* is a description of one of those problems.

Companies, which shareholders own but professional managers manage, feature two sets of interests. The shareholders' interest is for the firm to make as much profit as possible. The managers' interests, however, may include having as big an office as possible or as great a chance of staying in the job as possible. How do shareholders manage this problem?

Commonly, they choose to reward management with shares in the company, which has the advantage of *aligning* the interests of shareholders and managers. Steve Jobs, famously, was only paid $1 in salary when he returned to Apple as CEO in 1997: the rest of his salary was paid in shares.

The evidence on management share schemes or employee share schemes is mixed, with the variation in schemes making it hard to draw an overall conclusion on whether or how they benefit firms.

Another, more subtle, aspect to this debate is that shareholders and managers aren't the only people with an interest in a company: customers, civil society groups, unions, government and others can all claim some degree of ownership of the company. This situation results in two competing types of model for companies:

- ✔ **Stakeholder model:** Sees the firm as being the nexus of all these interests.
- ✔ **Shareholder model:** Sees only shareholders as being relevant or important.

Fashions for describing firms have changed several times in recent history. The American Academy of Management, for instance, pronounced in favour of the stakeholder model in the 1970s, changed to the shareholder model in the 1980s and then back to the stakeholder model in the late 1990s.

Currently, management and firm theorists prefer the stakeholder model. However, to begin analysing the firm and for quite a long way on the journey to understanding the firm, the shareholder model is likely to be all that you see in microeconomics. The reason is that understanding the conflict between shareholders and managers is generally difficult enough without adding other entities into the mix.

Part II

Doing the Best You Can: Consumer Theory

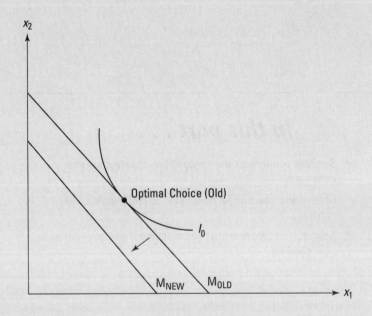

What can psychologists teach economists about consumer choice? Find out online at
www.dummies.com/extras/microeconomics.

In this part . . .

↙ See how economists use utility to investigate consumer behaviour.

↙ Understand how budget constraints affect people's best options.

↙ Appreciate how price changes make consumers re-evaluate their choices.

Chapter 4

Living a Life without Limits

· ·

In This Chapter

▶ Seeing what people choose when unconstrained

▶ Recognising the importance of marginal utility

· ·

Sometimes you just can't seem to choose what you want – limits are everywhere: speed limits, calorie limits, height limits on rollercoasters designed to drive the child who's just 1 millimetre short of the restriction wild with frustration. Well, not in this chapter. Here we look at unconstrained consumer choice. This situation may not be very realistic, but it allows economists to examine consumer behaviour with no nasty intrusions to get in the way of what people want, such as lack of time or money (don't worry, we cover constraints in Chapter 5).

In Chapter 2, we look at the consumer choice model that economists use to investigate people's preferences and introduce some of the key tools of analysis, for instance indifference curves and the concept of *utility* (the value a representative consumer gets from consuming something).

In this chapter we look at utility in a more mathematical way, in particular in terms of something called the utility function. This tool occurs frequently in economics, and is one of the keystone concepts behind looking at demand and supply in a given market, and so it's a tool with much utility (groan).

We build up a mathematical picture of the way a representative consumer treats utility, and for that we need to build up a picture of how people choose when they don't have constraints (see Chapter 5 for more on what the constraints are and Chapter 6 for how the picture in this chapter changes when you introduce them). We set up ways to evaluate the amount of utility consumers get from their choices (including *marginal utility,* which is the amount of utility gained by consuming an extra unit of something), keeping things straightforward by assuming that these choices aren't constrained.

If you're new to the concepts of utility and consumer choice, we highly recommend that you read Chapter 2 before this one.

Eating Until You're Sick! Assuming that More Is Always Better

In general, economists assume that, if given a choice, people prefer more goods to less. This assumption holds, up to a limit, because at some point people get satiated by their consumption of a good and don't want to consume any more of it.

If you've ever been unable to consume a tenth bar of chocolate, you've experienced this phenomenon. Economists call it *diminishing marginal utility*, meaning that as you consume increasing amounts of something, the utility gained from each extra amount is smaller as the amounts get larger. At some point marginal utility falls to zero and you desire no more of the good – it can even turn negative afterwards (yes, it's true, you can eat so much chocolate that eating any more causes displeasure rather than pleasure!).

However – and this is quite a big however – up to that point the more-over-less assumption operates. We look closely at this issue in the later section 'Deciding How Low You'll Go! Marginal Utility'. But here we begin from this assumption and define some terms that economists commonly use 'in the field'. The key starting point is the concept of a consumption bundle, something we touch on in Chapter 2 but examine in more detail in this section.

When you get the idea of what utility is to the economist (Chapter 2 is invaluable!), you can start putting together the building blocks that economists use for modelling. In this section we go through the terminology, showing you how economists represent preferences in a special shorthand that you can then use to ensure that models are consistent.

Making your choice: The consumption bundle

A *consumption bundle* is a set of goods that a consumer may choose to consume. Suppose that the only goods available in the world are tea and coffee. Then a consumption bundle is any set of cups of tea and coffee that the person may choose, and you can write:

(tea, coffee)

For the bundle containing one cup of tea and one cup of coffee, the bundle would be written as

(1 tea, 1 coffee)

Now imagine that the items in the brackets can represent any goods whatsoever. We call them x_n, where n is an index identifying the good in which you're interested. You can then rewrite the bundle as follows:

$$(x_1, x_2, \ldots x_n)$$

Here n is all goods whatsoever.

Although this expression is more realistic (in that at some level every good competes for your wallet with every other good), it's also very complicated. Instead, for simplicity economists often use two goods: the one they're interested in and everything else. We follow this two-good layout for now, but if you're interested in doing so you can eventually generalise the simple model to all goods.

The two-good layout leaves the consumption bundle as being

$$(x_1, x_2)$$

Here x_1 is usually plotted on the horizontal axis of any graph or space and x_2 on the vertical axis.

Consumption bundles have to follow the normal rules of preference (which we discuss in Chapter 2), which means that, for instance, with three bundles, A, B and C, and where A is preferred to B, and B to C, A must be preferred to C.

Provided that you can satisfy the rules of preference of well-behaved preferences (completeness, reflexivity and transitivity – see Chapter 2), you can represent any consumption bundle on an *indifference curve*. This depicts consumption bundles that yield an identical level of utility on the same curve so that if you were to take any bundles (call them P and Q for the moment) on the curve you'd be indifferent between them (and can write, as we do in Chapter 2):

$$P \sim Q$$

Thinking about utility in another way: Possible sets

Another way to think about consumption bundles and preferences is to think about them as things that fit inside a set of possible choices. The advantage is that showing in a diagram which sets people would prefer is easy. For instance, in Figure 4-1 we draw an indifference curve for all the consumption bundles for which Bob gets the same amount of utility. We mark up two

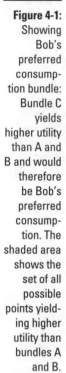

Figure 4-1:
Showing
Bob's
preferred
consump-
tion bundle:
Bundle C
yields
higher utility
than A and
B and would
therefore
be Bob's
preferred
consump-
tion. The
shaded area
shows the
set of all
possible
points yield-
ing higher
utility than
bundles A
and B.

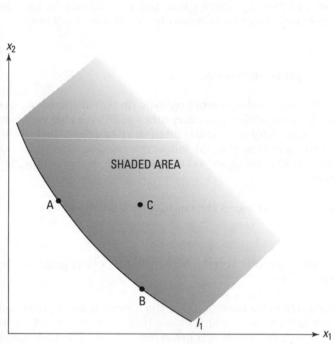

equivalent bundles A and B. He's now offered a bundle that offers more utility than these two, call it bundle C, and we translate this into microeconomist speak as follows:

$$C \succ B, C \succ A$$

This expression confirms that C is strictly preferred to B and A. In Figure 4-1 we picture C as being a member of the set of points that are strictly preferred to A and B, and we shade the area covered by that set. Because we specify that that relationship is *strict preference* (see Chapter 2), it can't include the indifference curve itself, because that would mean Bob gets at least as much utility from something we've already said yields *more utility!*

Drawing a utility function

In the preceding section, we draw curves for levels of utility, where that level of utility is the same along all the points of the curve. But suppose you want to compare bundles that are on different levels of utility. Easy! You draw a set of indifference curves moving away from the origin. Each individual curve has the same level of utility along the curves and each curve expresses a higher level of utility, the further away from the origin it is! Check out Figure 4-2.

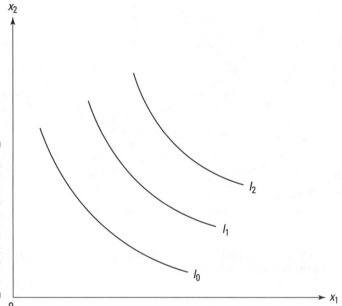

Figure 4-2:
Indifference curves further away from the origin yield higher utility for Bob.

The great thing about this depiction is that if you connect a line going through the indifference curves, and the indifference curves are derived from well-behaved preferences, any point on the new line is part of a nice, well-behaved, utility function. We show this in Figure 4-3, where the new line goes from the origin through the indifference curves.

But, you may ask, what if all those points are different combinations of goods? After all, imagine that you've shown that for indifference curve 1, Bob will be indifferent between the bundle of 3 cups of tea and 4 cups of coffee and the bundle of 5 cups of tea and 2 cups of coffee, but prefers the bundle on indifference curve 2 of 6 cups of tea and two cups of coffee. What is this telling you?

The answer is something very important about utility functions, which is that if preferences are well-behaved, almost anything that satisfies those rules could be part of a utility function! (In fact, a near infinite number of possible, consistent, utility functions could satisfy those rules. You just wouldn't know which particular one any individual consumer is on until his behaviour reveals it in some way!)

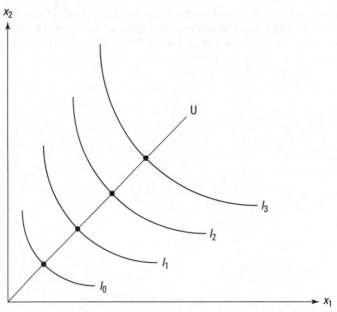

Figure 4-3:
Drawing a
utility func-
tion through
indifference
curves
shows how
Bob gets
more utility
as he moves
to a higher
indifference
curve.

The absolutely crucial point to take away is that *well-behaved preferences
make well-behaved utility functions.*

Deciding How Low You'll Go!
Marginal Utility

One really big thing to get clear is the difference between total and marginal
utility. *Total utility* (the amount of utility gained in total from consuming
something) is a useful concept, but economists far more commonly look at
how utility changes as consumption changes. For that, they use the concept
of *marginal utility* – the utility gained only from consuming one extra unit
of a good.

Considering the last in line:
The marginal unit

The concept of the marginal unit is one of the most important items in the
economics toolkit; economists use it to analyse pretty much all production
and consumption decisions. For instance firms, as we point out in Chapter 3,
optimise their production based on the relationship between marginal revenue

and marginal cost. For a consumer, the concept of marginal utility is key in looking at consumption decisions. But what is this mysterious marginal unit of which we speak? We're glad you asked!

The *marginal unit* is defined as only the last, incremental unit of something, whether cost, benefit, utility or revenue.

In Table 4-1, we show the utility gained by chocoholic Ray from consuming bars of chocolate. As in the preceding section, we plot the points on his utility function, but we now add an extra column, which tells only the gain (or loss!) in utility from consuming an extra unit of chocolate bars (or an extra bar if you want it put in human speak). This is the marginal utility yielded from only the incremental last extra unit of chocolate, and ignores the consumption of all the other bars in favour of looking just at what happens to Ray's utility as he consumes that last extra unit.

Table 4-1	Ray's Total and Marginal Utility from Consuming Chocolate Bars	
Bar of Chocolate	*Total Utility*	*Marginal Utility*
1	5	5
2	11	6
3	16	5
4	19	3
5	19	0
6	17	−2

We begin by using cardinal measures of utility (flip to Chapter 2 for an explanation), so that you can see what happens with some simple numbers. Suppose that Ray gets 5 units of utility from his first bar. The second bar is even more enjoyable than the first and he gets 6 units of utility from it. The third, however, is starting to cause icky chocolate tummy and he gets less utility from that and the fourth is really not giving all that much more utility. By the time he's on to the fifth he's feeling queasy and not enjoying it as much as suffering it.

Quantifying all the utility, we draw up a table for Ray (Table 4-1).

We plot the table in Figure 4-4 and, as you can see, utility rises to a peak level – something that economists call *satiation* – and then becomes disutility. Peak utility is found somewhere between the fourth and fifth bars (and we hope that these are fun-sized rather than full-sized bars!); assuming that Ray is economically rational (and doesn't have any other constraints), he stops eating there.

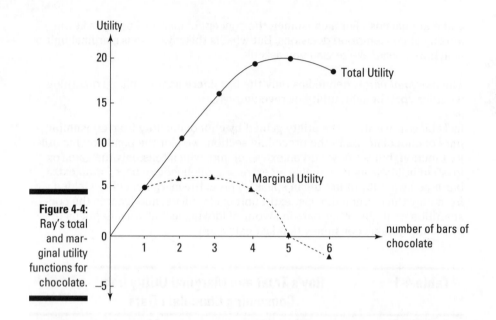

Figure 4-4:
Ray's total
and mar-
ginal utility
functions for
chocolate.

Don't confuse marginal utility with the marginal rate of substitution (MRS –
see Chapter 2). Marginal utility is the gain in utility associated with an extra
unit of something, whereas MRS tells you how much of one thing you have to
give up in order to get an extra unit of something else!

Creating a formula to model utility

We say in Chapter 2 that utility gets revealed from behaviour rather than
measured upfront. Well, if you know how a person exchanges one good for
another along the indifference curve, which you can infer from behaviour,
you can use the formula we present in this section to reconstruct the ratio
of his utility functions so that you know something about the marginal utility
gained from consumption of an extra unit!

You can write the formula for marginal utility when the quantity of a good
changes. Start by writing a utility function (U) for the utility gained from consuming quantities of two goods, x_1 and x_2:

$$U(x_1, x_2)$$

Note that if you write $U(x_1, x_2)$ equals a constant, you've written a mathematical description of an individual indifference curve (that is, you've gone
through the earlier 'Making your choice: The consumption bundle' section,
but in reverse, generating an indifference curve from a utility function!).

Now, you take the changes in the utility achieved when x_1 changes. To do so you write, first, that marginal utility (*MU*) is the change in total utility when x_1 changes. Using a formula, that makes it:

$$MU_1 = \frac{\Delta U}{\Delta x_1}$$

Okay, now you expand the top of the equation using the formula for a utility function. Replace *U* with the original expression for utility (x_1, x_2) and then the new utility when *x* changes becomes:

$$U = u\left(x_1 + \Delta x_1, x_2\right) - u\left(x_1, x_2\right)$$

This means that *MU* equals all the right-hand side of the equation, all over Δx_1!

Here's an interesting bit. We warn you in the preceding section not to confuse marginal rates of substitution and marginal utility, but the two do have a special relationship: first, the marginal rate of substitution is also the slope of the indifference curve; and second, points on the same indifference curve grant the same level of utility. Now think about a change in the consumption of both goods that leads to utility staying the same, so that both the before and after consumption bundles are on the same indifference curve. That change means that the marginal utility gained from the change equals zero, and so you can re-write the equation for the MRS so that:

$$MU_1 \Delta x_1 + MU_2 \Delta x_2 = \Delta U = 0$$

This doesn't seem all that Earth-shattering . . . until you solve it for the slope of the indifference curve (which is the MRS, and you can write as $\Delta x_1 / \Delta x_2$):

$$MRS = \frac{\Delta x_2}{\Delta x_1} = -\frac{MUx_1}{MUx_2}$$

So here, using a little bit of simple, but clever, maths, you can reconstruct information about what you'd like to know (utility) from something you do know (MRS). Now that's microeconomics!

Ray is in conformity with the rules of choice, which makes his preferences well-behaved and therefore workable with. If he isn't, it becomes a far more challenging task to infer anything about his behaviour. Compare Ray, for instance, to Cookie Monster. As we're sure you know, Cookie Monster is 'monster', and Cookie Monster 'eat cookie', irrespective of how much utility 'Cookie Monster get from cookie'. Cookie Monster, therefore, doesn't behave like it has well-behaved preferences, and you can make no inferences whatsoever about marginal substitution or utility!

Chapter 5

Considering the Art of the Possible: The Budget Constraint

In This Chapter

▶ Affecting consumer choice with a budget constraint

▶ Seeing how consumers push utility to the maximum

▶ Modelling consumer behaviour in two ways

*I*n Chapter 4 we discuss economics in terms of what we call *unconstrained optimisation,* where the only limiting factor is the amount of utility a person achieves. Ah, such freedom!

In the real world, of course, you never quite have 'world enough and time' to accomplish all the things you want to. You could always achieve something else if it wasn't for those pesky constraints, such as buy an item if you weren't just so short of moolah. So, in reality, satisfying your wants can never be as simple as Chapter 4's model: in practice you may be unable to consume anything up to the point that you gain further utility.

Therefore, almost nothing in economics works on an unconstrained model. At some level, everything is constrained, if not by money then by time. When you're deciding how much of something to consume, your utility isn't the only important aspect; you also need to consider the availability of resources.

Fortunately, economists are very comfortable with the idea of scarcity! They've thought about this problem for over a hundred years and have a number of tools for describing the process of choosing when some kind of constraint is involved. In fact, at the heart of most of the basics of microeconomics is a model of constrained optimisation, which deals with precisely this conundrum.

To make the model from Chapter 4 more fitting to the real world, in this chapter we add another piece of the puzzle: the budget constraint. We describe what this does to the feasible level of consumption that an individual consumer undertakes and how economists use it to look at the way choices get made in reality by introducing you to the budget constraint and showing you what it means. We explain what you can tell from the budget constraint and how you can play with it to show how people's choices are affected by changes in budget. We also use the indifference curve from Chapter 4 to show how economists model a constrained choice, and show you one important implication of the model – that the ratio between prices is the same as the rate of substitution between two goods!

Taking It to the Limit! Introducing the Budget Constraint

The key to moving from unconstrained optimisation to constrained optimisation is the introduction of a *budget constraint*. This is a method of conceptualising all the ways that the choice of doing or buying something is held back by the availability of resources, whether in terms of money, time or something else. It also provides some insights that help economists put a bit more flesh on the utility model, giving them a little more help in modelling the real world.

In this section, we present the budget constraint, and because we expect that your time and effort is constrained, we do our best to keep things simple!

Introducing the budget line

Imagine, as in Chapter 4, that you have two goods x_1 and x_2 (you can think of them as coffee and tea, or season tickets to see Bolton Wanderers and a new car, or even just one good and all other possibilities). We assume that you have a fixed amount of resources, which we call M for now. The two goods have prices p_1 and p_2 respectively.

The maximum amount you can spend on both goods is M and so the budget constraint has the following formula:

$$p_1 x_1 + p_2 x_2 = M$$

This equation is known as *the budget line*.

If you're mathematically aware, you may have picked up that this expression describes a straight line, and that it slopes downward. Doing a little substitution in the equation, you can give the slope of the line by the price ratio of the two goods:

Slope $= -p_1 / p_2$

Anything up to the budget line is feasible; anything beyond it is unfeasible and so ruled out. We plot the shape of the budget line in Figure 5-1.

Figure 5-1:
The budget line, or budget constraint, splits an area into affordable (or feasible) and unaffordable (or unattainable) sets.

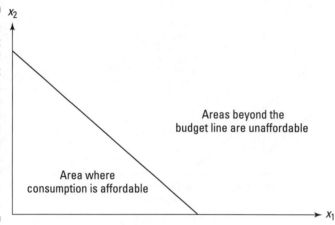

Note that points beyond the budget line, that is, those farther away from the origin than the budget line, are now ruled out. This means that when we re-introduce utility curves, the highest possible utility curve that you can be on is the one that's tangent in one place only to the budget constraint (assuming, that is, that the curves are strictly convex as in Chapter 2).

We demonstrate this point again in the later section 'Getting the Biggest Bang for your Buck'. For the moment we show you some ways of manipulating the budget constraint and a couple of the points you can glean quite simply from doing so.

Shifting the curve when you get a rise

Suppose that one day your boss calls you into her office and announces that you're going to get a rise. Of course, you're delighted, but far more importantly, you've gained an opportunity to put your microeconomics to use. The way you do is by understanding that the M (the fixed amount of resources) in the budget constraint is now bigger than it used to be, and so you can use this fact to manipulate the budget constraint to show your new purchasing possibilities.

A budget constraint maps the relative availability of two goods to a fixed amount of resources, which we call *M*. In the utility model, this means that you can take account of income by moving the budget constraint away from the origin so that the new curve is parallel to the old, as in Figure 5-2.

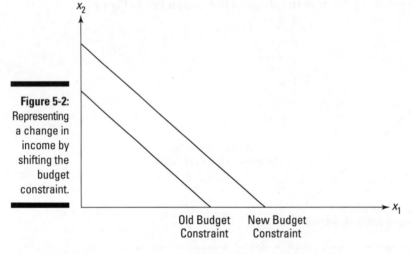

Figure 5-2:
Representing a change in income by shifting the budget constraint.

You can look at this issue another way too, as meaning that the availability for consumption of any of the bundles in your utility function is now increased. Therefore, you can shift the constraint in the same way when you want to model the effect of a rise in prices that's constant across goods (shifting the budget constraint in to rule out any level of utility beyond the constraint).

A shift in the budget constraint means that some bundles of utility are now either available where they hadn't been before (if the change is positive) or ruled out (if the change is negative).

Twisting the curve when the price of one good changes

Although economists can model some situations, particularly those relating to changes in income, by just shifting in the budget constraint, having some prices changing more than others is quite a normal phenomenon. Changing income shifts the budget constraint, but because prices are part of the constraint (the p_1 and p_2 in the earlier 'Introducing the budget line' section), any change in prices also changes the constraint. If all the prices you're interested in change at the same rate, you can model the effect by shifting the constraint as in the preceding section.

But suppose that some prices change more than others, or that you're interested in what happens when some prices change and some don't. In that case you need to look again at the formula for the budget constraint to see how that affects your feasible consumption.

For instance, take the current consumer price income for the UK. The latest data available indicates that the average index of prices for the UK fell by 0.5 per cent over 2014. Breaking the figures down into goods and services, however, as the ONS headline data does, the price of goods fell by 1 per cent and that of services *rose* by 2.3 per cent over the same period!

This example is just on a very broad sector-based approach to breaking down the figures. If you look further into the raw data, you find that some goods rose in price, some fell and the overall average picture hides these changes in *relative prices*.

Relative price changes have another effect on top of the effect of a change in overall prices: they cause substitution between goods. Suppose that you're deciding to take a break from work for a nice hot beverage. Suppose further that coffee has become relatively more expensive. Then, under some circumstances (which we explain more fully in Chapter 6, we promise!) you may want to substitute some of your consumption of coffee for tea, preserving utility overall at a cost of reducing some consumption of your preferred option.

What does all this mean for the model? Well, we have a very simple way of describing changes using the budget constraint. Instead of shifting the constraint, economists rotate it a little, so that it becomes steeper when the price of the good economists are interested in has risen.

In Figure 5-3, we show you how we'd take account of a rise in the price of coffee.

A rise in the price of any particular good is the same as a fall in income, because it reduces the number of opportunities to consume. However, a rise in relative prices of one good (relative to another or all others) also means some substitution away from the more expensive good towards the cheaper one.

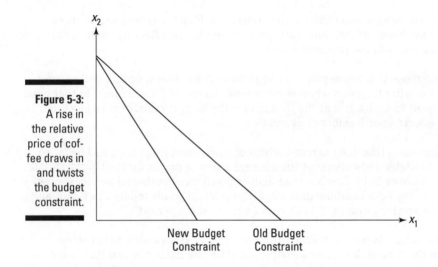

Figure 5-3:
A rise in
the relative
price of cof-
fee draws in
and twists
the budget
constraint.

Pushing the line: Utility and the budget constraint

The budget constraint divides up the utility map into feasible and unfeasible areas, and so we can now use the utility model and take a look at what a consumer will do to optimise her utility when a constraint exists. To do so, we have to take a look at what happens when we put the indifference curves from Chapter 4 together with the budget constraint in this section.

As we describe in Chapter 4, a consumer would, up to a point of satiation (and we assume that we're some way within that point), try to consume so that she's on the highest available indifference curve: that is, one farthest away from the origin. We show this on Figure 4-2 in Chapter 4. Each of the indifference curves has the same level of utility at all points along the curve, and the only way to be at a higher level of utility is to be on a higher indifference curve.

In Figure 5-4, we reintroduce the budget constraint. Okay, now, we look at three indifference curves (and associated consumption bundles on each curve):

✔ **Indifference curve I1:** Lies entirely within the budget constraint and therefore is available. But would the consumer choose it? The answer is no, because higher levels of utility would be available by consuming right up to the budget line – all the areas above the indifference curve but within the constraint are still affordable but all yield higher utility than any point on I1.

> ✔ **Indifference curve I2:** Also has points that are inside the constraint – although some are outside it.

REMEMBER

Clearly the consumer would have to prefer points on I2 to those on I1, because they all confer a higher level of utility. But even though some combinations on I2 are unfeasible, the feasible points all lie away from the budget constraint, meaning that utility is available, as long as we restrict ourselves to combinations of x_1 and x_2 that are away from the extremes.

> ✔ **Indifference curve I3:** Has a multitude of unavailable points, but notice also that this has one very important available point – the point D – which is exactly on the budget line (mathematically, you say that it lies on a tangent to the line). This point yields higher utility than any point on I1 or I2, and is available, though you'd have no change from your M (fixed amount of resources) if you spent it on point D!

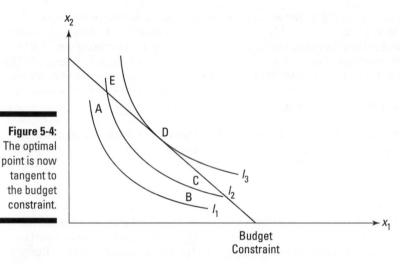

Figure 5-4:
The optimal point is now tangent to the budget constraint.

REMEMBER

When looking at utility given a budget constraint, the best available point must lie on an indifference curve tangent to the budget constraint, because that's when the consumer has spent to the last penny available!

Getting the Biggest Bang for Your Buck

The shape of the budget constraint itself (see the preceding section) is of great importance to microeconomists. In and of itself, the nature of the constraint provides information that's useful for looking at consumer behaviour.

One of the key ways in which a tax, subsidy or rationing constraint affects consumers is through lowering (or, better, raising!) the budget constraint. Economists manipulate the budget constraint into showing you those kinds of points in a number of ways – we look at two here.

Economics assumes that consumers want to get as much utility as possible for the least possible cost. Changes in relative prices of goods change the budget constraint and therefore the highest level of utility a consumer can get. So if anything affects the budget constraint, it also affects how consumers will choose which bundle of goods to consume!

Exploring relative price changes with the numeraire

Sometimes economists prefer to move away from absolute prices – for example £1.29 for a cheeseburger – to relative prices that express prices for one good in terms of how much something else costs – for instance, that the same cheeseburger costs 1.29 times the price of a hamburger costing £1. The reason is that prices are often in different units, and in some cases, it makes everything simpler to calculate if you just look at the ratios of prices rather than the prices themselves.

The *numeraire* price is what you get when you fix the price of one of the goods on the budget line to 1. Doing so is useful when you want to strip out the effect of the level of the price and just look at the effects of changes relative to the price of a good.

To get the numeraire price, start by considering that setting one price to 1 and allowing the other variables to change around it doesn't change the properties of the budget set at all. In the original budget line we use earlier in this chapter (in the section 'Taking It to the Limit! Introducing the Budget Constraint'), the formula is as follows:

$$p_1 x_1 + p_2 x_2 = M$$

But if we fix things so that p_2 is 1, we still get exactly the same budget line, except with the intercept for x_2 (M/p_2) now just being M. The key thing is that the relative price of everything else is now expressed holding the numeraire price of x_2 at 1!

If everything in the budget set changes at the same rate, the only effect on the consumer is to shift in or out the budget line as a whole. If you multiply the budget line by a number, the optimal choice of the consumer doesn't change. So if the price of all goods and services in an economy changes by exactly the same amount in a year, the inflation is *balanced* and doesn't affect consumers' purchases.

A numeraire is one way of fixing an economist's attention on relative prices. If you're unsure about the change in price of one good relative to another, the numeraire helps you to see how the ratio matters. Again, the slope of the budget constraint is the important factor, because it measures relative prices rather than absolute prices. If you use a numeraire price, you can quite simply see what's happening, because it sets one of the prices at 1 making the role of the price ratio clearer.

Using the budget line to look at taxes and subsidies

The budget line is normally a simple straight line. But if, for instance, a tax changes the cost of a good relative to others, this is tantamount to a price change and you can use the shape of the budget line to prepare some ways of looking at the tax.

Before we do so, we have to be a bit more specific about the type of tax, because they do different things to the shape of the budget line.

Two types of tax

We want to distinguish two types of tax (or their seemingly positive cousin, subsidies) that affect the constraint:

- ✔ **Quantity taxes:** A tax on units of something bought. Examples are the tax that government levies on petrol, expressed per litre, or the 'sin' taxes – also called *specific duties* – levied on certain goods, such as per unit of alcohol. These taxes simply change the price paid for that quantity: if x_1 is a litre of unleaded petrol, and the quantity tax is τ per unit, the price of a litre is $p_1 + \tau$, and you can treat this simply as a price change.

- ✔ *Ad valorem* **('to the value of') taxes:** Instead of being based on the quantity of the good, the constraint is affected via the effect of a price on a good, in much the same way.

  A common example is Value Added Tax (VAT), which is levied as a percentage of the purchase price of a good. In the UK this tax is currently 20 per cent of the final purchase price of all goods that aren't exempt – some countries levy at different rates by type of purchase, but with the exception of the zero-rated goods the UK doesn't.

  The former price of the good is p_1, but the post-tax price is $(1 + \tau)p_1$ where τ is the rate of tax. For the 20 per cent VAT that the UK consumer pays, therefore, τ equals 0.2 (convert the percentage to a decimal!) and $1 + \tau$ is 1.2, and so the price of any non-zero-rated good is 1.2 times p.

Again, you can treat the introduction of an *ad valorem* tax as being tantamount to an increase in the price of the good you're considering, and manipulate the budget constraint to show it. In this case it would draw in the quantity of x_1 that can be consumed, showing as a drawing in of the budget line!

A third type of tax: Stamp duty

An even more interesting case than the preceding two shows up on the constraint, and that's what happens when a tax is only levied on consumption of a good above a certain price.

This is the case in the UK for stamp duty – strictly speaking, *stamp duty land tax* (SDLT) – that people incur when buying a home. If that home has a market price of less than £125,000, the buyer doesn't need to pay any stamp duty. But above £125,000 (until the price reaches the next band at £250,000), buyers have to pay 2 per cent of the purchase price to the government. So, the microeconomics question is: how do you look at this aspect using a budget constraint?

The answer's easy! One slope of the line for purchases goes up to the threshold and then the line bends at that point (see Figure 5-5).

Figure 5-5:
The effect on the budget constraint of a stepped tax.

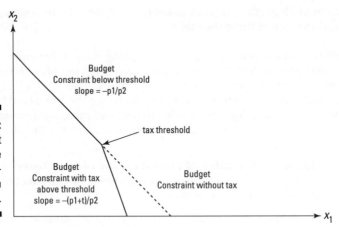

To make everything easier, think about it as a quantity rather than a value tax for a moment. Suppose, for argument's sake, that the first house takes no tax and a second does (actually differential taxes apply for second homes, but they strangely work to make the second home pay less tax in the UK!). Now, while you're deciding to buy a first house, the budget constraint is the constraint for x_1 up to the point where $x_1 = 1$. Here, the slope of the budget constraint is $-p_1/p_2$ as it was earlier (see 'Taking It to the Limit! Introducing the Budget Constraint'). However, beyond x_1 the slope changes to become $-(p_1 + \tau)/p_2$. As you can see in Figure 5-5, the budget line is steeper beyond the threshold!

You can do the same type of graphing with subsidies, too. A subsidy, in this case, is just a negative tax, and so instead of adding it to the price you subtract it. Therefore, if good x_1 is subsidised, the budget slope is $-(p_1 - \tau)/p_2$. We show this in Figure 5-6.

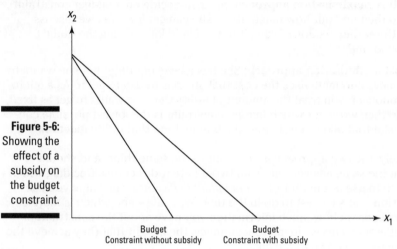

Figure 5-6:
Showing the effect of a subsidy on the budget constraint.

Budget Constraint without subsidy   Budget Constraint with subsidy

Rationing too appears on the budget line. If a good is rationed, one area of the budget set becomes unavailable at any price – the set is *truncated* in economics speak.

To show this, cut a vertical line in above the maximum rationed consumption of good x_1. To the left of the line, the budget set behaves as normal. To the right, where the maximum consumption is greater than the rationed amount – we call it r for the moment – the set consists of goods that the consumer could afford, but can't get. We present this example in Figure 5-7.

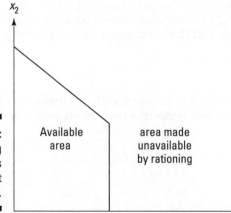

Figure 5-7:
Rationing truncates the budget constraint.

Available area   area made unavailable by rationing

Putting the Utility Model to Work

In essence, a consumer can optimise in the classic choice model in two ways:

- ✓ **Utility maximisation approach:** She can decide on a budget constraint and then find out how much utility she can get for it (as we discuss in the earlier section 'Taking It to the Limit! Introducing the Budget Constraint').

- ✓ **Cost minimisation approach:** She has a level of utility that she wants to achieve and minimises the cost that she has to pay to get it. As a micro-economist, you treat the amount of utility that she wants to get as fixed, and then work out which budget constraint is the lowest possible constraint that allows her to afford a bundle from that utility function.

Ultimately, the two approaches work out to the same thing, and should arrive at the same answer, but from two different directions. Deciding which approach to use is a matter of *computational efficiency* – meaning you use the version that's easiest to do in the time available – and which is more efficient depends on how much information you have about the constraint or the indifference curves. In microeconomics, the insight that they achieve the same answer is known as *the dual*.

What's most important is a conclusion that you can derive from knowing something about utility (see Chapter 4) and something about the budget constraints (check out the earlier section 'Taking It to the Limit! Introducing the Budget Constraint' in this chapter) and something about how the two have to be related. The relation between the two that's important in this case is that the highest level of utility possible for a constrained consumer occurs when the indifference curve is tangent to the budget constraint. Therefore the slope of the utility curve and the slope of the budget constraint are equal at that point.

The slope of the indifference curve is the marginal rate of substitution (MRS) as in Chapter 4 and the slope of the budget constraint is the relationship between the two prices ($-p_1/p_2$). Given that these have to be equal, you can assume the final implication, that the optimising consumer's best point occurs when:

$$MRS = -p_1 / p_2$$

You need to know this equation for Chapter 6's full discussion on optimisation and for Chapter 9, which looks into the famous supply and demand model.

Chapter 6

Achieving the Optimum in Spite of Constraints

In This Chapter

▶ Breaking down price-change effects into income and substitution

▶ Revealing consumers' preferences

▶ Comparing income and substitution effects

*T*he single most important part of microeconomics is the *constrained optimisation* model, which is that people act to achieve the best they can given some kind of constraint upon their choice. This way of looking at people's decisions runs through most of the microeconomic syllabus, finding its way into all sorts of things from consumer choice to environmental or industrial analysis. Yet its roots lie in the way economists look at individuals.

To microeconomists, people optimise. When prices change, people respond to the information and react. Suppose that you have £1 in your pocket to spend on a treat. You have two types of available treat, chocolate bars and biscuits, and you start by getting your best mix of the two: that's two of each to begin with. Now imagine that the price of the biscuits goes up. What do you do? Well, if you're behaving as microeconomists suggest, you switch some of your consumption from biscuits to chocolate bars so that you can keep your level of utility as high as possible!

Putting the constrained optimisation model into place means dealing with the effect of prices on utility. We lay the foundations in Chapters 2 and 4 on utility functions and Chapter 5 on the budget constraint, which give you the framework's starting point. In this chapter, we start from the optimum point in Chapter 5, where utility is exactly tangent to the budget constraint, and show you what happens when something changes.

We hope that, given your time constraints, you find that this chapter helps to maximise your utility!

Investigating the Equilibrium: Coping with Price and Income Changes

When investigating the effect of price changes, a good place to start is by thinking about what the changes do to the behaviour of a representative consumer. Indifference curves (see Chapters 2, 4 and 5) excel in this situation!

Start at a given equilibrium, to give a sense of what happens before you make changes. In this case the plot in Figure 6-1 is an equilibrium with well-behaved indifference curves and a standard budget constraint, and so, as desired, the price ratio equals the marginal rate of substitution between goods x_1 and x_2.

Figure 6-1:
A parallel shift in the budget constraint simulates a change in income (makes the old optimal choice unavailable, given the new constraint M_{NEW}).

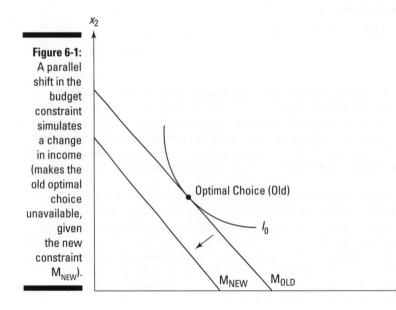

Now, imagine some situation that affects your income calamitously (such as losing your job, getting a new job that doesn't pay as much or a national economic disaster like those affecting Greece, Ireland or Portugal recently). The details don't matter; the important thing is that it reduces your income.

Starting at the equilibrium, you can draw in a new budget constraint, one that's parallel to the original one, but to the left of it. Of course, this means that the original equilibrium level of utility is now unattainable, and so you, as the representative consumer, react by reducing your consumption of goods x_1 and x_2 (see Figure 6-1).

Suppose that just one price changes (remember that you can treat x_1 and x_2 as though x_1 is the good you're interested in and x_2 as all other goods). This is an interesting situation, because the effect on your purchasing opportunities isn't just experienced through an overall fall in income, but also through the *relative price* effect whereby x_1 is now more expensive relative to the price of all other goods available. This situation is where indifference curves fully unpack their awesome power – check out the next section.

Dealing with Price Changes for One Good

In this section we explore what happens when a relative price changes. In reality this tends to happen when people talk about price rises. Only very rarely do all prices change at the same rate, but in those rare cases the budget line merely shifts in and out in parallel with the original. More often, the price of one good changes when others don't, or changes at a different rate to other goods. We take you through this scenario so that you can see its importance.

When the price of one good changes, you can say two things within the context of the *utility function* (which represents mathematically the consumer's preferences; see Chapter 2 for more):

- ✔ The budget line, whose slope is the ratio of the two goods' prices, changes.

- ✔ The equilibrium condition requires that the marginal rate of substitution (MRS) is equal to the ratio of the two prices. So the slope of whatever indifference curve the consumer is now on must be different to its original (at the point where the ratio of prices and MRS are the same).

Don't worry if all this seems a little complicated. In this section, we break it down into a set of stages to make the whole process clearer.

Pivoting the budget line

In the optimisation model, you take account of situations where one price changes by pivoting the budget line.

The budget line shows the maximum you can buy at the prevailing prices. For example, you have £100 and a new tennis racket costs £40 but a tennis lesson £20 per hour. You could buy one racket and have three lessons for the maximum, or two rackets (one for you and one for a tennis partner) and one lesson. Or you could buy five lessons and hope that your old racket holds out! All these options are possible. But if the tennis lessons go up to £25, your options for substitution change. Now the maximum number of lessons you can buy while keeping your old racket falls to four.

In Figure 6-2 we show the old equilibrium (with indifference curve U_1 tangent to the budget constraint, M). To this, we add the initial price change, which is illustrated by pivoting the budget line (as we discuss in Chapter 5), so that the good whose price changes (x_1) becomes more expensive, drawing in the line along the x axis (representing the ability a consumer has to purchase x_1). This is the shape of the final budget line, and the slope of this line is the same as the MRS on whichever indifference curve the consumer ends up. We label this M^{final} in Figure 6-2.

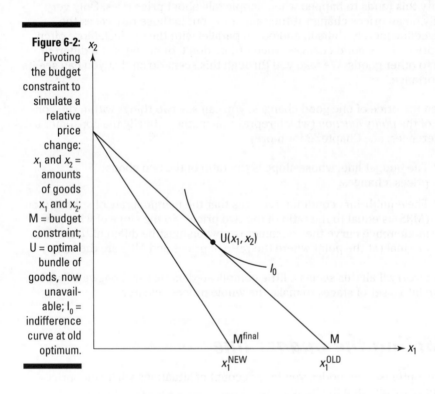

Figure 6-2: Pivoting the budget constraint to simulate a relative price change: x_1 and x_2 = amounts of goods x_1 and x_2; M = budget constraint; U = optimal bundle of goods, now unavailable; I_0 = indifference curve at old optimum.

Therefore, to simulate a rise in the price of good x_1, you draw in the budget line so that maximum allocation to x_1 is reduced from x_1^{old} to x_1^{new}. The optimal point on the old constraint ($U(x_1,x_2)$) is no longer available.

But you can't get to that point yet! You have to unpack a couple of new features first. Two effects occur when the price of a good changes:

- ✔ **Substitution effect:** Where a rise in price for a good relative to other goods leads to a substitution away from the more expensive good and towards the less expensive ones.

- ✔ **Income effect:** Reflects the fact that when prices rise, people have less income to spend overall.

The next stage of working through from the change in the price of one good is to work out the two effects in two stages so that you can see clearly how they operate, as we do in the following two sections.

Seeing substitution in practice

Economists are interested in how people make decisions when they want to consume up to their budget constraint, but a price rise means that their previous level of preferred consumption is unattainable. In other words, the situation when people substitute towards the relatively cheaper good.

Consider this example. A representative consumer – call her Kirsty – likes to meet up with her friends to watch art films and eat noodles. Suppose that she has a total budget of £60 for her entertainment activities. If a film costs £10 and a bowl of hot noodles costs £5, suppose that she maximises her utility – remember that she'll spend right up to the budget constraint if she can – when she goes to see a film four times a week and has a bowl of noodles each time. Now suppose that – horror! – the film price goes up to £15: the film becomes more expensive, relative to noodles. As a result she can't afford her optimal budget. But if she substitutes two visits to the noodle emporium for two to the cinema, she can maximise her utility relative to the new budget constraint!

Of course, economists need to set up the problem so that it's as general as possible and doesn't rely on in-depth knowledge about a particular person and a particular good. Kirsty makes these choices automatically, and economists need to set things up to make them formal enough to use them eventually for calculations.

To show how substitution takes place you need to know about the *slope* of the new budget line, but not its position. To illustrate it, you need to draw a *shadow budget line* that preserves the original *level* of price for x_1 while using the new slope.

Start with Figure 6-2 and draw a new budget line parallel to the final budget line but tangent to U_1 (though not at the same point of tangency – the slope of the budget line has changed, which means that the optimal point where MRS = slope of M will be different!). We do so in Figure 6-3.

The shadow budget line (M^{SHADOW}) shows how the effect of the change of price of x_1 must cause substitution, even in the absence of reduced budget overall.

Note that we don't shift the indifference curve U_1, because the intention here is to show the substitution effect. Consumption of x_1 falls and that of x_2 rises owing to the relative price effects, but income is (approximately) preserved!

Adding in the income effect

When a price changes relative to other prices, it doesn't just affect the amount consumed relative to other things: it also changes the amount consumed as a whole, because it generally makes your preferred amount unattainable.

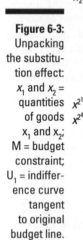

Figure 6-3: Unpacking the substitution effect: x_1 and x_2 = quantities of goods x_1 and x_2; M = budget constraint; U_1 = indifference curve tangent to original budget line.

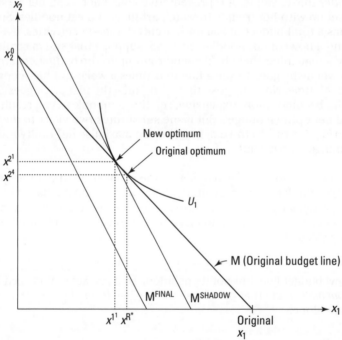

Here's an example of the income effect, where someone's original best bundle becomes unaffordable and the person consumes less in total. Inigo, a representative consumer, would like to spend his weekly disposable income on shoot 'em up video games and pizza. He has £50 to spare and initially a game costs £30 and a pizza £5, so he buys one game and has pizza four times a week. But – disaster – the price of video games goes up to £35. His initial consumption is no longer possible, and so he now gets only three pizzas a week (assuming that he can't or won't substitute away his game!). Thus his total consumption must fall, from one game and four pizzas to one game and three pizzas.

Again, economists want to generalise away from specific numbers, and so they form a more general picture of the income effect. Follow along now as we show you the general model that economists use!

The income effect occurs because the price change (and the corresponding shift in the budget constraint) means that the level of utility associated with U_1 is no longer available. Thus, the economically rational consumer optimises by shifting down to a new utility curve parallel to the original U_1 (denoted U_2 in Figure 6-4). As we discuss in the preceding section, M^{SHADOW} covers the relative price changes, and so the move from M^{SHADOW} to M^{FINAL} just deals with the reduction in overall income.

In Figure 6-4 we indicate the new optimum as U* (the best available position for the consumer after accounting for income and substitution). U* is at a different point of substitution between x_1 and x_2, and so less x_1 is consumed, and it's on a lower utility curve, U_2. This is the 'final' equilibrium point, where utility is as high as it can possibly be given the constraint.

'It takes different strokes': Different goods have different income and substitution effects

The relative size and (in some cases) direction of the income and substitution effects (see the two preceding sections) depends on the type of good you're examining. For instance, if a good is supplied by a competitive market with many close substitutes, the substitution effect is likely to be large (infinitely so in the case of perfect competition). But if the good has no close substitutes, the income effect is likely to be much larger compared to the substitute good.

Figure 6-4:
Shifting
back the
shadow
curve to
investigate
the substitu-
tion effect
gives a new
optimum U*:
x_1 and
x_2 = quan-
tities of
goods x_1
and x_2;
M = budget
constraint;
U_1 = indiffer-
ence curve
at original
optimum;
U_2 = final
indiffer-
ence curve
tangent to
final budget
constraint
M^{FINAL};
U bar =
chosen con-
sumption
bundle after
substitu-
tion effect
tangent to
M^{SHADOW};
U* = final
best opti-
mum after
accounting
for income
and
substitution
effects.

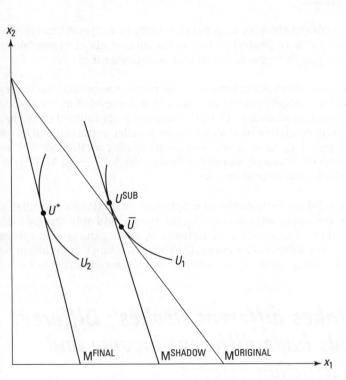

Several factors determine the size of each effect, including the following:

- **Income elasticity:** Measures the responsiveness of purchasing to a change in income. Normal goods have income elasticities – see Chapter 9 for a full account – around 1, meaning that if income rises by 10 per cent consumption of those goods also rises by around 10 per cent. But some goods (such as luxuries) respond more dramatically to income changes and some respond negatively (the consumption of inferior goods falls as incomes rise).

- **Existence and closeness of substitutes:** When substitutes are perfectly interchangeable, the indifference curve is a straight line and a rise in the price of one substitute results in substitution away to the cheaper option. (Strictly, the slope of the indifference curve is the price ratio the whole way along the curve, and not just at the optimum.)

- **Ability of a consumer to switch:** An implicit assumption here is that switching from one option to another is free and costless, which isn't always true (as you know if, say, you've tried to switch operating systems on your computer!). Economists dealing with markets in technology frequently have to adapt models to add in *switching costs,* which are derived from, among other things, the cost of learning to use a technology or of giving up a network of software users.

Discerning a Consumer's Revealed Preference

Given what we state in the preceding section, you can say a few more things about the relationship between preferences and the budget constraint. Advanced models have many things to say, but you need to consider a couple of steps first: the principle of revealed preference and how it impacts upon what we can say about a representative consumer; and how you can use some maths to decompose a change in prices showing how much is due to the income effect and how much is due to the substitution effect.

One of the frustrations with building models out of the utility behaviour of consumers is that utility isn't usually measured, but found out *after* someone makes a choice. It's revealed from the impact upon prices and quantities and then inferred from working out what that would do to a consumer's choice.

This somewhat back-to-front way of looking at things makes sense when you realise that economists know nothing about the consumer until he participates in a situation where inferences can be made regarding his behaviour.

We're not saying that the constrained optimisation model has no power, just that when looking at it, you have to think about how anyone knows anything about the consumer's preferences – which is via a revealed preference.

To put *revealed preference* as simply as possible, if a consumer chooses a bundle of goods – call it A – over another bundle – B – given that both B and A are affordable, you can say that the consumer prefers A to B. In other words, the act of choosing the bundle A *reveals* that the consumer preference is for bundle A over bundle B.

In Figure 6-5, we plot two such bundles: A lies on the budget constraint line and so is an optimal choice; B lies in the region below the budget line, and so is a feasible choice. However, the consumer chooses bundle A.

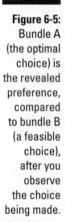

Figure 6-5:
Bundle A
(the optimal
choice) is
the revealed
preference,
compared
to bundle B
(a feasible
choice),
after you
observe
the choice
being made.

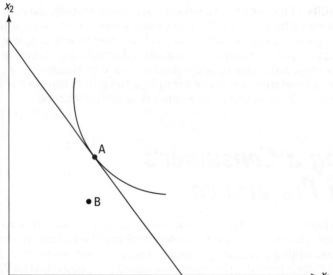

Until the consumer does something, microeconomists have no way of knowing his preferences for these bundles. Although you may be able to deduce the existence of A and B using axioms, you can't know for sure a consumer's preference. In the act of him consuming A, rather than B, therefore, you gain information about his preferences that you didn't previously possess. Thus, you can infer that bundle A is preferred to B from the choice made by the consumer.

With that done, you can directly break down the income and substitution effects for a change in price of a good, as we show in the next section.

Decomposing Income and Substitution Effects

The income and substitution effects of a change in prices occur simultaneously when someone makes a choice. When introducing these two effects in the earlier section 'Pivoting the budget line', however, we break them down so that the changes occur sequentially – pivoting the budget constraint indicated the substitution effect and shifting it indicated the income effect.

Although a good way of looking for both effects and considering their magnitude, here we go deeper and delve into the maths of what's going on. To do so microeconomists use a construction called the Slutsky equation to consider the relative magnitudes of the two effects, which allows them to say a little more about the merits – in terms of utility – of the two goods.

Remember that when a price changes, it causes two effects on the consumer:

- ✔ A substitution effect, which emerges when the budget line pivots, which shows how much of the change in consumption of one good changes relative to the other good.
- ✔ An income effect, which emerges when the budget line gets shifted to take into account a change in the total amount of money a consumer possesses.

Unpacking the effect of a price change in a model with two goods

In this walkthrough, we consider a change that allows a representative consumer to afford more of the two goods (see Figure 6-6).

The most important thing to note is that the consumption bundle indicated (x_1, x_2) is optimal in the sense that it's the highest utility available on the original budget line M_{old} and the pivoted budget line M_{new}.

Now, the equation of a budget line is (from Chapter 5):

$$M = p_1 x_1 + p_2 x_2$$

At this point two things have changed from the original optimum point: the price of good x_1 (p_1) and M (now associated with a new budget line and so must have also changed). This step in building the constrained optimisation model has, however, held utility constant by saying that the bundle (x_1, x_2) is available and works on both M_{old} and M_{new}.

Figure 6-6:
A change in consumption when a price falls. The consumer substitutes towards the cheaper good: $x_{1\ OLD}$ = old level of consumption of good x_1; $x_{2\ OLD}$ = old level of consumption of good x_2; $x_{1\ NEW}$ = post change consumption of good x_1; $x_{2\ NEW}$ = post change consumption of good x_2, I_1 = original indifference curve; I_2 = new indifference curve; M_{old} = old budget constraint; M_{new} = new budget constraint.

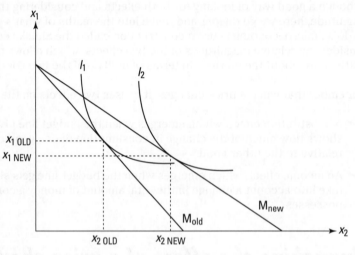

(x_1, x_2) works on both budget lines, and so you can write two equations describing its relationship to the original budget line and the changed one:

$$M = p_1 x_1 + p_2 x_2 \qquad \text{: original equation}$$
$$M' = p_1' x_1 + p_2 x_2 \qquad \text{: pivoted budget equation}$$

For consistency, the equations show M as the original sum of money and M′ as the changed sum, and p_1 as the original price of good x_1 and p_1' as the changed price.

Now subtract the first equation from the second and you get:

$$M' - M = x_1(p_1' - p_1)$$

Use the shorthand of Δ to indicate a change so that $M' - M = \Delta M$ and $p_1' - p_1 = \Delta p_1$, and substitute into the equation so that $\Delta M = x_1 \Delta p_1$.

Getting what you prefer

From the preceding section, you have a (slightly abstract) equation for determining what happens to income (M) and price (p_1) when a representative consumer wants to keep the quantity of x_1 he's consuming at the same level.

Here's an example to show how a consumer substitutes to keep utility at an optimum level. Carol has a bit of a coffee habit. Every week she allocates £10 of her disposable income to getting coffees at work. Each coffee – her choice is a vanilla latte – costs £2 (and she consumes up to her budget line, a maximum of £10, and has five coffees a week). Now suppose that her coffee rises to £2.20 – that's inflation, folks! – and she wants to keep her consumption at five delicious vanilla lattes a week. What must happen to her income to do so?

As the famous local microeconomist, Doug is asked to look at her purchasing patterns. Given her declared preference, he realises that she wants to keep x_1 (five lattes!) as a constant and he applies the formula from the preceding section. He knows that the price of a latte has risen by £0.20 (expressing the unit in pounds rather than pence). So Doug has two knowns, x_1 and Δp_1, and he can figure out M from the formula.

$\Delta M = x_1 \Delta p_1$ and so 5 (value of x_1) times 20 pence equals the change in income that Carol must gain to keep the value of her consumption constant. She does a quick piece of mental arithmetic to see that if her income rises by £1 a week she can keep consuming five lattes a week.

Developing the substitution effect in numbers

The model in the preceding section demonstrates the changes in M that keep the consumption level of x_1 static given a change in price. But when the budget line pivots, the bundle that was optimal usually is no longer optimal, because the relative prices of the two goods have changed, making one relatively dearer than before. Thus, the consumer is most likely to optimise by substituting towards the relatively cheaper option.

To talk this situation through in numbers, you start by making the amount of x_1 that the consumer wants to consume the subject of the equation, so that you have an expression for the consumer's demand.

Meeting the useful demand function

The demand for a bundle of x_1 is generally given as a function. A *demand function* relates the quantity of something consumed to the price of the good and the amount of income a consumer possesses.

Not specifying exactly for the moment the relationship between money and prices, here's the demand function for good x_1 given p_1 and M:

$$x_1 = x_1(p_1, M)$$

Discerning the change in demand

The purpose of the exercise is to evaluate x_1 (the old optimum) and x_1' the new optimum when p_1 and M change. The old level of demand is in the above equation and the new one is:

$$x_1 = x_1(p_1', M')$$

The substitution effect therefore measures the effect of the change in demand when the budget constraint pivots and is given by:

$$\Delta x_1{}^s = x_1(p_1', M') - x_1(p_1, M)$$

From this equation, you can see that when you know the change in demand and the level of money required to keep x_1 the same, you can work out the substitution effect (see the next section).

Calculating the substitution effect from a demand function

Here we make an assumption about the shape of a particular demand function and take a look at the substitution effect. Adam needs to use his car for transport and buys petrol in litres from the local garage. His demand is given by the simple form:

$$x_1 = 20 + M / 10 p_1$$

His allocatable income, M, is €240 and we assume that petrol costs €3 a litre. Prices for benchmark crude oil have plummeted and – somewhat implausibly – all that fall is being passed on to consumers – happy days! – meaning that Adam now pays a price of €2 a litre. As his microeconomist friend, you're fascinated by this change in his fortunes, and you want to calculate how large the substitution effect is as Adam changes consumption in response to price (as his demand function tells you he will).

You know from his choices which of two bundles Adam would prefer, because that was revealed when he chose. But to make a calculation, you need an idea of the general relationship between the price of petrol and the quantity demanded. Derived from knowing how much gets bought at any particular price, this is an example of a demand function (see the preceding section).

You're in a quandary: you want to show how much of the change in quantity consumed depends on substitution and how much on change in income, but you can't know that until you know the relationship between price and total change in demand. As we describe in the earlier section 'Discerning a Consumer's Revealed Preference', microeconomists never know what preferences exist until they're revealed by a consumer making a choice. You can't know until you've worked out that general relationship, but you need an understanding of the substitution and income effects in order to build the general relationship model. As a result, you have to start by gaining intuitions about how Adam may behave and then building up a consistent picture of the relationship between price and quantity.

Therefore, learning consumer theory is a little circular and requires you to use a demand function. In this example, Adam's demand function relates quantity consumed (x_1) to the price of good x_1 (p_1) and the amount of income he had M (€240). So you can start performing your clever calculations given a very simple relationship to work with!

To evaluate the size of Adam's substitution effect you go through a four-stage process:

1. **Take Adam's demand function and evaluate x_1 for M and p_1.**

   You know Adam's original demand, and so you calculate X_1 for the demand function. Plugging in 240 for M and 3 for p_1 you get 28 litres of fuel bought per week.

2. **Find the value of M′ that keeps x_1 the same when p_1 changes.**

   You apply the formula $\Delta M = x_1 \Delta p_1$. You know that x_1 equals 28 and that $\Delta p_1 = (2 - 3) = -1$, and so M must change by €–28. That means the value of M′ must be 240 – 28, which equals (ta-da!) €212.

3. **Plug M′ and p₁′ back into the demand function to evaluate new demand.**

   Going back to the original equation for Adam's demand for petrol, you put in the new numbers for M (€212) and p_1 and now calculate: $X_1 = 20 + 212 / (10 \times 2) = 30.6$ litres.

4. **Apply the formula for the substitution effect.**

   You use the equation

   $$\Delta x_1^{s} = x_1\left(p_1',M'\right) - x_1\left(p_1,M\right)$$

   and plug in 30.6 for $x_1\left(p_1',M'\right)$ – the new compensated demand from Step 3 – and 28 for $x_1\left(p_1, M\right)$ – the original demand. Therefore, the substitution effect is responsible for 2.6 litres extra of fuel being purchased per week.

If you simply plug in a value for p_1' in the original demand function you get an answer for the total change in demand (which you can verify by plugging in the numbers comes to 4 litres). But this way, you identify that of the 4 litre increase in demand, the substitution effect is responsible for 2.6 litres, or 65 per cent of the total change in demand!

You calculate the substitution effect by stripping out the effect of income (in other words, Step 2): finding the level of income that compensates for the change in price is key! If you don't find the compensated demand, you're looking at total change in demand and not the size of the substitution effect.

Totting up the income effect

The other effect of a change in price is to change the level of income. If the price of a good changes, it's tantamount to arguing that a consumer's income has also changed, because the budget line now either restricts the level of demand or allows consumption of goods that were previously unavailable.

In the preceding section, you model the change in income by shifting the budget line out. But you can also use some clever adaptations to that process to make a calculation of the income effect on Adam's demand – and of course adapt them to other demand situations.

To do so, define the income effect as the change in demand for a good when income changes from M to M′ and price is held constant at p_1'. This definition keeps the mathematical treatment in line with the graphic example in Figure 6-4 where the budget line first pivoted and then shifted.

To express the income effect mathematically, write:

$$\Delta x_1{}^n = x_1(p_1',M) - x_1(p_1',M')$$

Here p_1', the new price post-change, is held constant and you evaluate the demand for x_1 given that M changes to a new value M'.

Now plug in Adam's numbers from the preceding section. For the expression $x_1(p_1',M)$ calculate his demand using the changed price of 2 but the uncompensated level of income, 240. You get:

$$X_1 = 20 + 240/(10 \times 2) = 32$$

Evaluate demand given the compensated income from step 2 in the preceding section

$$X_1 = 20 + 212/(10 \times 2) = 30.6 \text{ litres}$$

and apply the formula for the income effect, taking the second answer from the first to get an answer of 1.4 litres of petrol.

The sum of the two effects comes to the total change in demand, and so although his demand changes by 4 litres overall, the income effect is responsible for 1.4 litres and the substitution effect for 2.6.

Putting the two effects together using the Slutsky equation

Put simply, the Slutsky equation says that the total change in demand is composed of an income and a substitution effect and that the two effects together must equal the total change in demand:

$$\Delta x_1 = \Delta x_1{}^s + \Delta x_1{}^n$$

This equation is useful for describing how changes in demand are indicative of different types of good. Indifference curves are always downward sloping, and so the substitution effect must always turn out to be negative. But the income effect may not be, depending on how consumption of a good changes with income. A normal good has a negative income effect, and so as income goes up demand goes up and as income goes down so does demand.

But not all goods are 'normal'; some are inferior in an economic sense. We don't mean that they're of poor quality, but that they have a negative income profile, so that for instance, as income goes up a person consumes less of them. Instant noodles, for instance, aren't generally held to be a product that people consume unless they're constrained in terms of money; as you get richer, you consume less of them. In this case, the substitution effect is negative but the income effect is also negative! For the opposite situation, see the nearby sidebar 'Giffen goods'.

Giffen goods

Although unusual, some cases exist where extreme trading down occurs so that as income goes down, the income effect is positive and the total change in demand turns out to be positive. These goods are known as Giffen goods after the economist who first investigated their existence during the Irish famine. They're often thought of as curiosities, but do exist, albeit as a small subset of the total set of inferior goods.

Part III
Uncovering the Alchemy of Firms' Inputs and Outputs

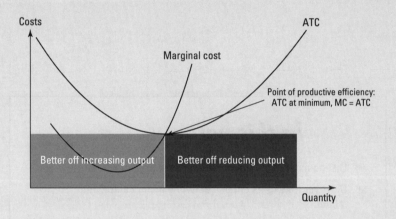

To see how firms decide on ways to reward their shareholders and how they go about it, visit www.dummies.com/extras/microeconomics.

In this part . . .

- ✔ Distinguish the different types of costs that firms face.
- ✔ Discover how firms choose between using capital and labour.
- ✔ See how firms and individuals come together to make markets.

Chapter 7

Working with Different Costs and Cost Curves

. . . .

In This Chapter

▶ Discovering two different views of costs

▶ Distinguishing average, total and marginal costs

▶ Connecting costs to staying in business

. . . .

*P*retty much all private production in an economy comes from firms. These firms make their decisions based on an indicator, *profit,* which expresses the difference between the revenues the firm takes in and the costs it expends in obtaining those revenues. To understand how a firm makes such decisions, as well as how economists look at them, you need to examine more closely the relationship between the different types of cost a firm faces – what economists call its *cost structure.*

In a market economy, and certainly in an economically liberal society, a firm can't simply march people to its showrooms, lock the doors and force them to buy its product (shame!). So although a firm may know a lot about prices and quantities, it doesn't necessarily know how much a consumer will want to buy at that price, at least until it starts to get data from transactions. Plus, it certainly can't control how much people will buy at that price (though it may have a good basis for guessing). Instead, economists look at the aspects of a firm's operations that it *does* control, which means looking seriously and carefully at its costs.

In this chapter we examine a firm through its *cost curves,* which provide a relationship between a given cost of production and how much a firm will produce for that cost. We define and investigate total, marginal and average costs, see how they interact within a firm and discuss their importance in firms surviving and continuing to trade or going under.

Understanding Why Accountants and Economists View Costs Differently

Economists look at costs in a particular way, which may not be what you expect. Every firm in every industry in every country incurs costs of one kind or another, and accounting systems provide a way of measuring and recording them. But economists aren't so interested in the record of what firms have done in the past but in the decisions that they may take in future. Therefore, economists have to look at costs in a different way.

In a set of company accounts, you find many items that describe costs, from costs of goods sold to overheads to general expenditure (these are *accounting costs*). Company accounts are produced to a set of standards that reflect the accounting profession's view of how best to describe the costs of a company, given that those costs are incurred in different ways and at different stages of production. As a result they report many different cost measures, and accountants know how to interpret these measures as needed.

Economists treat costs in a slightly different way called, unsurprisingly, *economic costs*. Whereas an accountant needs to know what costs *have accrued* over the past year, an economist wants to examine costs as they relate to the firm's decision-making. This involves some key subtleties, the most important of which is that economic costs account for the opportunities the firm had to give up in order to do what it's doing. Economists call these *opportunity costs*. In principle a firm has to account for them before going on to make any decisions about production or investment so that it knows it's making the decision on a rational basis.

If you're scratching your head a little, here's an example to relieve that itch.

Suppose that you gave up a decently paying job to start a business and at the end of your financial year your accountant sends you a statement saying that your revenue was in excess of your costs by £25,000. You're happy with this, considering that an accounting profit of £25,000 is a decent return on your business. But then your economist friend points out that the job you gave up was paying £35,000, which means that you gave up an opportunity to make £10,000 more than you received from your new business.

In fact, your *accounting profit* of £25,000 was an *economic loss* of £10,000 when you factor in the opportunity cost of giving up your old job to start your business. (Economics is called the dismal science for a reason!)

The upshot is that when looking at the individual types of cost a firm incurs, you can assume that we (and economists in general) are talking about *economic costs* that include *opportunity costs!*

Looking at a Firm's Cost Structure

When considering a firm, economists place emphasis on its cost structure – which means looking at what different types of cost contribute to the overall costs of the firm. As we discuss in this section, they tend to break down costs in different ways, depending on the parts of the picture they're looking at.

Typically microeconomists use three different ways to express the costs of a firm:

- ✔ **Total costs:** These look at the least level of detail.

- ✔ **Average costs:** These provide a view on how much producing a given level of output will cost *per unit.*

- ✔ **Marginal costs:** These tell economists something about how expensive adding an extra unit of output is going to be.

Economists also tend to break down costs into the following components, and use these relationships to discover something about the structure of a firm or the type of production it engages in:

- ✔ **Fixed:** Don't depend on the size of output.

- ✔ **Variable:** Depend on the size of output.

Taking in the big picture: Total costs

When talking about the types of cost a firm faces, economists start with the biggest and least detailed view of costs and then break them down in ways that make sense for economic decision-making.

The most global view of a company is in terms of its total costs (TC), which economists use quite simply to arrive at a number for total profits (you don't need to worry about gross or net terms here!). *Total costs* are simply the overall cost of making a product and serving it to a market after all those relevant cost elements are accounted for.

If you start with a number for total revenue received (TR) and then subtract all those costs, you arrive at a figure for profit. We write that as an equation here:

$$\Pi = TR - TC$$

The Greek symbol Π in the equation stands for profit, so that economists don't get confused with price (generally denoted with a P).

When you have that simple view as a firm owner, you may want to start looking at aspects of the total cost a little more closely. The simplest way to break down total costs is into two categories:

✔ **Costs that depend on the amount you've produced:** Includes all things that are ongoing in the sense that the more you produce – or for a service the more activity you undergo – the more you pay, which means things such as costs of each input used or the cost of utilities. These are called *variable costs* and economists usually denote them VC when talking about variable costs as an aspect of total costs.

✔ **Costs that don't depend on the amount you've produced:** Includes all the elements that your firm would have to pay regardless of how many items it produces. These may be the cost of premises, or licences if needed, or even the cost of advertising that the firm has to buy to let people know about it. Economists call these *fixed costs* and usually use the abbreviation FC for them.

Together, the two types of cost must sum to the total cost at which the firm operates, so we can say:

$$TC = FC + VC$$

Here's an example. A bicycle manufacturer makes bikes using labour, materials and utilities costing £10 a bike. Assuming that she makes 100 bikes, the variable costs of bicycle manufacture that she faces will be 100 bikes times £10 a bike, which equals £1,000. However, in order to do this she needs a factory with the capacity to make the bikes: that costs £10,000. So her total costs are fixed costs (£10,000) plus the variable costs of making 100 bikes (£1,000), which equals £11,000 total costs.

Here are two important points to bear in mind:

✔ You have to pay fixed costs even if you produce absolutely no output whatsoever. If, for instance, you take out a rental contract for an office, you have to pay the cost of rent irrespective of whether you produce anything at all.

✔ Variable costs depend on the amount of output you produce. If you have a pizza restaurant and you make no pizzas, you don't need any flour, tomatoes or even the power for a pizza oven. But the more pizzas you make, the more you spend on these inputs.

Measuring by unit: Average costs

By itself total cost doesn't say much about the firm and still less about how it makes its decisions. Economists want to discover a little more about how the firm operates and so they look at the relationship between total cost and the number of units produced. To do so, they divide the cost of production by the number of units produced to derive the *average costs*.

Making use of average costs

Average costs are useful things to know in and of themselves, but they also have some important properties that economists use to find out about the efficiency of production. To get them, you divide total costs (TC) by the quantity produced (Q)

$$ATC = TC / Q$$

where ATC is average total costs.

Now here's an interesting thing. As we describe in the preceding section, total costs break down into fixed costs (FC) and variable costs (VC). Therefore you can divide these components through by quantity to get average fixed costs (AFC) and average variable costs (AVC), which is the amount of fixed cost per unit and the amount of variable cost per unit. Or to put it another way:

$$ATC = TC / Q = (FC + VC) / Q = AFC + AVC$$

To discover the interesting thing, take a look at average fixed costs. Fixed costs don't change whatever the level of production, but as you go on producing more and more, the average fixed cost per unit falls as you divide by a bigger number each time.

Here's a very simple example. A baker needs to incur a cost of £100 for set up, premises and so on, and can then make a cake for £2 per cake. The total cost is the sum of fixed and variable costs. We use the more usual economics form and replace 'per cake' with Q (quantity produced) to get a formula for her total costs:

$$TC = 100 + 2Q$$

Now divide through by quantity to get average cost:

$$AC = 100 / Q + 2$$

We now plot some numbers for the average cost. In Table 7-1, we compute total and average costs according to this formula.

Table 7-1	Seeing the Relationship between Total, Average, Fixed and Variable Costs					
Quantity Produced:	*1*	*2*	*3*	*4*	*5*	*6*
Fixed cost	100	100	100	100	100	100
Variable cost	2	4	6	8	10	12
Total cost	102	104	106	108	110	112
Average total cost	102	52	35.333	27	22	18.667
Average fixed cost	100	50	33.333	25	20	16.667
Average variable cost	2	2	2	2	2	2

Take a look at the average total cost row. If you notice that the costs fall as we add more units, that's good! Now look at the costs broken down below (into fixed and variable components) and you see that the average fixed costs are particularly falling. Why? Well, a fixed cost doesn't depend on how much a firm produces: it still has to pay the same cost. In this case, though, because it's making more units, the fixed cost is being *divided* by more units each time, which means that as the firm makes more, the fixed cost gets smaller!

This fact is a key principle behind the concept of *economies of scale*. As the baker produces more cakes, she does so for a lower cost per cake!

Visualising economies of scale by plotting average costs

One way to see how this works is to plot the average cost over a range of production. The average cost curve is U-shaped. Over the range of output, as more gets made, the fixed costs get split into smaller parcels and average costs fall. (This may not always be the case in reality, but it's commonly seen in real firms, and it makes a decent enough working assumption for most models.)

This works well up to a point, beyond which the increase in variable costs from adding an extra unit is greater than the decrease in average fixed costs by adding more units. At this point economists say that the firm has fully exploited economies of scale and is experiencing *diseconomies of scale*.

Figure 7-1 shows that average fixed cost is always falling, because the same number is divided by a bigger number each time, but that average variable costs start to rise beyond a certain point. That point, where the average cost of production rises again, is the *minimum efficient scale* and is important for considering the efficiency of a firm. Just note it for the moment: we say more about what efficiency means in this context in Chapter 8.

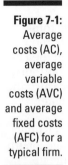

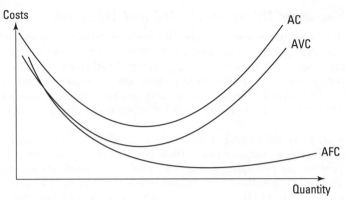

Figure 7-1:
Average costs (AC), average variable costs (AVC) and average fixed costs (AFC) for a typical firm.

Adding only the cost of the last unit: Marginal cost

The breakdowns we use in the preceding sections reveal the level of total cost or what that cost computes when attached to an individual unit of production. But economists also use another important measure to consider production: marginal cost.

Meeting marginal cost

Put simply, *marginal cost* is the cost of adding only one extra unit of production to your output. Imagine that you produce ten beach balls for £10 in total cost. If you add an extra beach ball to your production and make the total cost £11, the marginal cost of the 11th beach ball is £1, because that's how much producing an extra beach ball adds to your total costs.

Economists express marginal costs in terms of the *change in total costs,* which means that they're a change in total cost for a given change in quantity. Thus marginal costs are a measure not of how much something costs but how much those costs are changing as you do something to production.

'Marginal anything' in economics is important, because only the last incremental unit is relevant when making a decision. If you've already made 100 units, for example, those units are irrelevant for your next decision because you already made that decision! The relevant factor is the marginal cost of producing the 101st unit, because that's the next decision you face.

You can calculate marginal cost (MC) fairly simply, even across a number of units by remembering that it's the change in cost for a given change in quantity (Q). So quite simply taking the change in total cost (TC) and dividing by the change in quantity gives you an answer:

$$MC = (\text{Change in TC}) / (\text{Change in Q})$$

Tracking where MC crosses the AVC and ATC curves

Marginal cost curves always cross the average variable and average total cost curves at the minimum of those curves: that is, at the bottom of the U-shapes that make up both curves! (Average fixed costs are different: they can fall over the whole of the production range and therefore not have a bottom of the 'U'). This intersection has to happen, because marginal costs are also the thing that determines whether or not average costs are rising or falling.

To see why, we move away from costs and think about worms for a while (say what now?). Suppose that a biologist is working out the average length of wiggly worms in a sample. Suppose she's measured ten and come up with an average length of 10 centimetres. Now imagine that she's given an 11th sample. If the 11th worm is longer than 10 centimetres, the *average* length of the worms in her sample goes up. If it's less than 10 centimetres, of course the average in the sample goes down. But if the *marginal worm* is exactly 10 centimetres long, the average stays at exactly 10 centimetres.

Back to costs. Suppose that the average cost of producing ten units is £1. If the cost of adding an extra unit is greater than £1, the total cost of producing all the units is more than £11, and the average cost of production is more than £1. But suppose that the marginal cost of an extra unit is 90 pence. Then the total cost is £10.90 and average cost is 99 pence: average cost has fallen! On the other hand, if the marginal cost is exactly £1, average cost is also exactly £1!

So we have three cases:

- ✔ *Average cost falls* when the marginal cost of producing an extra unit is less than the average cost of producing all previous units.

- ✔ *Average cost rises* when the marginal cost of the extra unit is greater than the average cost of producing all preceding units.

- ✔ *Average cost stays the same* when the marginal cost of producing an extra unit is exactly the same as the average cost of producing the previous units.

You can see this effect illustrated graphically in Figure 7-2. These 'typical' average curves are split at their minimum points (bottom of the U) by a marginal cost curve!

Here's a key implication. To minimise costs, you want to be at the minimum of the average total cost curve. You're at that point when the marginal cost of adding an extra unit of production is exactly the same as the average costs of all the preceding units. So, to produce for the lowest possible cost, you know not to produce when the marginal cost is greater than average cost, and that if your marginal cost curve is below average cost you're better off in terms of cost when you expand your production up to the point where they're equal!

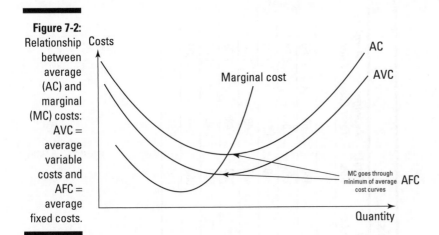

Figure 7-2:
Relationship between average (AC) and marginal (MC) costs: AVC = average variable costs and AFC = average fixed costs.

Putting it together: Cost structure of a simple firm

In this section we consider a simple firm example to show you how microeconomics looks at the cost structure of firms in general.

Zio Enzo's Pizza makes authentic Italian-style pizzas, and is considering how to minimise its costs. Enzo asks his daughter, Maura, to use her first-year microeconomics training to look at the firm's cost structure. She deduces the following:

- ✔ Fixed costs will be £100 per week, no matter how many pizzas are produced.

- ✔ A pizza-maker is paid £10 per hour for an 8-hour day.

- ✔ Enzo's has no variable costs other than the labour that goes into making them (implausibly, out of all the pizzerias in the world!).

- ✔ The variable cost that's relevant is the number of pizza-makers employed to produce the firm's output.

- ✔ The output initially improves as the firm hires more pizza-makers, because two can produce more output than one. But soon enough a bench full of pizza-makers start getting in each other's way as they fling dough around and reduce the net contribution of each successive pizza-maker.

Maura collects all the data together and summarises it (see Table 7.2).

Table 7.2   Cost Structure of Zio Enzo's

Workers	Output	Output per Worker	Fixed Costs	Average Fixed Costs	Variable Cost	Average Variable Cost	Total Cost	Average Total Cost	Marginal Cost
0			100	0					
1	50	50.0	100	2.00	80	1.60	180	3.60	1.60
2	140	70.0	100	0.71	160	1.14	260	1.86	0.89
3	220	73.3	100	0.45	240	1.09	340	1.55	1.00
4	290	72.5	100	0.34	320	1.10	420	1.45	1.14
5	350	70.0	100	0.29	400	1.14	500	1.43	1.33
6	400	66.7	100	0.25	480	1.20	580	1.45	1.60
7	440	62.9	100	0.23	560	1.27	660	1.50	2.00
8	470	58.8	100	0.21	640	1.36	740	1.57	

Here's what she can tell about the business from this breakdown of the cost structure. From the output per worker column she notices an interesting, but entirely normal phenomenon: more gain in output comes from adding the first incremental worker than from adding the eighth! As she suspected, the firm gains *increasing returns* from the first additional pizza-maker joining the team. But after adding the third, they start to get in each other's way, making their additional contribution to output decrease. The more workers she adds, the more their contribution to output falls.

Economists call this a case of *diminishing returns* to adding extra labour.

Now we plot the data points for average and marginal costs in Figure 7-3.

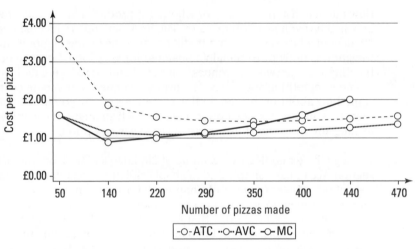

Figure 7-3:
Cost curves
for Zio
Enzo's: ATC
= aver-
age total
costs; AVC
= average
variable
costs;
(MC) =
marginal
cost.

Although both average cost curves are shallow (because of the low numbers of workers relative to the number of pizzas produced), they are, more or less, the U-shaped curves we talk about in the earlier section 'Tracking where MC crosses the AVC and ATC curves'. Also note that the marginal cost curve goes through both of those minimum points.

Applying microeconomic thinking to the cost-minimising level of production, therefore, Maura can tell her father that he makes himself best off at the point where he's employing three pizza-makers to do the work. (Clue – the lowest average variable cost of making pizzas is, as you can see from Table 7.2, at three workers. When you increase the number of pizza-makers by one, the marginal cost added is greater than the variable cost, and so you can see that you've passed the sweet spot and costs are now increasing again.)

Relating Cost Structure to Profits

The motivation for a firm staying in business is that its revenues exceed its costs (including opportunity costs – see 'Understanding Why Accountants and Economists View Costs Differently' earlier in this chapter for a definition): in other words, the firm is making profits. Therefore, we need to consider a firm's revenue side. In this section we introduce the ideas of profit maximisation and shutdown conditions.

Looking at firm revenue

How much a firm produces – or whether it produces at all – also depends on how much revenue a firm takes in. The firm can control its costs better than it can control its revenue, but it still needs to be taking in money in some way, or it is unlikely to remain a business for very long! Because profits are the difference between revenues generated and costs expended, you have to know something about how the firm's revenue relates to its costs to know something about profits. So, in this section, we show you how to manipulate revenue equations to see how much profit a firm might make and when not making anything and shutting down is the wisest option.

We begin by extending the example of Zio Enzo's Pizza from the preceding section. We make a simple and probably ridiculous assumption that Enzo's is a strict price taker (check out Chapter 10 for more on price takers and their opposite, price makers). Being a *price taker* means, quite simply, that Enzo's has no influence on the price that the market is willing to pay for the delicious, imaginary pizzas that Enzo makes. Instead we assume that the market is willing, in general, to pay £2 a pizza (perhaps it's a student area!), and that no relationship exists between Enzo and any competitors.

We introduce the formula to work out profits earlier in this chapter (in 'Taking in the big picture: Total costs'), but we restate it here:

$$\Pi = TR - TC$$

Now we take the term for total revenue and expand it. Total revenue (TR) received for selling Q units of a product at price P is:

$$TR = P \times Q$$

So how can the firm discover whether $P \times Q$ is greater than total costs, and if so by how much? Here's a trick: average total cost (ATC) is TC divided by Q, and so ATC multiplied by Q is TC. Therefore:

$$\Pi = (P \times Q) - (ATC \times Q)$$

The two terms for revenue and costs contain Q, and so we divide both sides by Q to drop it out. For profits, the result is an unwieldy formula; instead, we focus on the two terms on the right-hand side of the equation.

Doing so tells you that if P (the price a firm receives for its output) is greater than average total cost, the firm supplying that good makes economic profits greater than zero. If the price is less than average total cost, the firm is taking losses. When the two are equal, revenues are equal to economic costs, and the firm makes economic profits of zero. The optimal condition for how much a firm should be willing to supply (the best that it can possibly do given its costs and revenues) is satisfied when the marginal cost of producing an extra unit is equal to the marginal revenue received from it.

Hitting the sweet spot: When MC = MR

When the marginal revenue gained from an extra sale is equal to the marginal cost incurred in making the good, the producer is maximising its profits. Put another way, if supplying an extra unit costs more than it receives for doing so, a firm's better off not doing it!

When making a decision, the firm is interested only in the last incremental unit of the product, whether talking about revenues or costs. All previous production is irrelevant: the firm just needs to focus on whether to make the last unit and, given that, whether producing the unit yields a profit.

Take a look at Figure 7-4 and you can see that we add a new line (compared to Figure 7-3) for the marginal revenue (MR) gained from selling an extra pizza. The assumption we make in the preceding section – Enzo's is a strict price taker – means that in this case marginal revenue is a horizontal line at a price of £2.

Figure 7-4:
Optimal
production
decision for
Zio Enzo's:
ATC =
average
total costs;
MC =
marginal
costs;
MR =
marginal
revenue.

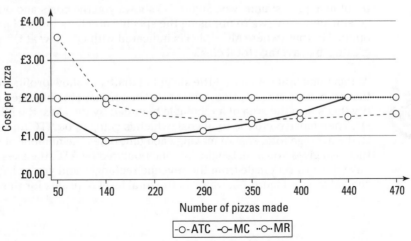

Notice that the marginal cost line crosses this line only where MC = MR, which is exactly at 440 pizzas (yum, breakfast!). So Enzo's will be making the optimal production decision where it produces 440 pizzas – where exactly as much is yielded from selling one more pizza as it costs to make.

This concept is so important that we now think about it in another way. Look at the earlier Table 7-2 and notice that the marginal cost of all the pizzas before the 440th is less than £2. Now look at the 400th pizza, which Enzo can make for a marginal cost of £1.60. If he were to make 400 pizzas, the marginal pizza would yield revenue of £2 but have a cost of only £1.60, which, you'd suppose, would make for one happy Enzo.

But he'd be forgoing all the positive revenue he could make by selling pizzas numbers 401 to 440. Therefore, he'd be better off expanding his production to the level where the cost and benefit are equal. But if he were paying more than £2 to make a pizza that only yields £2, he'd be better off reducing his output until the two were equal!

The very best production decision a firm can make is when MC = MR.

Viewing profits and losses

Here are two observations concerning profits and losses for a firm under the condition of producing optimally:

- ✔ Setting Q so that MC = MR allows the firm to make the optimal output.
- ✔ At Q* (the optimal amount of production) where MC = MR the firm isn't guaranteed a profit, but if it can make profits, it maximises them (and if it must take losses, this output minimises them).

We now walk you through understanding whether a firm will or won't make a profit in a quite simple way. Figure 7-5 shows you the costs and output for a generic company (we're not using the specific numbers for Zio Enzo's). The optimal output (where MC = MR) is indicated with Q*. Now at Q*, price is greater than average total costs.

At this point you can use a little sleight of maths to show profits: remember that revenue is simply price × quantity. On our mapping of price and quantity that's also the area of a rectangle bounded by the axes, the MR line and Q*. Then move on to the total cost, which is going to be ATC times Q*, that is, the average total cost of making each unit times the number of units: that also gives you a rectangle, but one bounded by ATC, the axes and Q*. Take the cost rectangle from the revenue rectangle, and you're left with the shaded area in Figure 7-5, which is the total level of profits for this firm!

Figure 7-5:
Profits for a
price-taking
firm when
P > ATC:
ATC =
average
total cost;
AFC =
average
fixed cost;
MC =
marginal
costs; MR
= marginal
revenue; Q*
= Optimal
amount of
production;
P = price.

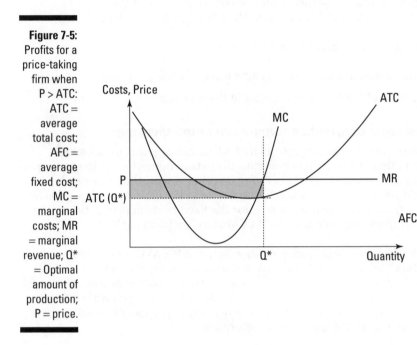

Peer deeper into the cost and revenue equations and you see that the only difference between the size of the rectangles is the difference between P and ATC. Taking P – ATC gives you the height of the box and multiplying by Q* provides its width, and there you have it – profits and another nice new formula for it:

$$\Pi = (P - ATC) \times Q$$

If, of course, the price received by the firm is less than average total cost of producing the good, the firm isn't making profits but taking losses. We use this important condition for the firm in the next section, where we talk briefly about why a firm may want to stop producing and under what circumstances.

Staying in business and shutting down

The simple fact is that if a firm doesn't make profits it doesn't tend to stay a firm for long. Even companies that are well run, well capitalised and innovative, or have other advantages can find themselves in this position, which is one reason why exiting a market is as important a consideration to an economist as the decision of whether to enter one or not.

In Chapter 10 we describe a specific model you can use for *perfectly competitive* market structures, but here we look briefly at this issue in a much simpler way (and refer you to the juicy details in Chapter 10!).

Economists are interested in two cases:

- ✔ What would induce a firm to exit a market in the short run?
- ✔ What would induce a firm to exit in the long run?

Not making a contribution? Shut down in the short run

In the short run, the assumption is that a firm can operate, for a limited amount of time, without fully covering all costs of operation, as long as it's covering the variable cost of operating. In other words, the price received for a sale covers the cost of producing the item. If you're doing this, you can at least get forbearance from people for the fixed costs of production in the hope that times improve and you'll be able to pay them back.

Thus the short-run shutdown condition is that if P < AVC then continuing to produce isn't rational. If you do continue producing at this level, everything you receive from an extra unit is less than the cost of producing it and therefore every unit you sell makes a loss! At this point, because you can't sell negative quantities of anything, the best thing you can do is *not* produce, because the more you produce, the more you lose!

Factory gets the blues

You rarely find a business operating when the price is less than average variable cost (P < AVC). One cherished example, however, comes from the celebrated record label Factory, which agreed to produce a single, 'Blue Monday' by New Order, in an extremely expensive laser-cut sleeve. The packaging was so expensive that the first pressing lost money on every copy sold (eventually the firm twigged, and came up with cheaper packaging for future releases).

A lot of copies were sold and so Factory lost a large amount overall, taking greater losses the more it sold. The single is often regarded as a classic, both in music and design, but Factory is never cited as a positive example in business textbooks!

Not covering all costs: Shut down in the long run

In the long run, a firm needs to cover all its costs of operation, even those for which it can get short-term forbearance. For instance, if you borrow money for a business loan, when times are hard you may be able to get your bank to agree to you deferring some of the payment or making reduced payments.

Suppose that the fixed costs of operation were $1,000 and that the firm is producing, optimally, Q*. Suppose further that the variable costs at Q* are $500 and the revenues coming in are $800. In this case, the firm is covering its variable costs of $500 and so doesn't have to shut down in the short run. It can make a bargain with its creditors to pay only $300 of the fixed costs back, for a while, and depending on their grace they may agree to that bargain. The result to the firm is an overall loss of $700 rather than a loss of $1,000 if it produces nothing, and so producing is better than not producing.

These payments can't be put off forever, however, only deferred temporarily. As a result, the long-run shutdown condition is met and the firm would still be better off not accruing losses. Instead, the firm operates for a while on the grounds that it's better off producing than not producing, but eventually accrues losses that it can't restructure away and has to shut down.

Chapter 8

Squeezing Out Every Last Drop of Profit

● ●

In This Chapter

▶ Examining whether a firm really is a profit maximiser

▶ Looking at how a firm maximises profits in the short and long run

▶ Understanding how firms minimise costs

● ●

*E*conomists tend to begin their analysis of firms with the assumption that the firm is a *profit maximiser* – that is, the firm's ultimate aim is making the most profit it can. Although microeconomics doesn't stop there (and has produced a number of analyses of firm motivation and results that don't rely on this assumption), the profit-maximising firm is the basic building block of microeconomic analysis.

In this chapter we justify the idea that a firm is in practice a profit maximiser. We also look at profit maximisation more closely, showing how it rests at the heart of economists' conception of efficiency and how profit-maximising firms choose the optimum amount of stuff to produce. In addition, we also discuss the opposite approach to achieving the same end: minimising costs while maintaining the desired output.

Take a moment to catch your breath as you've quite a ride ahead!

Asking Whether Firms Really Maximise Profits

In most cases, economists assume that firms want to maximise their profits and that, as a result, they make their decisions on this basis.

Here's a possible objection to this assumption: economists are thinking about a firm as a very simple thing, quite unlike the complex entities that firms are in reality. All the following conditions may not be ones that can or will exist in reality:

- ✔ No shareholders
- ✔ Management has unified interests
- ✔ No internal issues between departments
- ✔ People turn up on time and do the job for which they're employed
- ✔ No hidden incentives not to make profit in the tax system

But suppose that you know nothing about a company and that you don't know that all those things are the stuff of working life. How would you then make a representation of a firm? What goals, behaviours or practices would you guess that this non-representative firm would engage in?

In this scenario, profit maximisation is a reasonable assumption to make. Of course, if you know about particular reasons why a given entrepreneur has made a decision, you can guess at a lot more information about the firm. But if you know next to nothing about the individual case, the only assumption that makes sense is that the firm intends to maximise its profits.

None of this, of course, means that profit maximisation is always the goal of the organisation. As a simple example, think of a company whose shareholders want to receive the highest possible level of returns whereas the management of the company wants to hold on to their jobs or take as many of the potential returns for themselves. If the managers have sufficient bargaining power over the shareholders, they can affect the decisions of the firm in their own interests.

Talking about efficiency, in the long and short run

When a firm maximises its profits effectively, it's acting efficiently. Economists like efficiency and deplore waste. Whatever you do in business, they prefer that you make efficient use of your capital and other resources. If you take the lowest point of the average cost curve – where the marginal cost curve crosses the average cost curve – you've found the most efficient level of production and at the point where marginal revenue equals marginal cost (that is, MR = MC: see Chapter 7). We take a moment now to explain – ahem, efficiently – why these two efficiency conditions are so important.

When economists discuss efficiency, they're most likely talking about the following two conditions:

- **Productive efficiency:** Exists when a firm can't increase output without increasing the quantity of inputs used to make that output.

- **Allocative efficiency:** Exists when making one party better off is impossible without making another party worse off (also called *Pareto efficiency* after celebrated Italian economist Vilfredo Pareto).

These two definitions are distinct, meaning that satisfying allocative efficiency without satisfying productive efficiency is possible. To see why, we look at the two concepts in a bit more detail.

Productive efficiency: Producing for the lowest possible cost

Productive efficiency is satisfied when a firm can't possibly produce more output without increasing the quantity of inputs needed to produce that output. It's met when the firm is producing at the minimum of the average cost curve, where marginal cost MC equals average cost AC.

Why is that? At the minimum of the average cost curve, economies of scale are at their highest possible level and production at its cheapest possible level. If a firm expands production beyond that point it incurs a marginal cost higher than the revenue received and is therefore better off reducing its output until it hits the lowest possible cost point (at the point where MC = AC). But if the firm is producing less than the optimal point, it can make itself better off when it increases production to a level where MC = AC.

These conditions are exactly the same as the profit-maximising conditions that we talk about in Chapters 3 and 7! So you can go a bit further and say that, at the point where a firm is maximising its profits, it's also productively efficient!

In Chapter 13, you can use the concept of productive efficiency to tell you a lot about how a market is operating. One application we mention here is in considering how society should treat natural monopolies – those companies that yield sufficient economies of scale relative to the size of the total market that they're unlikely to ever face a direct competitor. One thing economists notice is that these companies tend to operate inefficiently; that is, that they don't tend to operate at the lowest possible cost (and that consumers are consequently hurt by this, as inefficiencies get pushed on to the consumer in the form of lower quality or quantity and/or higher prices.)

We summarise productive efficiency in Figure 8-1: the two shaded areas reveal how the firm can become better off by making itself more productive.

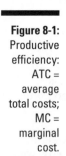

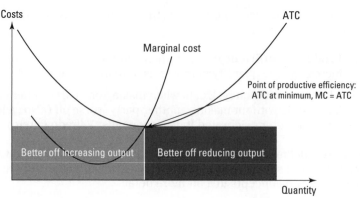

Figure 8-1:
Productive
efficiency:
ATC =
average
total costs;
MC =
marginal
cost.

Allocative efficiency: Can you make one party better off without making another worse off?

Allocative efficiency is related to the concept of Pareto efficiency that econo-mists use to look at social welfare – see Chapter 12, but it has important aspects that are driven by efficiency in production. Essentially, if something is allocatively efficient one party can't possibly be made better off without making another party worse off. Here's a simple example to illustrate the point. Suppose that Alice and Bob are allocated money from a central pot of £100, and you record the allocations twice:

✔ In the first round you allocate the whole £100 and Alice and Bob get half, £50, each. Now within this framework, you can't give either Alice or Bob more without making the other worse off, and so the distribution is allocatively efficient.

✔ If, however, you hold back £1 and distribute £99 to Alice and Bob, any distribution between the two isn't allocatively efficient, because you can simply release the £1 and make either party better off, *without making the other worse off!*

In the context of production, when a firm is operating at lowest possible cost, it's also allocating efficiently its budget for inputs between capital and labour. This occurs – you guessed it! – when the average cost of the firm is at a minimum!

We use this concept of efficiency in Chapter 12, when we talk about welfare in general. For the moment, we just want to introduce the idea that when all firms operate at their minimum cost, welfare in society is maximised.

Checking the long and the short run

Economists distinguish between the long- and short-run position of a firm. They do so because a firm can find itself in a number of positions where it can't fully react to change immediately and therefore makes slightly different decisions to the optimal one, until it's fully capable of reacting to whatever change – pricing, technological, demand or whatever – has taken place.

Economists want to be more precise about what the terms long and short run mean, without specifying a particular time interval (for example, a month) that will be different for firms in different industries: for example, finding an exploitable oil deposit may take longer than writing a couple of lines of code. The definition economists use is simple: in the long run the firm is able to change its use of all factors of production – labour, capital, land – whereas in the short run the firm's limited to imperfect adjustment, usually of only one factor.

As an example, imagine that a firm employs ten people to do a job working on ten machines. Suppose that the lease it pays for the machines becomes more expensive, so that the firm would be better off employing only eight machines and eight people. Suppose, further, that it's able to return the machines to the lease company without any further ado, but that making a person redundant involves a process that can take up to a month:

- ✔ **In the short run:** The firm adjusts its use of machines – capital – without adjusting its use of labour. Thus, over this short-run period the firm isn't operating at its long-run most effective use of resources.

- ✔ **In the long run:** After the firm negotiates all relevant legal redundancy conditions, it can operate even more cheaply. Assuming profit maximisation is its aim, it moves towards doing so.

Microeconomists express this situation by looking at costs in the short and long run. To an economist, any short-run average total cost (SRATC) curve must be by definition less *elastic* – that is, price responsive – than a long-run average total cost (LRATC) curve. Therefore, in a diagram, a SRATC curve is steeper, reflecting the lower ability to adjust in the short run (as costs go up, output doesn't change as much as in the long run). Because a profit-maximising firm wants to operate at the best point in the short run, the minimum of SRATC, the LRATC curve connects all the best short-run curves together, so that all the minimum points of all the SRATC curves join to form one single LRATC curve.

We illustrate this condition in Figure 8-2. Remember that a short-run marginal cost curve goes through the minimum of each of the SRATC curves, and the long-run marginal cost (LRMC) is more elastic – price and cost responsive – than in the short run.

Figure 8-2:
Costs in short and long run: SRATC = short-run average total costs; LRATC = long-run average total costs; LRMC = long-run marginal cost.

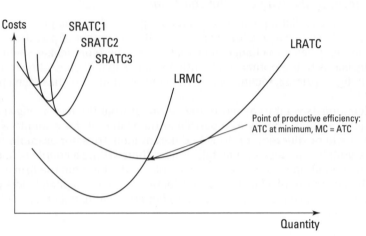

Going Large! The Goal of Profit Maximisation

In the preceding section, we explain why economists assume that firms seek to maximise their profits. Here, we tell you a little more about that profit-maximising process. To do so we need to make a few little extensions to the model of the firm we use in Chapter 7 to take account of how the firm changes its decisions when inputs change. The most important of them is that we're going to express output in terms of two inputs, capital and labour, and their respective prices, the cost of capital and the wage rate.

Firms can use two methods to work out how to use their inputs to make outputs: the profit-maximising approach of this section and the cost-minimising approach (see the later section 'Slimming Down! Minimising Costs'). Although eventually they lead to the same place – assuming you do the relevant calculations right! – they arrive via slightly different journeys. Wherever you're going though, you need a place to start and we begin with something called a production function.

Understanding a production function

A *production function* is a mathematical description of how a firm makes its output. For a simple firm with only one input a production function may be:

$$f(x_1)$$

Here, f is the firm's production function and x_1 is the amount of an input – for example labour. If you know the amount of the input x_1 and the shape of the function f, this equation shows that you know how much the firm will output. We now add the second input – we hold it constant because we're going to look at the short run first – and then use a little maths to say something about how much the two inputs cost.

We call the production function f, the two inputs x_1 and x_2 and their respective costs w_1 and w_2. We begin by spelling out the production function:

$$f(x_1, x_2)$$

That shows a relationship between inputs and outputs but not profit: the f part of the expression explains that it's a relationship, the x_1 and the x_2. For the moment, we're not spelling out exactly what that relationship is mathematically! To know about the firm's profits, we need to know about the revenue gained from the outputs and the cost of obtaining the inputs. The revenue side is very simple. If you know the output level, multiply it by price (P) and you have total revenue (TR):

$$TR = P\,f(x_1, x_2)$$

And for total costs (TC):

$$TC = (w_1 x_1 + w_2 x_2)$$

Because we're holding the second input constant in the short run, we call it $\bar{x}_2$. It won't be changing, and so we can treat it as a constant.

From the original production function we can combine the two above equations to make a profit function that we want to maximise:

$$\max p - f(x_1, x_2) - w_1 x_1 - w_2 x_2 \text{ with respect to } x_1$$

Meeting the isoprofit curve

We now substitute output, y, for the production function for a moment and use that to draw a picture. Again, we'll use the Greek letter π for profit. The equation is now:

$$\pi = py - w_1 x_1 - w_2 x_2$$

We make output the subject of the equation to get an *isoprofit* curve, which is a curve on which all points yield the same level of profit. In the equation above, profits could change if p, y, or one of the ws or one of the xs changes. On an isoprofit curve, we hold π, profits, constant for any point on the same curve, and plot the relationship between inputs and outputs for a given level of profit. We rearrange the equation to make y the subject:

$$y = \frac{\pi}{p} + \frac{W_2}{p} x_2 + \frac{w_1}{p} x_1$$

This equation shows that the expression on the left-hand side, all those terms that don't include an x_1, is constant and where the curve intercepts the y axis. The expression on the right, referring to x_1, gives the slope of the line, $\frac{w_1}{p}$.

Looking at profit maximisation using isoprofit curves

Now we turn to the concept of the *marginal* – the incremental change (see Chapter 7). In this case the incremental change we're interested in is the change in production at the margin. The slope of the production function is the measure of how production changes as x_1 changes. In general, the marginal change in output is called marginal product, but here the relationship only exists between x_1 and output, because we kept x_2 constant!

In Figure 8-3 we illustrate maximisation using these expressions. You can see three isoprofit curves, but only isoprofit 2 is possible and optimal. Why?

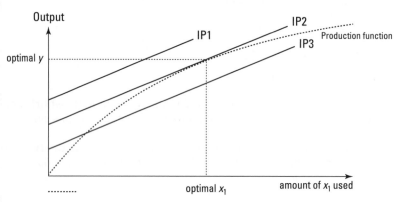

Figure 8-3: Profit maximisation for one factor using three isoprofit curves: IP1 = isoprofit 1; IP2 = isoprofit 2; IP3 = isoprofit 3.

Well, at isoprofit 2 the marginal product (MP, slope of the production function) is equal to the cost of the input used divided by the price received at market for your output. Or to put it more succinctly:

$$MP = w_1 / P \text{ or } P - MP = w_1$$

To discover what this means, we ask Jeph the Joiner, proprietor of Jeph's Joinery. He has a job on at the moment making chair legs for an interior designer. He wants to know, given that all the equipment he could use is fixed in the short run, how many people to employ at what wage in order to make as much profit as possible. His cousin Emma the Economist takes a look at his figures and says that he should employ up to the point where the contribution of the marginal worker is such that multiplying output by price equals the wage that Jeph will pay.

Jeph knows his hardwoods but not his margins and asks for the answer with less jargon. Emma says: suppose that you're making your chair legs and you know that the next one – the marginal one – is going to yield £10 in revenue. Now suppose that you have to hire someone for a cost of £11. If the cost is greater than the marginal revenue, you make yourself better off by *not* producing that unit (£11 is greater than £10 and you'd lose £1 on the output). If the cost of hiring is only £9, however, you'd make a surplus of £1. But you make yourself better off still, assuming that you can sell the product, by hiring up until the cost of hiring equals the value of the marginal product – that is, the marginal revenue – you yield from selling the output!

Microeconomics lays great stress on the concept of the margin for exactly this reason. The best that a firm can possibly do is when the marginal benefit it gets is equal to the marginal cost of achieving it.

Maximising profit in the long run

Here's a quick question for you: what's the difference between the short and the long run to an economist? If you say that in the long run all factors are variable, you're correct! If not, take a look at the earlier section 'Talking about efficiency, in the long and short run' before reading on. When you're clear on this issue, you can go on with the next bit, safe in the knowledge that extending the model to two inputs isn't so difficult.

I wonder if, after reading the preceding section, you want to say 'hang on a minute; that situation's unrealistic – only one factor changes!' You're right, because in the example Jeph's Joinery is considering only the short run. What happens in the long run?

Essentially, if a position minimises average costs in the short run, it must lie on the long-run average cost curve (see the earlier Figure 8-2). We use that fact to point out that the only thing that has changed when moving to the long-run equilibrium is that now the last equation in the preceding section must apply *to each input* and not just one. Thus for two inputs x_1 and x_2 you get a pair of conditions:

$$p \, \mathrm{MP}_1\left(x*_1, x*_2\right) = w_1$$

$$p \, \mathrm{MP}_2\left(x*_1, x*_2\right) = w_2$$

Here, * denotes that these values of x – the quantity produced – are the optimum – the levels that are the best we can do – for x_1 and x_2!

Profit-maximisation problems tend to follow these forms, though they can get more complicated than our simple presentation. Sometimes economists are interested in a different, though related, type of question, such as what to do if the price of one input changes and not the other, or what happens when firm technology changes. We discuss an adaptation of the model for that – the cost-minimisation model – in the next section.

Slimming Down! Minimising Costs

In the preceding section, we discuss a firm maximising its profit by choosing a level of inputs that allows it to produce a given level of profit. Now we rearrange the problem slightly and assume that the firm wants to reduce its costs to the minimum level while making a desired level of output. To do so, the firm chooses how much to use of two inputs, called x_1 and x_2, as we define them in the earlier section 'Understanding a production function'. But unlike in that section, we want to choose a way of minimising the cost – w.

Economists write this problem in a new way, using two equations to represent it:

$$\text{Min } w_1x_1 + w_2x_2$$
$$x*_1, x*_2$$
$$\text{Such that } f(x_1, x_2) = y$$

The min means choose values of x_1 and x_2 that make everything in the equation $(w_1x_1 + w_2x_2)$ as small as possible. The values we're choosing for x are optimal values, and we call those x^*_1 and x^*_2 with the * meaning an optimal value.

The second equation, which equates the production function to the level of output, is called an *isoquant* – meaning that all points on the same curve yield the same level of output, in this case y. Now we alter the first equation above to see another facet of the equation: we look *for a given level of cost,* which we denote C. We do so by rearranging a little so that:

$$w_1x_1 + w_2x_2 = C$$

Rearrange this so that we can put x_2 on the vertical axis in the graphs (see Figure 8-4) and we get:

$$x_2 = \frac{C}{w_2} - \frac{w_1}{w_2}x_1$$

In this rearrangement of the equation, the quantity of x_2 used is a function of the constant level of cost and the relative price of x_1. Given that the price of x_1 is w_1, the relative price of x_1 is w_1/w_2. Now, when plotted on a graph, it becomes a straight line with a slope of $-w_1/w_2$ and an intercept on the y axis of C/w_2.

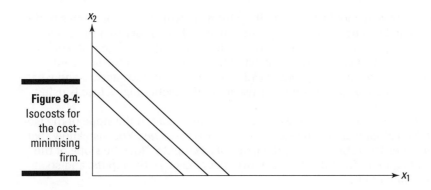

Figure 8-4:
Isocosts for the cost-minimising firm.

We allow C to change to create a set of lines, each of which has the same total cost, whatever that is, and the slope of $-w_1/w_2$. Called *isocosts* (see Figure 8-4), these are all downward-sloping parallel lines. Every point on an isocost has the same cost and higher isocost lines have higher costs.

The final step is to put the isoquant and isocost together. We restate the problem as finding a point on an isoquant line with the lowest possible isocost associated with it. This happens at a point of tangency between the isoquant and isocost, which is a more mathematical way of saying that at the optimal point the slopes of the isocost and the isoquant are equal (see Figure 8-5).

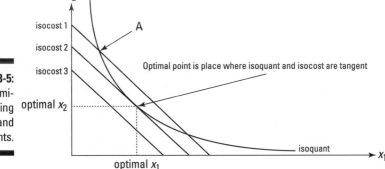

Figure 8-5:
Cost minimisation using isocosts and isoquants.

The only place that can be optimal is the point where the two curves are tangent. Taking a look at the isoquant, you can see that an infinite number of combinations of inputs can make up that fixed output. However, point A for example is on a higher isocost than the optimal and therefore wouldn't be chosen, because the same output can be produced for a lower cost, and the firm wants to minimise those costs.

You can derive a cool further condition from knowing about the slopes of the isoquant and isocost and how they must match. Remember that the slope of something is generally an indication of how much it's changing at a given point. Economists are interested in what the changes along the isoquant reveal about the marginal product (MP) of the two inputs x_1 and x_2, and what the ratio of the marginal products says about the technology a firm is using.

Here, remember that the slope of the isocost must match the slope of the isoquant. You already know the slope of the isocost: $-w_1/w_2$. You also know that this matches the ratio between the price of the inputs. Now the slope of the isoquant is the ratio of the marginal product of each of the inputs, and so at the optimum point:

$$MP_1 / MP_2 = -w_1 / w_2$$

The bit on the left side is the ratio between the marginal product of the two inputs at the optimum. It's also known as the *technical rate of substitution,* because it describes the rate at which a firm gives up one input in order to add increasing units of another input. Because economists generally assume diminishing returns when substituting, the isoquant must slope continuously downwards for this type of analysis to be what economists call 'well behaved' – this captures diminishing returns to substituting one unit of one input for one unit of another.

Chapter 9

Supplying the Demanded Information on Supply and Demand

· ·

In This Chapter

▶ Looking at the supply curve

▶ Demanding to see the market demand curve

▶ Seeing how a market equalises supply and demand

· ·

*I*f anything exemplifies microeconomics, it's the famous model of supply and demand in a marketplace. Aspects such as constrained optimisation (Chapter 6) or firm production decisions (Chapters 7 and 8) are of course important, but microeconomics really comes into its own with the supply and demand model. In many ways it's the most powerful tool in the micro-economist's toolkit.

The supply and demand model is a centrepiece of economics, because it adds to the understanding of the consumer and producer by letting them interact through the medium of exchange. This exchange is usually voluntary and likely to benefit both parties, though not necessarily to the same extent. The supply and demand model is also the bedrock of the discussions of different types of market that we cover in Chapters 10 to 12.

So if you – ahem – demand an explanation on supply and demand, and how the market seeks equilibrium between the two, we're happy to – ahem ahem – supply one!

Producing Stuff to Sell: The Supply Curve

Producers in a market are generally organisations of people. These firms set their levels of production to be optimal in terms of costs, seeking to produce (that is, *supply*) up to the point where marginal revenue equals marginal cost and attempting to get their long-run average costs down to as low a level as they can. The marginal (and indeed average) costs of production are related to the technology a firm chooses to get the best level of output for the combination of inputs chosen.

These features of production characterise the individual *rational* firm, which seeks to maximise its profits or minimise its costs – given the conditions in the marketplace.

But economists also want to analyse what a collection of firms does – that is, an industry – as well as the actions of just one. They want to aggregate the decisions of individual firms so that they can clearly see how this simple behaviour at the firm level influences the prices and quantities of things made and exchanged in a market. The supply curve is one way of going from an individual firm to an industry.

Moving from marginal costs to firm supply

You can go easily from an individual firm's supply to industry supply by adding up, horizontally, the marginal cost curves of the individual firms in the relevant industry. In this section, we describe how this process works.

Marginal costs

The *marginal cost* (see Chapter 7) of producing anything is the cost of producing only the last unit of that good; it tells you what happens to cost when adding one extra unit to production. At the margin, the firm produces up to where marginal cost (MC) of producing a new unit equals marginal revenue (MR) – the revenue gained from selling one extra unit. Thus, the rational profit-maximising firm chooses its production so that MC = MR.

If the market in which the firm operates is perfectly competitive – the firm is a *price taker* that accepts the market price without being able to influence it – the marginal revenue received is just the same as the market price, and so price equals marginal cost.

Another way of telling how competitive a market is in reality is by seeing whether the price at which producers can sell their product is at or close to the marginal cost. If it is, the market is very likely to be competitively supplied. If not, the market is likely to be dominated by one firm or have some other anti-competitive features. The firm in the competitive market uses this relation between MC and MR to solve the profit-maximisation problem, so that it can set its best – optimal – level of output given the price it can get in the market. That means maximising the difference between total revenue and total costs.

This problem features an important assumption: the price received by the firm isn't related to its strategic decisions. Therefore, whatever the firm decides with respect to its output, price doesn't change, which is another way of saying that a firm is a price taker.

We start by making the total costs of the firm a function of its output, meaning that as output changes, cost changes. We write that function as $c(q)$.

In other words, costs (c) are dependent on the output produced (q). This is called the *cost function* for the firm.

Revenue costs

For the revenue side, total revenue (TR) is given by the quantity produced, which is – again – q times the price of the good, p: TR = pq.

Profits equal the difference between cost and revenue, and so the firm wants to maximise: $pq - c(q)$. Plus, it wants to do so by choosing the best level of q.

If you look at the marginal terms as described here and in Chapter 7, you can see that marginal revenue is the rate of change of revenue when output changes. If a firm increases its output by a change in q (write as Δq) then the change in revenue, ΔR, is $\Delta R = p\Delta q$.

But at this point, price is assumed not to change as q changes and so price must be quite simply given as $\Delta R / \Delta q = p$.

Yet this expression is exactly the expression for marginal revenue – it tells you that you're to evaluate the change in revenue as output changes, which is exactly, by definition, what marginal revenue expresses! So until you change to build a model that allows price to change in response to firm decisions, price equals marginal revenue.

Cost side

We write marginal cost (MC) in this case as $c'(q)$, which tells you to look at the change in costs as q changes. Doing so, you can rewrite it as MC(q).

Firm supply curve

Okay. Now that you have an expression for marginal revenue and marginal cost, you can notice that if price isn't dependent on a given firm's output, it produces up to the point where $p = MC(q)$.

This relation is the foundation of the supply curve for a firm. It relates the price of a good to the marginal cost of supplying one extra unit of this good. Therefore, it expresses the firm's decision in terms of price and quantity, which is the relationship shown in a supply curve!

In Figure 9-1 we plot the marginal cost curve for a price-taking firm as a relationship between the cost or price of a good and the quantity that the firm will make of the good: this is the *firm supply curve*.

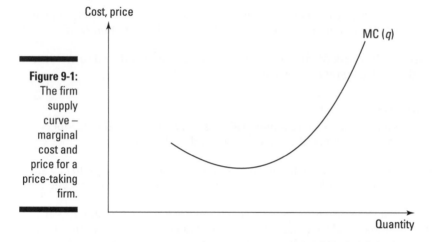

Figure 9-1:
The firm
supply
curve —
marginal
cost and
price for a
price-taking
firm.

Totting up the numbers from firm to industry

Given the information in the preceding section, you now need to aggregate the decisions of all the firms in the industry.

The firm supply curve is really just its marginal cost curve given an assumption of price taking (the firm can't individually influence the price of a product). Therefore, if you add up all the marginal cost curves of all the firms in the relevant industry you arrive at the industry supply curve.

You need to add up the firm supply curves *horizontally*. You have to add the quantity made by firms for a given level of cost in order to see the relationship between cost, price and quantity (remember: the firms are price takers acting optimally and so cost and price are the same!).

We summarise this situation in Figure 9-2, which shows two marginal cost curves added up for an industry of two firms. We set this out arithmetically for four prices in Figure 9-3.

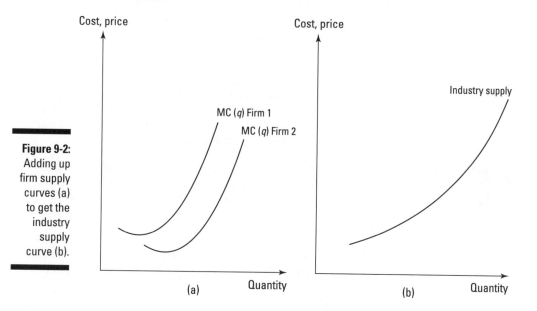

Figure 9-2: Adding up firm supply curves (a) to get the industry supply curve (b).

Figure 9-3: Adding marginal cost curves horizontally to make the supply curve.

Price	Firm 1 supply at price P		Firm 2 supply at price P		Industry supply
1	10	+	15	=	25
2	15	+	25	=	40
3	20	+	35	=	55
4	25	+	45	=	70

Giving the People What They Want: The Demand Curve

Supply decisions are important in and of themselves, especially in understanding how a firm chooses optimal production (see the earlier section 'Producing Stuff to Sell: The Supply Curve'). But it takes two to tango (as all *Strictly Come Dancing* fans know) and two sides to make a market; markets can't exist without customers because buyers need to exchange with someone!

The buyers in a market comprise the demand side of the market. Whereas looking at the supply side lets you see how producers produce more or less given the price that they receive for their goods, the *demand side* plots the relationship between the price of a good and the quantity that buyers purchase at that price. The *demand curve* summarises this relationship.

When deriving a demand curve, bear in mind that the demand curve plots the relationship between price and quantity, *holding other factors constant*. In other words, any individual demand curve holds income, the price of other goods and preferences constant in order to focus simply on the one relationship that matters in this model: between price and quantity. This condition also means that in contrast to the preference and choice model from Chapter 6, any given demand curve plots only the conditions for one good and not relative changes in consumption of one good with respect to another.

Going from preferences to demand

In Chapters 2 and 4 to 6, all the examples involve substitution with two goods. A consumer allocates a set of resources between consuming a quantity of good 1 and good 2, to achieve the best possible utility. A budget constraint sets a maximum level of consumption and the consumer chooses the best consumption bundle in utility terms. Figure 9-4 summarises the optimal choice given the budget constraint.

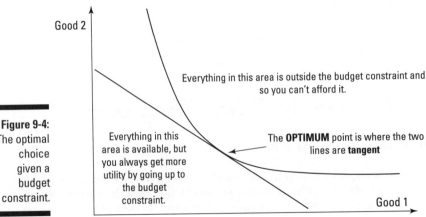

Figure 9-4:
The optimal choice given a budget constraint.

Good 2

Everything in this area is outside the budget constraint and so you can't afford it.

Everything in this area is available, but you always get more utility by going up to the budget constraint.

The **OPTIMUM** point is where the two lines are **tangent**

Good 1

The demand curve answers a slightly different question. Given that consumers behave as they do in the preceding paragraph, what's the relationship between the price of a chosen good and the quantity of the good demanded, not usually by one consumer, but by all participating in that particular market? To answer this question, you have to understand how the choices we present in Chapter 6 add up to make a demand curve. The simplest way is to consider a situation where the only thing allowed to change is the price of one good: money and the price of all other goods are held constant.

Here's an example using simple numbers. Carol has £10 and wants to allocate it to slices of pizza. We assume only one good (slices of pizza) and one sum of money allocatable to buying pizza (a disposable income of £10). With no other goods, you can take anything referring to the price or quantity of anything other than the slice of pizza to be zero.

If a slice of pizza costs £1, Carol can afford ten slices (assuming non-satiation, though that much pizza may not be experienced as utility but discomfort!). We show this and five other per-slice prices in Table 9-1.

Table 9-1	Pizza Slices Carol Can Buy with £10
Price per Slice	**Number of Slices Affordable**
£1	10
£2	5
£3	3
£4	2
£5	2
£6	1

We plot Carol's quantity demanded against price in Figure 9-5. You can see a nice clear, though in this case not quite straight, line denoting the relationship between price and quantity. As the price of a pizza slice rises, the quantity demanded falls! This relationship is a *demand curve*.

Now we take Carol's preferences and add them to the preferences of the only other patron of the pizza place, Doug. When you add up all the decisions of all the consumers in the market, holding constant their income and the price and availability of any other substitutes, you arrive at the market demand for pizza slices and you've derived the market demand curve (see Figure 9-6)! For this, we've assumed that Doug has similarly well-behaved preferences, although we haven't gone through the exercise of quantifying them in the same way as with Carol. The key point is that whatever they are, you derive market demand by adding them up.

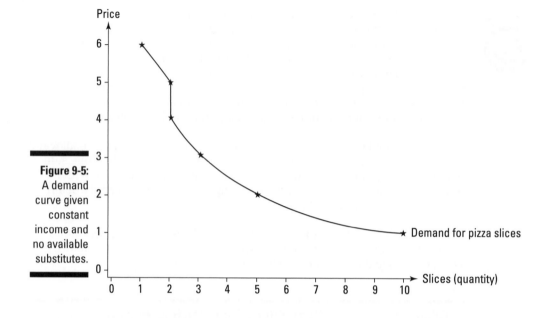

Figure 9-5:
A demand curve given constant income and no available substitutes.

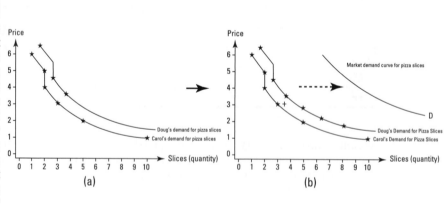

Figure 9-6:
(a) Adding up individual demands to get market demand: showing Doug and Carol's individual demands for pizza slices; (b) Showing the market demand is the sum of individual demands.

Economists are sometimes lazy about making the distinction clear, but strictly speaking at any point on a demand curve you're talking about the *quantity demanded* at a given price, whereas the term *demand for* is talking about a general relationship between price and quantity for a given good. So in this section's example, we discuss *the demand* for pizza by looking at the *quantity demanded* by Carol at different prices.

Seeing what a demand curve looks like

The demand curve in the preceding section maps only two variables, price and quantity, holding all other things, such as income and tastes and prices of other goods, as constants. Thus, the demand curve tells you that any point along the curve is a relationship between price and quantity: when price goes up, the quantity demanded of a given good goes down.

You can read price and quantity off the axes of the curve, but for some types of application starting with a demand function is more useful. In this approach you use numbers to describe the price–quantity relationship.

Quite simply, a *demand function* is any mathematical formula that describes a demand curve! Here's a very simple formula for a demand function: $x_1 = 100 - p$. This expression relates the quantity consumed of a good (x_1) to a price of the good and a constant (which you can interpret as income that may be allocated to the good). The key point is that the only variable that's allowed to change is price.

Despite some reasonably rare exceptions (see the nearby sidebar 'Exceptions to downwards demand curves'), *demand curves slope downwards*, indicating that any given point on a demand curve will have a lower quantity demanded where the price is higher. Two main interpretations follow:

- ✔ When looking at an individual consumer and aggregating, a higher price means that holding income constant an individual consumer will substitute away from the good whose price has risen and therefore consume less of it.

- ✔ When taking all the consumers in the market together, at a higher price fewer consumers exist who're willing to pay up to that price to receive the good.

The curve shifts when anything other than price changes

When looking at demand curves, you hold absolutely everything except price constant for any given curve, meaning that price changes are movements along a demand curve. If something other than price changes, you have to analyse the change by comparing different curves. To simulate such changes you shift the demand curve horizontally to show a change in one of the factors held constant.

We continue the preceding section's pizza slice example. If, say, Carol has £20 to allocate to pizza (rather than £10), her demand at £1 a slice is 20 slices and at £2 a slice, 10 slices. We illustrate that by shifting her demand curve to the right to show that she can now afford twice as many pizzas as before. Similarly, if a noodle bar opens up on her campus, we shift the curve horizontally to the left to show that her demand for pizza falls as a new rival opens (see Figure 9-7).

Exceptions to downwards demand curves

Sometimes a demand curve may not apparently behave as you expect. These exceptions tend to occur at the extreme ends of the income spectrum (or quality spectrum).

At the bottom end of the quality spectrum are Giffen goods, which are so inferior that as your income is constrained your consumption rises through an extreme trading-down effect. Because you can think of a rise in price as a relative fall in income, you can see Giffen goods as being so inferior that their demand curve at least partially slopes upwards.

At the top-quality end are Veblen goods, whose consumption also depends on the value of other people knowing that you're capable of affording those goods (rare artworks, couture fashion, supercars!). Here a rise in price can lead to an increase in demand precisely because a higher price increases your ability to boast about your consumption! This phenomenon,

identified by sociologist Thorsten Veblen, is called conspicuous consumption, and relates the utility gained from consuming a good to the fact that other people see you as 'well off' if you can.

Economists debate hotly the rarity or not of these phenomena. Giffen goods were often treated as a theoretical curiosity, but extreme trading-down does occur, such as among food prices in exceptionally constrained situations (in fact, the example was developed after looking at one such crisis situation, the Irish famine 1845–52). Veblen goods have received more attention recently as economists seek to explain consumption behaviour in developed societies where at least some percentage of the population is rich enough to base its consumption decisions on being seen to consume.

Figure 9-7:
(a) For changes in price, read off the same demand curve; (b) When something other than price changes, shift the demand curve.

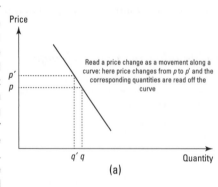

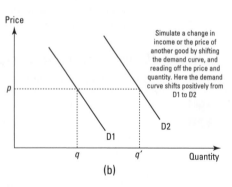

Don't confuse the two operations of *moving along* a curve and *shifting a* curve. If, for instance, you see a rise in prices and an increase in demand, most likely this happened because something shifted demand, such as income or tastes, as opposed to an individual demand curve sloping upwards. When you get the hang of distinguishing between movements along the demand curve and shifts in the demand curve, you can start to see how they work in the real world.

In the 1990s, the brewer of a somewhat generic lager repositioned itself in a more premium segment of the market: first it raised the price and second it advertised the lager as a premium brand. A microeconomist can look at the price movement along the curve and read off that quantity demanded was likely to be lower. But the second stage of the strategy created a taste effect that raised, in some way, the utility gained from consuming the lager so that at any given price the quantity demanded would be greater. Thus the demand curve *shifted outwards,* leading to a greater level of consumption for any given price! We depict the case in Figure 9-8.

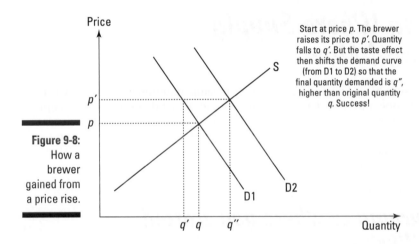

Start at price *p*. The brewer raises its price to *p′*. Quantity falls to *q′*. But the taste effect then shifts the demand curve (from D1 to D2) so that the final quantity demanded is *q″*, higher than original quantity *q*. Success!

Figure 9-8: How a brewer gained from a price rise.

Read the situation in two stages, bearing in mind that a demand curve holds everything except price constant. That means, if you're looking at something else – a rise in income or a change in tastes for example – you need to shift the demand curve to model the change!

What you can glean from supply and demand

When you know the shape of the supply and demand curves, you can manipulate them to investigate changes in price and quantity using a method called *comparative statics,* where you compare two states of the market at two different periods in time as if they're simple camera snapshots. Then you can compare how price and quantity change after your change has been enacted. The lager example above uses comparative statics to gain some insight into a process in the market.

Be aware, however, that comparative statics leaves out some detail of the adjustment process between the two states of your relevant market.

This omission isn't usually a problem in and of itself: you can discover a large amount about how a market behaves by comparing two moments in time. But sometimes *dynamics,* that is, adjustments and changes over periods of time like in a moving picture, are important and have to be considered. A change where a market adjusts suddenly and sharply to a change in price is very different to a change where a smooth path of adjustment occurs. At this point, pretty much all models you're likely to pick up are examples of comparative statics, but at more advanced levels you can add extra tools to your toolbox to compare dynamic adjustments.

Identifying Where Supply and Demand Meet

Plotting supply and demand curves on the same diagram gives an upward-sloping supply curve and a downward-sloping demand curve, and – except in rare circumstances – a point where the two cross. At that point, price and quantity have values that keep producers and consumers happy so that exactly as much is produced at that price as customers want to buy. That point is called *equilibrium.*

Returning to where you started: Equilibrium

In the supply and demand model, markets are *equilibrium-seeking,* meaning that after an adjustment everything ends up back at a point where prices and quantities are equal (no unsold goods and no running down of inventories). Typically, using supply and demand analysis, you start and end at an equilibrium, even if not at exactly the same equilibrium point as before.

Equilibrium and equilibrium-seeking are extremely important concepts to microeconomists. At the equilibrium, markets *clear:* exactly as much is produced as consumers need and producers have no *stockbuilding* (no *excess supply*) or running down of stocks and shortages (as would be caused by *excess demand*). In this model, equilibrium comes about because the price can adjust to ensure that quantities demanded and supplied are equalised.

To see this process in action, suppose (as in Figure 9-9) that a situation occurs where price is temporarily higher than the equilibrium. This case sees excess supply, because the quantity supplied at that price is greater than the quantity demanded. With excess supply the price adjusts, falling so that, first, more potential buyers are tempted back into the market and, second, the marginal producers decide that producing is no longer worthwhile and cut their production. These two effects lead to the equilibrium-seeking market returning to its equilibrium where the market clears.

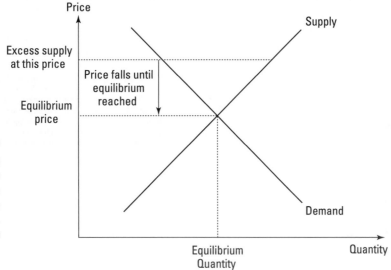

Figure 9-9:
Price falls
in response
to excess
supply.

This equilibrium-seeking tendency is one reason why economists require good evidence before recommending action to control a market. In the view of the majority of economists, unless proven otherwise, the price mechanism is sufficient to adjust markets until they clear. Examples of interferences in markets that have merely made things worse are many – often it comes about because any one policy maker knowing as much about a market as the people participating in it is difficult.

Not all economists prefer no intervention in all cases. We just mean that the profession wants to ensure that intervention doesn't make things worse!

One example of intervention going wrong is with a specific type of rent control in the 1970s in the UK, which allowed landlords only a maximum rent. The problem was that the maximum rent was in some markets below the equilibrium. Setting the price ceiling at that level led to an excess demand for rentals from potential tenants, while marginal landlords were unable to get as much in rent as they felt compensated them fairly for the value of their properties. As a result, many landlords left the market at exactly the same time, because more people wanted to rent from them and the rent controls prevented prices from adjusting to create an equilibrium that may have kept landlords and tenants happy.

The result was a collapse in the private rented market, and the knock-on effects included lower labour mobility (because private rents are often the most flexible way of being housed when a person moves from one town to another). Therefore, this style of rent control was abolished. Not that the government ceased all involvement in the rental market – it moved on to other adjustments. We walk you through this case in Figure 9-10.

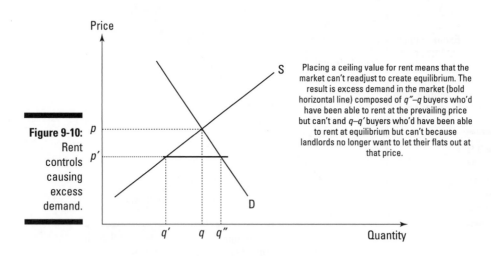

Figure 9-10: Rent controls causing excess demand.

Placing a ceiling value for rent means that the market can't readjust to create equilibrium. The result is excess demand in the market (bold horizontal line) composed of $q''-q$ buyers who'd have been able to rent at the prevailing price but can't and $q-q'$ buyers who'd have been able to rent at equilibrium but can't because landlords no longer want to let their flats out at that price.

Reading off revenue from under the demand curve

At the equilibrium, you can see on the supply and demand curves a unique price and quantity at the point where they intersect. The interesting thing is that, if you multiply price by quantity at a given point on a demand curve, the result is the revenue yielded from selling q units of a good at price p.

Total revenue always equals price times quantity and also corresponds to the area of a rectangle under the demand curve. When testing the responsiveness of demand using *elasticity* (a measure of how demand changes for a given change in price – we discuss it in the later section 'Testing the responsiveness of demand using elasticities'), one result shows whether a producer's revenue will be higher after a price change. You can find that by comparing the size of the rectangles before and after a price change. Later in the 'Testing the responsiveness of demand using elasticities' section we show you the simple formula for how that happens, but for the moment take a look (in Figure 9-11) at the rectangles under the demand curve for an old price of p and an old quantity of q and for a new price (after a change) of p' and a new quantity of q'. The change in revenue from p to p' and q to q' is:

$$(p \times q) - (p' \times q')$$

Figure 9-11:
Revenue changes after a price change. (a) Original revenue before the change is given by Price times Quantity; (b) After a price change the area under the demand curve changes – the revenue gained at the new price and quantity is shown by the shaded area, the dotted lines indicate the old amount of revenue for comparison.

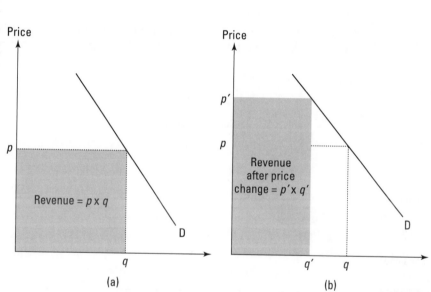

(a)

(b)

Summing the gains to consumer and producer: Welfare

The equilibrium price at which a market clears provides another useful thing to ponder when analysing a market: gains made simply by trading, which economists call the *gains to trade*. The idea is that for any given equilibrium in price and quantity, some consumers would be happy to buy for above the market price and some producers would be happy to supply for less than the market price. Both parties have made a trade that makes them better off, because they'd have been willing to buy (sell) at a higher (lower) price and don't have to; so each party captures some value from the trade.

The consumers' gain is called *consumer surplus* (see Figure 9-12), which comprises the gain for those willing to have bought at a price above the equilibrium and who don't have to. It's given by the area formed by:

- ✔ The equilibrium price and quantity in the market.

- ✔ The highest price that consumers are willing to pay on the demand curve ($p^{\max}$ in Figure 9-12).

- ✔ The point where a horizontal line from the equilibrium point crosses the vertical axis (the intersection with the line is p, equilibrium price).

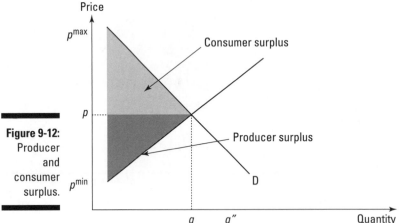

Figure 9-12: Producer and consumer surplus.

The length of the line between the first and third points in the list is q, and so the size of the area under the demand curve is the area of the triangle, given by:

$$\text{Consumer surplus} = \frac{1}{2}q\left(p^{\max} - p\right)$$

A similar reasoning applies to the area above the supply curve and below the market equilibrium price, which comprises producers willing to supply the good for a price lower than the equilibrium price, but who don't have to because the market clears at that equilibrium. Here, the only substitution is to use $p^{\min}$ for the price at which the cheapest producer is willing to provide (see Figure 9-12):

$$\text{Producer surplus} = \tfrac{1}{2}q\left(p - p^{\min}\right)$$

Welfare, the term used in this model, is the sum of the gains to trade between the two parties, and so is given by the sum of producer and consumer surpluses (we summarise this in Figure 9-12). Check out Chapter 12 for more on welfare.

Welfare has several meanings in economics and they get more tightly defined as the type of model does, but when you're using the supply and demand model, it means the sum of consumer and producer surplus. The same also applies to the model of oligopoly in Chapter 11 and monopoly in Chapter 13. In the perfect competition model in Chapter 10, all the welfare goes to the consumer (nice!).

Testing the responsiveness of demand using elasticities

The most direct calculation you can make from the supply and demand model relates to responsiveness to a change in price, or to a change in something else that has been held constant in the particular case you're considering. The number that you arrive at measuring responsiveness is called an *elasticity*.

In this section we discuss the three most important cases:

- ✔ **Own price elasticity of demand:** When the price of the good you're looking at changes. It measures the responsiveness of demand to a change that can be depicted as a movement along the demand curve.

- ✔ **Cross-price elasticity of demand:** When the price of something other than the good you're looking at changes. It measures the effects of shifts in the demand curve.

- ✔ **Income elasticity of demand:** When the amount of consumer income changes. Again, it measures the effects of shifts in the demand curve.

Effect of an own price change

The own price elasticity of demand measures the effect of the change in the price of a good on its associated quantity demanded and therefore of the revenue that producers gain or lose as its price changes.

You can arrive at the revenue change by reading off prices and quantities and comparing the size of the rectangles under the demand curve (see the earlier section 'Reading off revenue from under the demand curve'). But you can measure the size of the effect more simply by using the own price elasticity of demand formula. A change in price from p to p' is $p' - p$. Using the mathematical shorthand Δ to indicate a change, we write this as Δp.

Now we do the same for quantity, again reading off the change in quantity for the two points p and p' (whose associated quantities are given by q and q'), which gives Δq. We now divide Δq by Δp to find how much q changes as p changes. This gives, first, a measure of responsiveness of demand and, second, the slope of the demand curve.

A problem exists, however. Economic variables come in different collections of units from different currencies to different sizes of supply (diamonds, we hear, aren't generally supplied by the metric tonne and steel not generally supplied in troy ounces!). So, to get the final answer you need to fix those units so that they don't affect the size of the change (otherwise a change affecting millions of troy ounces would have a larger effect than a change affecting the same amount expressed in megatons!).

You can do this in two ways, using whichever is more convenient. One is to use the formula for changes and multiply by the inverse of the ratio at the original value, to fix units. That gives the own price elasticity of demand as

$$\text{P.E.D.} = (\Delta q / \Delta p) \times (p / q)$$

The other way is to start by using percentage changes so that

$$\text{P.E.D.} = \Delta\%q / \Delta\%p$$

Both ways are valid arithmetically and give the same number. Sometimes, percentage changes are given to you by the data you receive and sometimes you have to calculate them. But for both methods the sum, and more importantly the inferences you can make, are the same!

The own price elasticity of demand is almost always a negative number. This reflects the fact that an inverse relationship lies along a demand curve between price and quantity, and so it follows that as price rises quantity falls. Funnily enough, this is also a backhanded way of saying that a demand curve slopes downwards.

Three cases exist for the own price elasticity of demand:

- ✔ **Elasticity of demand is more negative than –1 (or its absolute value is greater than 1):** A rise in prices leads to a fall in revenue, but a fall in price causes a rise in revenue.

✔ **Elasticity of demand is less negative than –1 (or its absolute value is between 0 and 1):** A rise in prices leads to a rise in revenue, but a fall in prices causes a fall in revenue.

✔ **Elasticity of demand is exactly 1:** A rise in prices leaves revenue exactly as it was.

Economists don't always put the minus sign before an own price elasticity of demand, because in the overwhelming majority of cases they assume it to be negative. In these cases we're considering the mathematical operator absolute value and so we strip off the minus sign. Unless a very important reason exists why the own price elasticity may be positive, for instance in a Veblen good, general practice is to assume that own price elasticity of demand has a negative sign as the downward-sloping demand curve indicates.

In the case of a perfectly normal good, the elasticity of demand divides into cases where the elasticity is more negative than –1 (that is, the absolute value is greater than 1 as, for instance, in the elasticity of –1.2) and those where it's less negative than –1 (for instance, an own price elasticity of –0.8). If it's more negative than –1 you've found a case of elastic demand:

✔ **Demand is elastic:** A decrease in price results in greater revenue.

✔ **Demand is inelastic:** A rise in price results in greater revenue, but a decrease in price results in lower revenue.

At some point on the curve, demand is *unit elastic*. At this point any rise in revenue caused by raising prices is exactly counterbalanced by the fall in revenue from selling fewer units of the product. In numerical terms, this is the same thing as saying that the own price elasticity of demand is exactly –1 at that point. Examples of demand functions do exist that yield elasticities of –1 at all points along the demand curve: these aren't straight lines!

Effect of a cross-price change

The cross-price elasticity of demand measures the effect of a change in the price of another good. Typically, you calculate it by knowing the prices and quantities before and after the change for two goods, i and j. So the effect of a change in the price of good j on the quantity demanded of good i is:

$$\Delta\%q_i \, / \, \Delta\%p_j$$

The cross-price elasticity of demand measures the effect of a shift in the demand curve, not a movement along it (it's changing something other than the price of the good in which you're interested). Three basic cases exist here:

✔ **Cross-price elasticity of demand is positive:** A rise in the price of good j has a positive effect on the sales of good i and so the two goods are substitutes. The greater the value of a positive cross-price elasticity of demand, the more substitutable the two goods are (so an estimate of the cross-price elasticity of demand that finds a high and positive sign allows the inference that the two goods are in the same market!).

✔ **Cross-price elasticity of demand is negative:** A rise in the price of good j has a negative effect on the sales of good i and thus you can infer that the two goods are complements. An example is that when the price of petrol goes up, sales of cars that run on petrol fall because the two are complementary goods.

✔ **Cross-price elasticity is zero or very near:** The two goods have very little quantifiable effect on each other.

Effect of a change in income

The income elasticity of demand performs a calculation when income changes. Income is of course held constant along one demand curve, and so the income elasticity measures the effect of a shift in the demand curve caused when income moves from m to m'. (Check the earlier Figure 9-7(b) for an example of a demand curve shifting.)

Typically, economists use Δm or Δy for a change in income, more usually Δy. They then evaluate a percentage change in quantity caused by the change in income. Unlike the effect of an own price change, however, the income elasticity doesn't simply rely on the slope of the demand curve being negative, and so the income elasticity may be positive or negative. Here we evaluate the formula for the income elasticity of demand:

$$\Delta\%q \,/\, \Delta\%y$$

Here are the four general cases:

✔ **Quantity demanded rises as income rises:** Makes the income elasticity of demand positive (economists call these types of goods *normal goods*).

✔ **Quantity demanded rises by far more than income rises:** For example, when a 10 per cent rise in income yields a 20 per cent rise in quantity (so that the income elasticity of demand is 2). This is therefore exhibiting behaviour associated with a *superior good* (often associated with consumption of luxury products).

✔ **Quantity falls as income rises:** The income elasticity of demand is negative. This is associated with *inferior goods,* where demand falls as income rises.

✔ **Income elasticity is zero:** Consumption of the good is unaffected by income. Necessities generally have income elasticities between zero and +1 and you'd expect their consumption to rise as income rises but not by as much as the rise in income.

Chapter 10

Dreaming of the Consumer's Delight: Perfect Competition

. . . .

In This Chapter

▶ Introducing perfect competition

▶ Understanding the requirements for a perfectly competitive market

▶ Explaining the need for perfect competition as a benchmark

. . . .

*I*s perfection attainable? Although from time to time you may use the term casually ('I've made the perfect cappuccino', 'reality TV shows are a perfect nuisance' and of course 'this is the perfect book on microeconomics!'), most people understand that achieving perfection in the real world is impossible. But that doesn't mean that they can't imagine the perfect situation.

Perfect competition is the name economists give to a situation with many interchangeable firms, none of which can influence the market as a whole. This scenario isn't all that likely in the real world, because it depends on a set of conditions that may be impossible to achieve. But structures do get quite close to it in several specific markets (though, of course, not in many others). When they do get close, they bring a series of benefits, which are most likely to go to consumers.

In this chapter, we look at the equilibrium of output and price in perfect competition – an ideal situation that economists use as a benchmark. We go through some of the conditions that determine which markets are oh so perfect and which fall below the standard. We also discuss the important factor of firm entry and exit, which lies behind the model of the perfectly competitive market. Do we have your attention? Perfect!

Viewing the 'Perfect' in Perfect Competition

The word 'perfect' means something very specific to economists. In this section, we outline what exactly that is and some of the necessary conditions for perfect competition.

Defining perfect competition

Perfect in the sense of perfect competition means that it *fully satisfies a set of conditions that economists have placed on the model.*

By way of an analogy, economists mean 'perfect competition' in the same way as a perfect circle exactly satisfies a set of mathematical conditions regarding curvature.

The term certainly doesn't mean that in a real perfectly competitive market everyone's always happier all the time. In fact, for producers, a perfectly competitive market may be a difficult one in which to operate, because it places very strict limits on what they can do.

Identifying the conditions of perfect competition

A number of factors are required for a given market to be in perfect competition:

- ✔ Many firms
- ✔ Interchangeability of firms and products
- ✔ Interchangeability of consumers
- ✔ Perfect information about prices and quantities
- ✔ Free entry into and exit from the market for firms

We go through them all in a little more detail in this section.

If you fail to find any of these factors in a given market, it isn't in perfect competition.

Many firms

In a perfectly competitive market, no firm is individually able to influence the price or quantity sold of a given good. For this to be the case, many firms need to supply the market, none of which has a significant share of the market. This is obviously not always the case in reality, because many markets are *dominated* by one firm or a group of firms.

The 'many firms' condition leads to economists describing firms in the market as *price takers* (the opposite being *price makers* or *price setters*). None of them can influence market price or demand, and so firms have no option but to take whatever price is determined by the market *as a whole*.

Interchangeability of firms and products

Products in a perfectly competitive market must be *homogenous,* that is, indistinguishable from one another. If, for example, you're shopping at a fruit and veg market with many costermongers (so that none can influence the price paid for apples), the apples that each sells must be the same: no 'better' or 'worse' apples and no stalls specialising in selling only Bramleys or only Coxes. Instead, all must be selling the same, indistinguishable product.

Similarly, the firms must have the same production technology. If they don't, long-run differences between firms are possible, which leads to differences between the firms in the market. This would open up the possibility of one firm being different enough from the other firms to be considered as being in a different market altogether.

Again, these definitions aren't meant to reflect real-world conditions. Although some goods are entirely homogenous, they aren't necessarily always produced by firms with the same production technologies. Take commodities, which are defined by their homogeneity: gold is either gold or something else. An atom of the metal is either a gold atom or an atom of different metal, not a different kind of gold atom. But this isn't to say that people produce gold to the same level of efficiency everywhere in the world!

Interchangeability of consumers

A similar issue is the degree to which consumers are alike. In a perfectly competitive market, consumers don't value the products produced by individual firms differently from one another. Therefore, no competition on product quality is possible in a perfectly competitive market, but only on whether or not a firm is able to satisfy consumers in its little piece of the market at a cost it can sustain.

Economists use this property in particular to examine what happens when a firm is considering whether or not to produce for a given, perfectly competitive, market.

Perfect information about products and prices

A perfectly competitive market contains no hidden elements. Consumers are perfectly informed about products and prices. Thus they're immediately able to assess whether they want to purchase from one firm or another.

This information can't come at a cost. If consumers have to work to find out prices, the competition isn't perfect.

Free entry and exit

Free entry into and exit from the market is an extremely important condition. If an entrepreneur sees profits being made in a perfectly competitive market, he's able to enter that market immediately and begin competing profits away from the firms in the market. Similarly, if he's in a market and not making profits, he's able to pack up and leave without his leaving incurring any costs in and of itself.

This condition doesn't mean that starting up involves no costs – just that it doesn't involve any costs above and beyond those of producing whatever he's producing in that market: no fees for entering and no costs of closing.

Putting the Conditions Together for the Perfectly Competitive Marketplace

At equilibrium in a perfectly competitive market, firms make *economic profits* (those assessed after all costs have been reckoned) of zero and produce output at the minimum possible cost. To see why, in this section we consider the equilibrium conditions for perfect competition. (To read more about supply, demand and equilibrium, check out Chapter 9.)

Seeing the supply side

Firms in perfectly competitive markets are price takers – by assumption. This means that although you can read the market supply and demand – and therefore equilibrium in price and quantity – from market supply and demand (just as in Chapter 9), when you look at the competitive position between firms within the market, you have to adapt the way you look at the supply decisions an individual firm will make. Therefore, if you want to see what's happening within the market, you have to return to looking at cost curves (see Chapter 7 for a full explanation).

To go from firm supply to industry supply, as we do in Chapter 9, you need to add up the marginal cost curves of all the firms in the industry and read off the output that's produced. That gets you the industry supply curve that you use to find equilibrium output.

The thing is, in perfect competition the assumption that market entry and exit for firms is costless means that supply in a perfectly competitive market looks a little different. What we're going to do is show you how horizontal addition works to get the figure for industry supply, so that you can see how it gets treated when you look within the industry.

We use the example of the grommet industry. Table 10-1 shows the output of three firms in the grommet industry at 3 different marginal costs. At a marginal cost of 1, for instance, firm A makes 10 grommets, B makes 11 and C makes 12. To get the industry supply, you add up the output of A, B and C at each of the three marginal costs – so when all competitors produce at a marginal cost of 1, industry supply is $10 + 11 + 12$, which equals 33.

Table 10-1	Marginal Cost and Industry Output in the Grommet Industry		
	Firm marginal cost		
Output per firm	1	2	3
A	10	11	13
B	11	12	15
C	12	14	17
TOTAL	33	37	45

The supply curve for the industry gives the relationship between output and cost for the industry. Adding up the marginal costs for each of the firms provides the supply curve for the industry.

We're adding horizontally so that we have to add up the output for all the firms!

Now, economics proceeds from an assumption of price being equal to the marginal cost of production. Table 10-2 shows industry output for 3 different prices. (You may notice that industry output is the same as in the bottom row of Table 10-1 – the difference is that we're using the marginal cost equals price relationship to make the inference that makes up the supply curve.)

Table 10-2	Supply Curve for the Grommet Industry		
	Price		
	1	2	3
Industry output	33	37	45

When you plot the output for the three firms, you get the typical upward-sloping supply curve (see Figure 10-1). Using the relationship between marginal cost and marginal revenue, you can express supply with price on the vertical axis and quantity on the horizontal axis, and lo and behold, you can say that this industry would produce an output of 9 when the sum of the marginal costs of the firms in the industry is 45, for example.

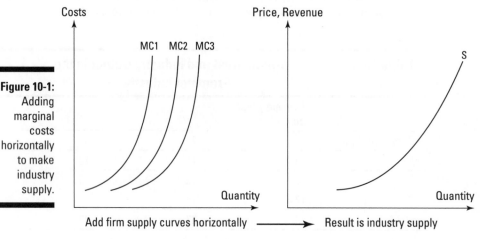

Figure 10-1: Adding marginal costs horizontally to make industry supply.

Add firm supply curves horizontally ⟶ Result is industry supply

This situation is fine for looking at most cases of industry supply and market demand, but the costless entry and exit condition (check out the earlier 'Identifying the conditions of perfect competition' section) places a new restriction on the model, one with a very powerful effect on firm supply.

Free and costless market entry and exit means that if any firm is making economic profits then that situation attracts a new firm to enter the market and that would compete away the profits made by firms in the industry. What matters, therefore, is what a firm would do when considering whether to enter the industry. Economists ponder that by considering something called the marginal firm.

Marginal, as usual in economics, means at the margin. At the margin, only one firm is deciding whether to enter the industry, stay in it or leave it. At equilibrium, the marginal firm will have no preference between those decisions. How can that possibly be the case? Well, given the rationality rule for firms – that production is set where marginal revenue equals marginal cost (see Chapter 3) – you know that this can happen only when a firm receives exactly as much for its last unit of output as the incremental amount it cost to produce. At equilibrium in perfect competition, therefore, economists look at the marginal revenue received by the last firm and find that it must equal the marginal cost of producing that output.

Digging into the demand side

The preceding section's discussion on supply is a start, but you also need to look at the other side of the market – demand – to get the market equilibrium.

Demand in a perfectly competitive market is infinitely elastic. As a result of the many firms rule and the price taking and perfect information rules (see the earlier 'Identifying the conditions of perfect competition' section), any attempt to cut prices below the market price leads to the entire market beating a path to your door. Plus, any attempt to raise prices above the market price leads to every potential customer running to your competitors. The upshot is that demand must be a flat horizontal line.

Here's an example to show what we mean. Imagine that you're in the middle of an aisle of many greengrocers in a market. They all sell identical cabbages, and tell you their prices by clearly barking them out so that getting that information involves no cost to you. They're all very near to each other too, so you incur no cost going from one to another to find a cabbage for your dinner (sounds yummy!).

For argument's sake, assume that all the cabbages on sale at the market cost £1 each. But then imagine that one greengrocer has the ability to get hold of cabbages for less and can therefore bring one to the market for 90 pence. You hear his price, and immediately realise (as a rational consumer) that his price being lower means that you can buy more (and following the model of the consumer in Chapters 4–6) can make yourself better off by doing so. You're economically rational and so it's a no-brainer. You buy from the cheaper producer.

But you aren't alone in this market – you're only one of many rational consumers. All the other consumers in the market have also heard his price and they all want to have more utility rather than less. So they all follow, leaving all the other greengrocers barking their prices to precisely no one.

When you get to the cheaper greengrocer, you find him looking absolutely exhausted. The entire market has come to him, and he can't possibly keep up with this rate of service and his stock is going to run out, leaving him scratching around trying to find cabbages to sell. What does he do? He has no choice. He's going to have to put his price back up to the market price – as we state in the earlier 'Identifying the conditions of perfect competition' section, he's a price taker! – and return to market equilibrium.

Returning to equilibrium in perfect competition

In this section we aim to put supply and demand together to get equilibrium (where, of course, supply equals demand). In the earlier 'Seeing the supply side' section we state why we consider the marginal firm. We now combine what we know about the marginal firm with what we deduced about demand (in the preceding section) to consider what happens when the marginal firm meets the rational consumer in perfect competition.

Economists are only interested in the marginal firm out of all the firms, and so microeconomics models output in the industry just using the cost curves for that one firm. (To revisit cost curves, pop over to Chapters 7 and 8. Don't worry, we'll still be here!) Figure 10-2 puts the equilibrium conditions into a picture.

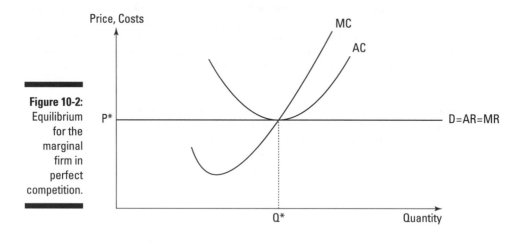

Figure 10-2: Equilibrium for the marginal firm in perfect competition.

The demand curve expresses not only average revenue, but also, because it's horizontal and perfectly elastic, the marginal revenue gained from selling an additional unit to a customer. Putting them together, as in Figure 10-2, the marginal firm sets output, assuming it is a rational profit maximiser, so that MC = MR, thus producing where the marginal cost curve crosses the demand curve.

Now here's an interesting thing. From Chapter 3

$$\Pi = TR - TC$$

where Π is profit. You can get TR (total revenue) and TC (total cost) by knowing that in the long run the marginal firm produces at the minimum possible average cost (AC). If you multiply AC by quantity (Q), you get TC. Similarly, if you multiply average revenue (AR) by Q, you get TR. Thus you can divide through by taking the quantity out of the cost and revenue terms:

$$\Pi = (AR - AC) \times Q$$

But you already know that in equilibrium for the marginal firm, average revenue equals average cost, that (AR – AC) has to equal zero and that if you multiply zero by quantity, you get zero. So there you have it: profits for the marginal firm in perfect competition have to equal zero.

Economic profits aren't the same as accounting profits. Many ways exist to assess accounting profits, but only one for economic profits, which is that they're assessed after *all costs have been reckoned*. This includes all wages, capital used and the opportunity cost of any alternatives.

Now we use the example of the greengrocer from the preceding section and put it into this model. Suppose the equilibrium is that the price of the delicious veggies is 10 units and the greengrocer prices at 9. What happens next? Well, first the firm is now pricing below equilibrium, so that TR < TC. If that's the case, it will make losses and have to take a decision about whether to go on producing.

But the lesson from the demand side is that, at that price, customers rush to the greengrocer's stall. In fact, because the curve is infinitely elastic, the entire market rushes to the greengrocer. Serving an entire market below cost isn't a sustainable position and the marginal greengrocer has to put prices back to the equilibrium in order to stay in business – if he decides not to shut down, that is!

Now what if the price is above average cost? Well, in this case you can work out from the equation that the firm now makes economic profits above zero. But then other entrepreneurs see the marginal greengrocer making economic profits and so are attracted to enter. They then compete away those profits until the point where the marginal firm is *indifferent* between staying in the industry and leaving it. In other words, after they enter, the marginal firm, again, makes economic profits of precisely zero.

Thus in the long run, which economists define as that length of time it takes for all production decisions to be changeable, the marginal firm in a perfectly competitive industry makes economic profits of zero.

Examining Efficiency and Perfect Competition

Economists derive two conditions for efficiency (check out Chapter 8 for more on profit maximisation):

- ✔ **Allocative efficiency:** That the market price for a product equals the marginal cost of producing it.

- ✔ **Productive efficiency:** That the firm produces for the lowest possible average cost.

Both these conditions are satisfied in perfect competition, which means that from the overall viewpoint of cost, equilibrium in perfect competition is allocatively and productively efficient. Thus, on the grounds of cost, perfect competition produces the most desired products for the lowest possible price.

This sounds wonderful, but for perfect competition economists place some very strict limits on what people want: they limit the consumer's desire for difference between products by saying that preferences were homogeneous (all identical to each other).

In a market with a strong desire for diversity of offerings, for example television programming, consumers would lose out by having a reduced range of options. In reality, consumer preferences in many, if not most, markets aren't homogeneous and that market couldn't arrive at this result.

Understanding that perfect competition is a boundary case

The best way to see perfect competition is as a maximum possible efficiency case, and not necessarily a depiction of the real world.

We draw an analogy with an engineer's concept of perfect efficiency, where 100 per cent of the energy put into a machine gets transformed into useful work. In reality, that's not true! But accepting the case where it does apply, as a model, the engineer is able to understand the degree to which his machine falls short of ideal and explore the reasons for it.

Economists use the idea of perfect competition in a similar way. Few markets in the world, if any, satisfy all the conditions of a perfectly competitive market, but that's not why economists are interested in its features. The real reason is to enable some comparison of the efficiency of a given market with that of the perfectly competitive market, and to assess the degree to which it falls short.

Also, although zero profits may sound nice in theory, in practice profits don't just get stacked in a bank vault! They can also be retained for investment, for instance in research and development (R&D) of new products. R&D is often an intensive and expensive process, and most economists point out that firms that don't make long-run profits have less capital to spend on R&D and less incentive to make that investment. Thus high levels of competition may have a drag effect on levels of R&D investment, and not be conducive to forming research-intensive companies.

Considering perfect competition in the (imperfect) real world

Many students ask whether the model of perfect competition really happens or whether it's just a textbook case. Our answer is that it *almost* does in some situations but not many, and although they're interesting, the primary interest in perfect competition is more normally as a benchmark for the effects of competition in other industries. Examples that we use in this chapter include a commodity market (because commodities either are or aren't something, and so they're homogeneous) with many buyers and sellers and a fruit and vegetable market.

Perhaps the closest example is something like the market for minicabs in a town, provided that the drivers aren't organised into companies taking significant shares of the market and are all well-behaved enough to be equally polite to customers and equally sure of reaching the destination safely and efficiently.

In this case, you'd expect to get quite close to the perfectly competitive situation even if it's only theoretically achievable. Confronted with a market like this, drivers would be making close to zero economic profits as a whole. They may be making a salary's worth of money, but remember that the salary is a cost from the perspective of the firm!

Part IV

Delving into Markets, Market Failure and Welfare Economics

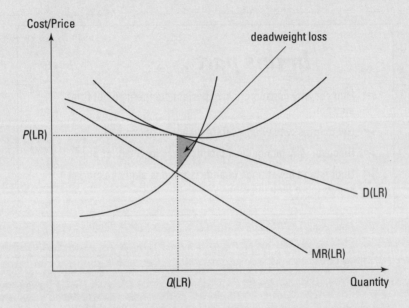

Many markets in information technology have unusual structures – find out what that means at www.dummies.com/extras/microeconomics.

In this part . . .

- ✔ Find out why consumers love perfect competition but firms may not.

- ✔ Get to grips with what welfare means in economics.

- ✔ Discover why monopolies produce less for a higher price.

- ✔ Understand how things change when one side of a market knows more than the other.

Chapter 11

Stepping into the Real World: Oligopoly and Imperfect Competition

....

In This Chapter

▶ Considering the criteria for an oligopoly

▶ Modelling firms' behaviour in oligopoly

▶ Differentiating products to tackle competition

....

*O*ligopoly is the name economists give to a type of market with only a few firms (it comes from the Greek word *oligos* meaning few). The classic example of an oligopoly is the supermarket industry, where a few supermarkets compete among themselves for customers and the bulk of the market is locked up between the four largest competitors: the names change – Aldi and Lidl are challenging now – but overall the market stays in the hands of few competitors. But oligopoly is visible everywhere, in industries as different as low-cost airlines and Internet services.

One of the ways in which economists analyse oligopoly is by comparing it with other market structures. Compared to perfect competition, which we describe in Chapter 10, consumers don't get as good a deal. But compared to monopoly (which has no competition, see Chapter 13), they do better.

Economists use the term *imperfect competition* to describe market structures with a few competitors, as in oligopoly, or two competitors *(duopoly).*

In this chapter, we discuss the basic attributes of an oligopoly, three ways of describing how firms operate in one and how firms differentiate themselves from their rivals.

Outlining the Features of an Oligopoly

The huge difference between the model of an oligopoly and the model of a perfectly competitive market is that firms carry out *strategic interactions* with each other, which means that they form beliefs about what their rivals might do in response to their acts. This behaviour makes oligopoly a useful jumping-off point for looking at even more complex markets, and for discovering the concepts of game theory, which economists use extensively when the models get really difficult. (We cover game theory in Part V.)

The first thing you have to do when looking at oligopoly is to describe the key characteristics that make a given market an oligopoly. In addition to it having only a few firms in the market, here are some more features to be aware of:

- ✔ **Entry into and exit from the market isn't costless:** The demand curve is downward sloping rather than a flat line (as for perfect competition: check out Chapter 10).

- ✔ **Firms, as ever, are rational profit maximisers:** They set prices or quantities to make marginal revenue equal marginal cost (see Chapter 3).

- ✔ **Firms interact by making guesses about how their rivals will react to their decisions:** These guesses about their rivals' behaviours determine the price that a firm will charge or the quantity they'll supply.

- ✔ **Prices tend to be 'sticky' in response to firm and consumer decisions:** Firms in an oligopoly don't tend to change prices as much as people guess and so oligopoly models look for a way of taking this tendency into account.

- ✔ **Consumers are rational utility maximisers:** Therefore, demand works in the same way as in Chapter 9.

The most important of these set-up conditions is the first. Oligopoly often comes about as a result of the existence of *barriers to entry*. In a perfectly competitive market, entry and exit are assumed to be costless (see Chapter 10). Changing this assumption makes a large difference, because rivals can base their behaviour on each other's actions without worrying about potential competitors who aren't currently in the industry. Thus firms in an oligopoly can make economic profits where competitive firms don't.

Barriers to entry are anything that imposes a cost on entering a market and they come in many kinds:

- ✔ **Innocent:** Such as high costs of capital. For example, setting up a manufacturer of aircraft costs a lot of money.

- ✔ **Strategic:** Such as entry deterrence by firms in the industry. For example, when an incumbent is able to cut prices to keep a rival out.

✔ **Prohibitive regulations:** Such as the result of government allowing only a few licences to trade in that industry. Examples include Finland having a state monopoly on distilling spirits and Britain's franchising system for rail operators.

Discussing Three Different Approaches to Oligopoly

A helpful way to start understanding oligopoly is to consider the special case of a *duopoly,* where only two firms are operating in the market. After you get the hang of thinking about how only two firms react to each other, you can adapt your modelling to think about the harder cases involving three or more firms.

Investigating how firms interact in a duopoly

When you restrict your modelling to two firms, the next complication is to think about how, exactly, these firms interact.

Two sets of possibilities exist here, giving you in total three ways of describing firm behaviour in an oligopoly. Each method focuses on a slightly different way of treating the interactions of the firm:

✔ You assume that both firms have approximately the same effect on each other, which gives two different types of behaviour:

  • *Cournot model:* Where quantity is the strategic variable.

  • *Bertrand model:* Where price is the thing that firms control.

Choosing to look at quantity has very different results from looking at price.

✔ You build on the assumption that one firm can make its choices first – in which case, economists say that it has *first mover advantage:*

  • *Stackelberg model:* Where a leader and a follower exist. This model explicitly treats one firm as having a leadership advantage over the other firm. Many variants of this model exist so as to take account of all the different conditions. We discuss a version where the firm has an advantage over choosing how much to produce, called *quantity leadership.*

Next you want to work out the equilibrium in each case so that you can compare them – the results are interesting even in a simple model!

Competing by setting quantity: The Cournot model

In the *Cournot model* of a duopoly, the two firms in the industry – which both make an identical product – simultaneously decide what quantity to produce for the market, given their beliefs about how the rival will react to its decision. You want to know how much each firm will produce in order to have the best chance of making maximum profits.

Imagine the simple scenario of two Canadian lumber companies, Fort William and Port Arthur. Lumber is a useful example because it's reasonably indistinguishable as a product – if one firm produces oak and the other pine you're looking at differentiated products and the equilibrium may be very different!

You solve the model by first considering just one company's decisions, calculating the *reaction function* – an expression for quantity or price for a firm explaining how it reacts given its beliefs about the production decisions of a rival. In Cournot oligopoly, the reaction function is expressed in terms of quantity.

Spelling out customer demand

Begin by looking at customer demand, which is something neither company can change – they can either set price (P) and read off the demand of consumers or set quantities (Q) and allow consumers to choose the price for which they'll buy. For a simple example, suppose a linear demand function:

$$P = 30 - Q$$

Fort William and Port Arthur produce Q_{FW} and Q_{PA}, respectively. The total market size depends on both firms' production and so:

$$Q = Q_{FW} + Q_{PA}$$

To make things simple, though a little unrealistic, set the model up with a marginal cost (MC) for both firms of zero (this keeps things a little simpler than reality, but as you progress with the model, you can change this assumption and see what happens!):

$$MC_{FW} = MC_{PA} = 0$$

The last thing is to find an expression for the total revenue of one of the firms. We choose Fort William and use the identity that total revenue equals price times quantity. Knowing the demand function you can write:

$$TR_{FW} = P \times Q_{FW} = (30 - Q)Q_{FW}$$

This gives the total revenue for Fort William as an expression of the total amount of lumber produced by the two firms – allowing you to move on to calculating the optimum production.

Finding the optimum production for Firm 1

The optimum is at MC = MR, and so finding the optimum level means setting MR equal to zero (as MC was assumed to be in the preceding section). MR is the change in total revenue when quantity increases by one. In order to find it, take the slope of the expression for total revenue for Fort William.

Beginning with the expression for TR_{FW}, multiply it out to see what all the parts of the expression are:

$$\begin{aligned} TR_{FW} &= (30 - Q)Q_{FW} \\ &= 30Q_{FW} - (Q_{FW} + Q_{PA})Q_{FW} \\ &= 30Q_{FW} - Q_{FW}^2 - Q_{PA}Q_{FW} \end{aligned}$$

Taking the slope of this equation with respect to a change in Q_{FW}, you get an expression for marginal revenue (MR). You can do so by plotting total revenue for Fort William against its output and taking the slope of the line (but if you trust us, you can go straight there by using calculus):

$$MR_{FW} = 30 - 2Q_{FW} - Q_{PA}$$

Now you know that MC = MR (because the firm is a profit maximiser) and MC is zero in this model, and so you know that if you set MR equal to zero and solve for Q_{FW} you get

$$Q_{FW} = 15 - \tfrac{1}{2}Q_{PA}$$

This result is the reaction function for Fort William that tells you what quantity Fort William will produce in response to what it believes Port Arthur is producing.

Plotting reaction curves for the two firms

You can go through the same reasoning as in the preceding section to get Port Arthur's reaction function – or you can trust us that it works out as being:

$$Q_{PA} = 15 - \tfrac{1}{2}Q_{FW}$$

The next stage is to plot the two reaction functions against each other. The axes are the quantity for the two competitors, and the two curves give the amount of lumber each will produce given the production of the other.

The two lines cross at one unique point (because they've been set up as straight lines – so this may not be true if they're curves of some form).

Figure 11-1 shows that point, which is called the *Cournot equilibrium*. To find it, set the two reaction functions equal to each other and solve to find Q_{PA} and Q_{FW}. In this example you get $Q_{PA} = Q_{FW} = 10$.

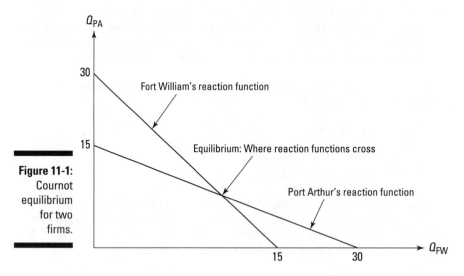

Figure 11-1:
Cournot equilibrium for two firms.

Therefore industry total production is 20.

Seeing why the equilibrium isn't as good as a competitive market

If you feed back the output of either firm into the demand curve, you can get an expression for the price each will receive. Market demand is given by $P = 30 - Q$ and total production is equal to 20, and so the price that the market is prepared to pay is 10.

This amount is greater than the assumed marginal cost – which was zero. So an oligopoly in Cournot equilibrium produces at a higher price than a competitive market, and firms in the industry make *economic profits* – that is, profits greater than zero. Solving for a price of zero (so that price equals marginal cost as in a competitive market), industry output is 30. So a competitive market produces a higher output than an oligopoly in Cournot equilibrium.

Seeing why the equilibrium isn't as bad as a monopoly

Suppose that the two firms co-ordinate their decisions so that you can treat them as a monopoly – a single firm that supplies the whole of the market. Then the firms together maximise their revenue based on combined demand.

Going through the scenario in the preceding section, marginal revenue is MR = 30 − 2Q, because now only one firm is in the game. Setting MR = MC, which is zero in this example, the output that maximises profits is 15. This amount is less than the Cournot equilibrium, and so an oligopoly in Cournot competition produces less than a competitive market, but more than a monopoly.

Collusion among firms in an oligopoly, to co-ordinate on the monopoly outcome, is therefore bad. When firms collude successfully, the result is a cartel and is highly illegal, precisely because it results in a lower quantity produced (and therefore higher prices). Check out Chapter 16 for more on cartels.

Following the leader: The Stackelberg model

The Stackelberg model differs from the Cournot model of the preceding section in that one firm is assumed to have the ability to set its quantity as market leader and the other firms can only follow its decisions. Economists call this condition *first mover advantage* and it exists whenever one company has an ability to lead the decisions of others. If – as happens in oligopoly in general – entry and exit are restricted in some way, this first mover advantage can persist for some time.

Deriving a Stackelberg model for the lumber companies means that you fix things so that firm 1 sets its optimal production and firm 2 just reads off and reacts to firm 1's decisions. Suppose that Port Arthur is able to be the first mover. What would it produce and how would Fort William react?

Start with the insight that in Cournot's model the two firms set their production simultaneously, but in the Stackelberg variant Port Arthur gets to input Fort William's reaction into its revenue calculation.

Suppose – as before – that the demand curve is given by

$$P = 30 - Q$$

Port Arthur makes its decision based on what it thinks its follower, Fort William, does, by substituting Fort William's reaction into its own total revenue function:

$$TR_{PA} = 30 - Q_{PA}{}^2 - Q_{FW}Q_{PA}$$

Next you substitute in the reaction function for Fort William, which you find from calculating the Cournot model as in the preceding section. Therefore, you substitute in

$$Q_{FW} = 15 - \tfrac{1}{2}Q_{PA}$$

This gives Port Arthur's revenue function given Fort William's reaction:

$$TR_{PA} = 30\,Q_{PA} - Q_{PA}{}^2 - \left(15 - \tfrac{1}{2}Q_{PA}\right)Q_{PA}$$

That looks unwieldy, and so we gather like terms to simplify:

$$TR_{PA} = 15\,Q_{PA} - \tfrac{1}{2}Q_{PA}{}^2$$

Find the slope of this line to get marginal revenue for Port Arthur:

$$MR_{PA} = 15 - Q_{PA}$$

You can now set MR = MC = 0, which gives production for Port Arthur as 15. Now, using Fort William's reaction function, you can plug Port Arthur's production back in and get 7.5.

Comparing to the Cournot results where both firms made 10 units (from the preceding section), you instantly see that Port Arthur makes 15 units of lumber and Fort William only 7.5! Also, summing the total output of the two firms you get 22.5 units rather than the 20 under Cournot conditions. So, if one firm gets to lead and move first, output for the industry as a whole is higher. Plug that into the demand function and you see that this is tantamount to price being lower!

The reason is that unless the following firm is willing to enter into cut-throat competition and take even lower revenue in the short run, it's taking the leader's decisions as read and playing off them. Thus the equilibrium that emerges favours the leader, but the result is better for the consumer than when both firms are equal!

Competing over prices: The Bertrand model

Firms competing in an oligopoly often do almost anything to avoid competing on price. One of the reasons for looking at oligopoly through the models in this section is that the lack of price competition is precisely what you want to explain! Both the Cournot and Stackelberg models with the simple equilibriums we show have points where both firms have a relatively stable output and no price competition.

But this isn't always the case. Sometimes in oligopoly you do see periods where one firm or another breaks the equilibrium and competes on price for a while. They may, for example, undertake a period of discounting or introduce a product at a low 'intro price'.

The *Bertrand model* of oligopoly looks at these situations, and explains what happens during a price war and why general price competition tends to be undesirable for the firms in this kind of market. You can illustrate this situation easily without calculating reaction functions, by considering what happens when the firms start in Cournot competition and one breaks to compete on prices.

At the Cournot equilibrium (see the earlier section 'Competing by setting quantity: The Cournot model' and earlier Figure 11-1), with undifferentiated products, the firms have no incentive to move. Each supplies half the market and customers are indifferent between the offerings of the firms. Now imagine that one of the two competitors – say Fort William – decides to cut prices by a small amount: what happens?

The answer is that because the goods are identical, all customers go to the lower-price supplier and Fort William takes the entire market! Of course, Port Arthur can't possibly let them and so it drops its prices, too. Suppose it cuts prices a small amount below Fort William's. Then it takes the entire market!

Each producer has an incentive to cut prices below its rivals and so each continues cutting prices until it reaches the limit. What's that limit? Well, it's when price equals marginal cost, which is – ta-da! – exactly the competitive price!

This finding bears out the important observation that price competition isn't in the interests of producers in this type of market. If each firm gets the competitive price, profits made are zero and neither producer gets to benefit from the lack of entry.

Comparing the output levels and price for the three types of oligopoly

We now take a look at what happens to price, output and profit under the three types of competition we describe in the three preceding sections:

- **Cournot competition:** The lowest output and highest price appears when firms are in this situation, reacting to their guess at what each other's output will be. The price here isn't quite as high as under a cartel or a monopoly, but higher than in other types of oligopoly.

✔ **Stackelberg competition:** Features not quite as high a price and not quite as low an output as Cournot, but it isn't quite as good as under a competitive market.

✔ **Bertrand competition:** Ends up with the same price as under a competitively supplied market (and therefore the highest quantity).

In reality, competition is often not as cut and dried as these models make out. An offer of a lower price isn't always a signal that the industry is about to enter into a frenzy of Bertrand competition. Take for instance a lowest price guarantee – far from being a signal that a company is willing to beat the best price in the market, it's more usually a deterrence strategy. If you offer to beat anyone else's price, it actually removes the incentive for anyone to try undercutting you!

In the Stackelberg and Cournot models, price exceeds marginal cost, which means that firms make economic profits. In the case of Bertrand competition with undifferentiated products, price hits marginal cost and therefore firms make zero profits in equilibrium – unless, of course, they're colluding.

Making Your Firm Distinctive from the Competition

In the hard-nosed world of competitive business, firms often differentiate their products to separate themselves from rivals. Car manufacturers, for instance, produce many different brands of car rather than a single generic item called a car! Even when the goods are relatively homogenous, for example, matches or sticky tape, identifying the products as different from each other in people's minds makes economic sense.

This practice raises a question – at which point are products different enough that thinking about them as being in the same market stops making sense? Economists examine this issue by looking at the cross-price elasticity of demand between two products (for details, check out Chapter 9): the more positive the cross-price elasticity, the more likely the two are in the same market. Looking at it from the perspective of a firm that wants to make as much profit as possible, branding and making its product different to competitors reduces the cross-price elasticity of demand.

Economists look at these behaviours in two ways:

✔ They adapt oligopoly models to allow the products to be differentiated.

✔ They use a model called *monopolistic competition,* which assumes that differentiation works in the short run, but not in the long run (because if you hit on a winning formula, someone is bound to copy it!).

Reducing the effects of direct competition

Companies reduce the effect of direct competition in many ways. These methods all seek to reduce the degree of direct competition faced by firms making similar products. They include:

- ✔ **Integrating their supply chains:** For instance, selling through preferred partners or through retail networks that they themselves own. Legal limits prevent firms with dominant positions from doing this, but if a business holds only a small share of a market, that's fine. A Vauxhall dealership that only sells Vauxhall cars and vans is an example of a producer owning a retailer – what economists call forward vertical integration.

- ✔ **Branding products:** So that consumers identify the products as being different. Sometimes this supports a product being different – think of tomato ketchup where brands and formulas are interlinked. But sometimes branding exists where products are minimally different – petrol, for instance.

- ✔ **Competing on some other dimension of customer need:** Location is one such example.

In the mid-1990s the supermarket industry in the UK transformed its operations. The competitors in the industry did so because improved data from the stores showed that the most important thing determining whether customers went to one store over another was the convenience of the location. In the 2000s they did so again, as Internet shopping and deliveries became the important factor!

Economists deal with these strategies by adapting the oligopoly models that we present in the earlier section 'Discussing Three Different Approaches to Oligopoly'. You can take account of differentiation in two basic ways:

- ✔ **Adapt the oligopoly models when significant barriers to entry exist.** In particular, if goods are differentiated in some way, Bertrand competition (which we describe earlier in 'Competing over prices: The Bertrand model') settles into an equilibrium where neither party has an incentive to change its price and both continue to make economic profits.

- ✔ **Use a refined model called monopolistic competition when no barriers to entry exist or they exist only in the short run (they may erode in the long run).** This approach looks at competition from the perspective of a firm that can make economic profits in the short run, but not in the long run (check out the next two sections).

A consequence of barriers to entry is firms making long-run economic profits in an oligopoly, which is one reason economists tend to dislike them. The thing is that, in reality, many industries show a turnover in membership.

Although some industries are nice examples of oligopoly with little entry – think of high-street banking – others show significant amounts of entry and exit. The car manufacturing industry, for example, has lost names such as Austin or Innocenti over the years, but gained a Lexus or Kia along the way.

Economists call the possibility of entering an imperfectly competitive market *contestability.* When markets are contestable, potential rivals exert pressure on the incumbent firms in the market and keep prices down and behaviour a little more competitive. The overthrowing of firms in these types of industry is a process called *creative destruction.* New entrants see the behaviour and work out new ways of making the product better or doing it cheaper. They enter the market and gain advantage over the already-present firms, growing bigger while rivals decline. That leads to a constant turnover of firms in the market and continual improvement in quality and novelty.

The average lifespan of a corporation, according to US research, fell from 67 years in the 1920s to 15 years today. Over that period, the economy became more complex and innovation happened at a greater pace, leading to more competition and more entry and exit!

Competing on brand: Monopolistic competition

When firms face open entry but are able to differentiate their products, economists turn to the *monopolistic competition* model. As its name suggests, it takes competition as a given and so firms are in a competitive market. But unlike in perfect competition they're able to do so by differentiating their product. Hence the monopolistic part of the name – each firm is trying to be the sole supplier of its 'flavour' of product.

This situation applies to many industries, from soft drinks – which are a relatively generic product with some degree of differentiation on brand – to broadcast television in the US and some other countries. These industries have in common the fact that the firms have to invest continually in their product or their brand – or both – or risk losing their profits to an entrant.

Seeing how brands compete

In monopolistic competition, the market demand curve is downward sloping. (The difference from the other models is that the demand curve for the individual firm is too – in perfect competition the firm faces a perfectly elastic demand curve and in oligopoly firms respond to market demand, not their own.) The demand faced by an individual firm is more elastic in the long run than in the short run, because entry is possible only in the long run. But it's downward sloping, reflecting the limitations on entry and the way a firm in monopolistic competition competes, which is by making its product or brand different from other entrants.

Firms, as usual, operate where marginal revenue equals marginal cost. They use that to set quantity, and receive the price the market is willing to pay (from the demand curve).

Demand is downward sloping and so the firm makes profits in the short run (see the shaded area in Figure 11-2(a), with markup being the difference between price and average cost). In the long run in Figure 11-2(b), entry has shifted the firm demand curve downwards and as a result the new equilibrium, though still having the firm producing where MC = MR, results in the firm making no economic profits!

The firm in monopolistic competition therefore has to deal with the continual threat to its profitability from entry. It can do so by investing continually in the value of its brand, perhaps by advertising – more advanced versions of the model consider the optimal amount of advertising for the firm to do – but also by investing in the quality of its product.

Trading efficiency for diversity: Monopolistic competition for consumers

Compared to a perfectly competitive market, some welfare loss (which we describe in Chapter 13) occurs under monopolistic competition. The monopolistically competitive firm produces less than under a competitive market, which means a deadweight loss – a loss of consumer surplus in particular. We depict this as a shaded triangle in Figure 11-3 (the area under the demand curve but above marginal revenue).

Although consumers may lose out through lower quantities and higher prices compared to a competitive market, they also gain something else: diversity of products. Each firm in monopolistic competition wants to be the monopolist of its own particular segment of the market, and so two firms in this structure avoid releasing identical products.

Some biases exist in monopolistically competitive firm production, though, and so not every possible desire on the part of consumers is met. In particular, monopolistically competitive industries have a bias against any product with a very high elasticity of demand, because this makes maintaining the premium of the brand difficult.

Figure 11-2:
Monopolistic competition – firm equilibrium. MC = marginal cost; AC = Average Cost. (a) In the short run: P(SR) = price in the short run; Q(SR) = quantity in the short run; MR(SR) = marginal revenue in the short run; D(SR) = demand in the short run. (b) In the long run: P(LR) = price in the long run; Q(LR) = quantity in the long run; MR(LR) = marginal revenue in the long run; D(LR) = demand in the long run.

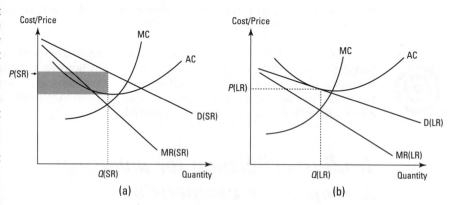

The price premium that a firm gets when it competes in this way is, in itself, part of the measure of the value of its brand. If you take the difference between the price of a branded good and a generic product, and multiply by quantity sold, you have a simple method for evaluating the value of a given brand!

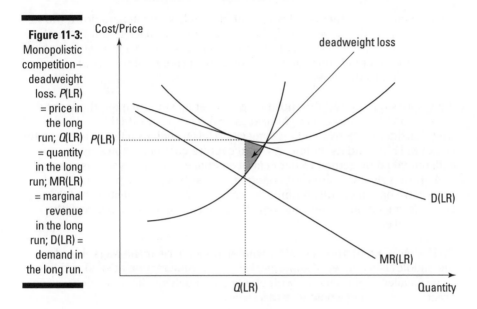

Figure 11-3:
Monopolistic
competition –
deadweight
loss. _P_(LR)
= price in
the long
run; _Q_(LR)
= quantity
in the long
run; MR(LR)
= marginal
revenue
in the long
run; D(LR) =
demand in
the long run.

Understanding differentiation:
The median voter

Many people think that simply deciding to be different to your competitors is
sufficient . . . wrong! In fact, boundaries apply to the amount of difference: too
little and you end up with no brand advantage; too much and you're really
not in the same market as competitors.

In 1929, the great economist Harold Hotelling came up with an observation,
now known as Hotelling's law – though it's less a law and more something
observed in many but not all cases. _Hotelling's law_ says that eventually markets that have differentiated products tend towards a position with minimum
differentiation. Products that are a little different adapt to each other and
eventually converge on a space in the marketplace where neither is especially different from the other.

To see Hotelling's reasoning, consider a simple example. Holloway Road in
North London runs south-east from Archway to Highbury. It's a long, major
thoroughfare and attracts many potential shoppers: locating a supermarket there is desirable because of the big potential market. Assuming that
you're the first person to think of this idea, where would you put the first
supermarket?

Well, if you assume that the throughput of people going up and down the road is roughly the same in both directions, the best place to put the first supermarket is right in the centre! Exactly halfway (given a little geographical latitude for planning constraints!) maximises the share of the people walking from one end to the other.

But where would a rival firm position a competing supermarket, the second in this road? The answer is right next to or directly opposite the first! To see why, consider if the rival built it somewhere else, such as halfway between the end of the road and its middle. It would capture customers towards the one end, but you'd be getting 75 per cent of customers because yours is nearest! Therefore, a rival will situate its offering as near to yours as possible – and successive openings will continue to open as near to this cluster until the centre is 'mined out'. Then, and only then, will entrants open between the middle and end.

On Holloway Road, this is exactly what happened. Near the Nags Head (in the middle) is a cluster of supermarkets: each tube station at each end has some smaller supermarkets, with one or two much smaller ones in between, exactly as Hotelling would've expected!

Also informally called the *median voter theorem,* this result is used to identify why political parties tend to cluster their offerings around the centre of the political spectrum. The reasoning is much the same as with supermarkets. If the voter that matters is the swing voter, parties tend to cluster around those voters found in the centre of the political spectrum.

Chapter 12

Appreciating the Fundamental Theorems of Welfare Economics

● ●

In This Chapter

▶ Thinking about social welfare

▶ Creating a framework for a general equilibrium

▶ Moving towards efficiency

● ●

*S*ome things just seem wrong, don't they? Joan Collins being a dame, Adam Sandler starring in a serious film or Boris Johnson wearing a backwards baseball cap and rapping. Well, microeconomics has its own 'just doesn't feel right' moment!

When studying any particular market, you arrive at a point called a *partial equilibrium* where supply and demand are equal for that particular good. But what happens when you ask the question about *all* markets rather than just one? Can economists find a general result that holds so that all markets are in equilibrium together? Although it seems to jar with everyday experience and often just doesn't seem right, surprisingly such a result does exist – given special circumstances. Economists call it a *general equilibrium* and it's one of the most startling and least understood parts of microeconomics.

A general equilibrium is needed so that many of the models that macroeconomists use to describe an economy make sense. It can also, if used carefully, inform policy decisions about the best way to shape an economy.

Along the way to a general equilibrium model, you arrive at two other results, which are also quite startling. These are called the *fundamental theorems of welfare economics*. Now *welfare economics* is the part of microeconomics that looks at how people can be made better off and it is tied to the idea that making things for the lowest possible cost and use of resources makes people better off. Economists in general also assume that people in a society as a whole gain more utility, and are therefore better off, if some people gain utility and none lose – economists call this a *Pareto improvement* – and would say that welfare is increased when a Pareto improvement happens. (We explain welfare and its multiple meanings in the following section.) The two fundamental theorems are an important stage in learning about welfare and without them most modern economic modelling would be impossible to do. The mystery is how to get to those results and how to interpret them. If you enjoy mysteries, join us as we show you what's really going on!

Getting the Welfare Back into Welfare Economics

Welfare is a difficult thing to define in general. People inquire as to other people's welfare, talk about a 'welfare state' or discuss different types of 'welfare benefit'. This vagueness is unfortunate, because welfare needs to be tied down a little more closely in order for people to put it to use in economics.

Economics is concerned with things that you can ultimately measure – so the meaning of welfare has to be related to prices and quantities. These, in turn, are things that economists hope capture the concept of utility (see Chapters 2 and 4–6 for a fuller discussion of utility). When economists talk about *maximising welfare* they're relating the concept of utility to groups – whether producers, consumers or society as a whole.

Economics also has to use more than one type of definition of welfare – depending upon whether you're talking about a partial equilibrium model or a general equilibrium model:

- ✔ **In a partial equilibrium model:** In this context, *welfare* is the sum of the areas bounded by the supply and demand curves for that particular good – the consumer surplus and the producer surplus.

- ✔ **In a general equilibrium model:** In this context, *welfare* means social welfare, the aggregate level of utility across all people in the economy. Therefore, seeking the highest level of welfare means making the aggregate level of utility as high as possible.

Pareto efficient contract curves are continuous and so an infinite number of points can satisfy the efficiency criterion. They all *could* be chosen, but they have very different degrees of equity – that is, equality between individual members of that society. If an economy can make 100 units worth of utility, a distribution that gives 100 units to Charlie and none to Victor is as Pareto efficient as one giving both 50 – though both distributions are preferable to, in terms of total utility, one giving 40 to Charlie and 40 to Victor.

Meeting two social welfare functions

Economists consider equity through a *social welfare function,* a curve drawn to reflect different valuations among people for different degrees of equity in distributing utility. These in turn tend to be drawn from the standpoints of ethical philosophies. Therefore, many views exist with interesting properties.

Figure 12-1 shows two different types of social welfare function:

- ✔ **Utilitarian function – Figure 12-1(a):** Sums the level of utility for each individual, and so it's entirely indifferent between Bill having 100 per cent of the utility and Ted having 100 per cent.

- ✔ **Rawlsian function – Figure 12-1(b):** Seeks to maximise the welfare of the least well off, and so it has only one unique sweet spot, at the corner of the L shape!

Figure 12-1:
Two social
welfare
functions:
(a) Utilitarian
and (b)
Rawlsian.

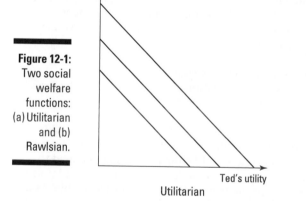
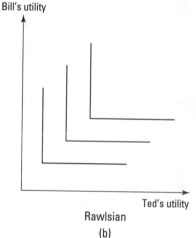

Understanding why markets tend towards one price

Economists talk about many of the implications of a general equilibrium framework in terms of welfare. But you don't need to go very far into welfare to see some interesting real-world applications. One is in terms of the observation that prices in any one market tend to be the same all through that market. You can use the general equilibrium framework to get into the logic of why this may be the case.

The general equilibrium framework has one other interesting point up its sleeve. If a competitive market achieves a Pareto optimal outcome, the price of any commodity must be the same. This is a consequence of all Pareto optimal points being on the contract curve, and the contract curve being points where everyone's MRS and the price ratio are the same. So, if a point is on the contract curve, it must be associated with the same relative price.

This is known as the *law of one price,* and interestingly (unlike much of the general equilibrium framework) you can test it in practice.

Suppose that you grow apples in Kent and sell them in Kent and Yorkshire. If the law of one price is true, the price in Yorkshire can be no higher than the price in Kent plus the cost of transporting those delicious Coxes to Yorkshire. If the prices in Yorkshire were higher, someone could make money by buying apples in Kent and driving them up to Leeds to sell them.

This practice is called *arbitrage:* buying something at a lower price in one market and selling on for a higher price in another market.

Now the law of one price suggests that if arbitrage can take place, entrepreneurs use it. In this situation, the supply of apples in the more expensive market would go up, lowering the price, leading eventually to the two markets being in equilibrium with each other!

Of course, in certain circumstances arbitrage may not be possible, for instance if people can't get hold of information about the prices or transactions costs are involved, so that the law of one price doesn't hold.

In a remarkable study, economist Robert Jensen looked at the availability of information in the market for fish in the Indian state of Kerala. He found that the law of one price only started to hold after 1997. What changed to allow this to happen? The introduction of mobile phones meant that information about prices in all the local markets became much more available! As a result, the arbitrage process kicked in and eventually all markets in the area converged on one price for each type of fish! When convergence between these markets occurred, no further arbitrage opportunities were possible and arbitrage stopped working – people could no longer buy in a cheaper market and sell in a more expensive one!

Understanding Why Partial Equilibrium Isn't Enough

The equilibrium in any given market – for instance, for shoes or fish – is a partial equilibrium, because it applies only to that one market. But economies are complex things and if something affects one market it affects many others as well through income or substitution effects. For example, a rise in the price of fish affects the amount of money that consumers spend on fish, which affects the equilibrium in strongly connected markets – perhaps they see substitution towards other foods. More generally, because everything competes at some level for consumption spending, the rise also affects the equilibrium in all other markets!

So to describe an economy in all its complexity, you need to have a way of describing a general equilibrium where all markets are considered. The problem, of course, is that doing so for a complex economy is a nightmare task! Imagine the amount of effort necessary in describing every partial equilibrium and extending that analysis to every market in an economy!

Instead, economists use a framework to simplify the process of getting to a general equilibrium. The framework we describe in this chapter is about as simple a version as anyone can use – but don't worry, you can extend it later as you get more confident with using your knowledge of microeconomics!

You need two things for the framework:

- ✔ **An Edgeworth box:** A tool for depicting exchange between people.

- ✔ **Pareto efficiency:** A concept for categorising which equilibrium results are efficient.

Modelling exchange with an Edgeworth box

In the constrained optimisation model (see Chapter 6) you depict levels of utility based on the preferences of one person for two goods. But here your task is to look at exchange, and so you need two people making choices (including whether to exchange with each other) based on their preferences.

Microeconomics deals with this situation by using the *Edgeworth box* (see Figure 12-2 for a generally applicable example), which effectively depicts utility for two people on the same diagram. This generalised Edgeworth box has two origin points depicting areas where one person gets zero utility and the other person 100 per cent of the available utility. At the bottom left corner is the origin for the first person, here Wesley, and at the top right the origin for the second, Buttercup. For this example, we imagine that the two goods are fish and shoes.

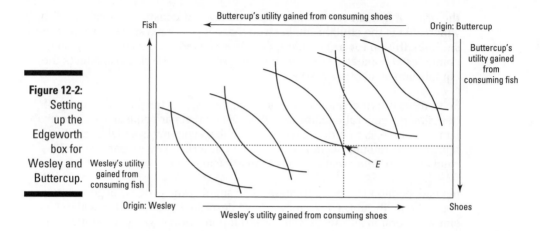

Figure 12-2:
Setting
up the
Edgeworth
box for
Wesley and
Buttercup.

Each participant has well-behaved preferences and so you can depict their utility with utility functions (as we describe in Chapters 4–6). You get a series of utility functions going away from the origin in both directions. Point E in Figure 12-2 is special: it specifies an initial endowment of fish and shoes for both Wesley and Buttercup so that:

- ✔ E_W^F is Wesley's endowment of fish
- ✔ E_B^F is Buttercup's endowment of fish
- ✔ E_W^S is Wesley's endowment of shoes
- ✔ E_B^S is Buttercup's endowment of shoes

Investigating Pareto efficiency

Having set up the initial endowment in the preceding section, you now want to know whether everyone is happy with it, which means using the concept of Pareto efficiency.

Pareto efficiency is a highly specialised version of efficiency for discussing distributions of things – income, utility, goods, wealth – between people. A distribution is Pareto efficient if the following aspects apply:

- ✔ You can't make all people better off.
- ✔ You can only make one person better off if you make at least one other person worse off.
- ✔ No potential gains can be made from trading.

Pareto efficiency doesn't mean that everyone has the same amount. A distribution where Buttercup has all the fish and all the shoes can be Pareto efficient, if you can't make Wesley better off without making Buttercup worse off!

So, to return to the question, is point *E* Pareto efficient? The answer is a resounding no! At point *E* both Buttercup and Wesley can have more fish and more shoes. Therefore, points in the 'lens' above *E* are all Pareto superior (although they're not all Pareto efficient: some of the points are closer to Pareto efficiency, without themselves being efficient points). For the points to be Pareto efficient, they must be points where no potential gains exist to trading, and so they must exist where the two people's utility functions meet at a tangent.

Connecting up all the points where Buttercup and Wesley's utility functions are tangent gives you a line that goes through every Pareto optimal point in the box – called a *contract curve* (see Figure 12-3). You know by looking at the contract curve whether any point is an allocation you'd end up with, because if it isn't on the curve you'd always make both parties better off by moving to the curve.

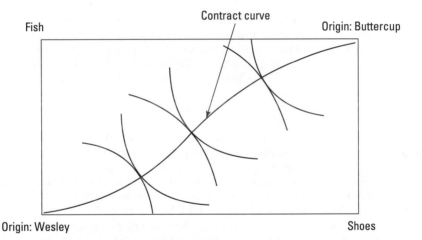

Figure 12-3:
Contract curve for Buttercup and Wesley.

Trading Your Way to Efficiency with Two Fundamental Theorems

Given the set up in the preceding section, we now need to investigate how you go from a Pareto inferior endowment to a final distribution. At the moment you have an initial endowment, *E*, which isn't on the contract curve, and so the potential exists to get to a better – Pareto optimal – distribution on the contract curve. We describe how in this section.

Bidding for the general equilibrium

The economist Léon Walras examined this situation with a thought experiment, in which an auctioneer is calling out prices for everything in an economy. He wants two things to happen: no excess supply or demand in that case. The place you want to get to is on the contract curve.

The auctioneer can, in theory, keep calling out prices until these two conditions are met! Seeing how this works isn't always obvious and so we walk you through an example.

You need two earlier results:

- ✔ At any point on a contract curve, Wesley and Buttercup's utility functions are tangent. That means that the marginal rate of substitution (MRS; check out Chapter 2 for details) of fishes for shoes must be the same for both.

- ✔ At any optimum position for any one consumer, the MRS must equal the price ratio between the two goods.

Calling out successive prices for fish and shoes, the auctioneer eventually finds an equilibrium that satisfies Wesley and Buttercup. At this price, they trade some of their endowments of fish for shoes or vice versa, until they arrive at the point where their MRS for fish and shoes are equal to the price ratio. This point is the *general equilibrium* for the – very simple – economy!

A general equilibrium model implies one simple result: all markets can't be in excess demand or excess supply simultaneously. If an excess supply of fish exists in this model, you must also see excess demand for shoes – otherwise both markets would clear! Even more startlingly, if one of the markets in this model is in equilibrium then the second must also be – if the market for fish clears then the market for shoes must also clear! This result is known in economics as *Walras's law*, which you can see in Figure 12-4. Here, 'E' represents an initial, non-optimal endowment. In this scenario, the process of tattonment (covered in the following section) will lead to an optimal point where Wesley and Buttercup's indifference curves are tangent to each other, and to the line measuring the price ratio of the two goods.

Grasping for efficiency: How markets set prices through tattonment

The auctioneer is a nice imaginary device but doesn't exist in reality and so Walras went further with his analysis.

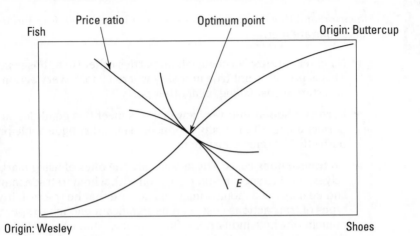

Figure 12-4:
The optimum arrived at by the Walrasian auction.

Markets have a tendency to equate prices with people's preferences all by themselves. Walras named this process *tattonment* (derived from the French for 'groping') to indicate that markets are consistently equilibrium-seeking – for instance, when excess demand exists prices rise until enough buyers drop out of the market and the market clears. They do so through participants' actions without any form of co-ordination at all, simply by continually responding to excess demand or supply in any of the individual markets within the whole economy.

Nobody 'knows' what that equilibrium may be, but markets find it by continually adjusting. That's tattonment, folks!

The first fundamental theorem: A free market is efficient

Walras's logic leads to the *first fundamental theorem of welfare economics:* a free market left to itself ultimately gives you a Pareto efficient outcome. (Flip to the earlier section 'Getting the Welfare Back into Welfare Economics' for more on welfare economics.) Another way of saying this is that eventually, through tattonment, the free market arrives at a condition where no more gains to trade are available. In this case all consumers have exchanged goods with each other to arrive at a position where no one wants to move any further or exchange any more.

However, and this is a huge 'however', it only does so if four fundamental conditions are met:

- ✔ **No externalities:** No costs fall on parties other than those exchanging. This is probably not true in reality where almost every action involves an external cost falling on another party.

- ✔ **Perfect competition:** Very few markets meet this condition in reality! In perfect competition, many producers sell indistinguishable products to perfectly informed consumers.

- ✔ **No transactions costs:** These costs are the ones of using markets themselves. For instance, finding a person with whom to trade may take time and he may need monitoring to make sure that he trades fairly. These types of transactions costs can be significant enough to spur the development of whole industries – for instance, comparison engines reduce the transactions costs associated with buying insurance.

- ✔ **Full information:** We devote a whole chapter to dealing with cases where people don't have full information (Chapter 15), and so you can probably guess that it's not a defensible assumption about reality.

We need to make one vitally important distinction. Although this first theorem is extremely important from a modelling perspective – in fact, you can develop very few of the advanced social welfare models without it – it doesn't necessarily hold in reality. Sometimes people – often, but not always, politicians – try to make this theorem hold as a real-world position. It doesn't. If you want to make a case for free markets, that's fine, but the first fundamental theorem doesn't make that case for you!

But what it does do is very interesting anyway! It says that a market is continually trying to get the best outcome given some constraints – trying in reality, succeeding in textbooks.

Those three constraints are worth stating clearly:

- ✔ No one can be worse off than his initial endowment (otherwise he'd simply refuse to trade).

- ✔ No one can be made better off without someone else being worse off – otherwise gains could be made by trading their way to equilibrium, which they can't.

- ✔ No overall excess demand or supply can exist.

If you make these three things constraints and solve, you would, given the four conditions, achieve a Pareto efficient outcome through the market alone. That's enough to ask the question of whether someone planning would *necessarily* be any better. The answer is quite probably not, because the market will continually be processing more information about people's desires, wants and needs than someone trying to plan centrally an economy, even given that you may not have a perfect economy!

The second fundamental theorem: Any efficient outcome will do

From Walras's argument, you can derive the *second fundamental theorem:* given well-behaved (convex) preferences, any Pareto efficient outcome is also a market equilibrium.

To see why, start with the first theorem from the preceding section – remembering that a Pareto efficient outcome doesn't mean an equal one; Buttercup getting all of both goods is still Pareto efficient! Now, all outcomes that are market equilibria must be on the contract curve, because they make utility functions tangent. But are all points on the contract curve market equilibria? The answer is that they must be because:

✔ Along the contract curve, every point is a tangent between two utility curves:

- The tangency point is equal to the price ratio.

- The price ratio must exist like this if the indifference curves are convex and don't cross.

✔ That price ratio is therefore the ratio of prices that must support a Pareto efficient equilibrium!

Putting the two theorems together: Equity and efficiency trade-offs

Put simply, the first fundamental theorem says that a free market wants to ensure that the overall size of the pie is as big as possible – if it weren't it couldn't be Pareto efficient because you could make both parties better off without making one party worse off. The second theorem says that if you have a Pareto efficient outcome, it can be a market equilibrium. Putting the two theorems together means that the question of efficiency and the question of distribution are entirely separate.

This result is another startling point, in itself. In essence, you can achieve any distribution you desire through a market system, as long as the distribution is Pareto efficient. Market mechanisms are neutral as regards distributions and so you can have any distribution you like or consider fair!

The result comes with some pretty big riders, though. The most important is that you're better off trying to achieve an equitable distribution – in this chapter that's in terms of fish and shoes – by lump sum redistribution than by doing anything that affects the ratio of prices. The reason is that, if prices are competitively set, every buyer consumes up to the point where the price ratio is a measure of the marginal benefit to the consumer. If you change the ratio of prices, you change the decisions of the consumer and you may not get to a Pareto efficient outcome at all!

Instead, if a government wants to make some people better off, it would be better taxing the endowment of one person and giving it to the other! That at least would be Pareto optimal and leave the important signals between relative prices alone.

In practice, of course, things are rarely as simple as this intuition supposes. Take a tax on someone's labour, for example. A person's endowment of labour is actually the total amount of labour that he *might have* provided, and not the total amount that he does provide. You can know the latter – it's how income taxes work – but can never know the former!

In reality, taxes are set for many reasons, from the noble to the downright awful. At some level, they're all fudges and compromises, sometimes because you can't work out the right thing to tax and sometimes because taxing the right things is unpalatable to an electorate.

Chapter 13

Controlling Markets with a Monopoly

*Y*ou can relax – despite its title this chapter is nothing to be with the board game and so you don't have to pick whether to be the dog or the car or whatever. You don't even have to explain why you didn't choose the iron – no one ever does! You may, however, come away with some better ideas for how to win the game, if you're ever forced to play it.

No, the kind of monopoly we're interested in is the opposite of a competitive market (which contains many firms in perfect competition): in a *monopoly,* one firm supplies the entire market. As you can imagine, supply arranged monopolistically has plenty of consequences, most of which make economists quake in their boots!

In this chapter we show you that a monopolist behaves differently to a firm in a competitive market so that consumers lose out as a result. We also have a word or two about some of the other consequences of monopolies and how people deal with them in the real world. Plus we describe the unusual case of when a natural monopoly arises.

The type of monopoly that we discuss in this chapter is a technical definition of monopoly that economists use to compare results against those in a competitive marketplace. When you hear about the authorities investigating monopoly they're almost certainly not dealing with a monopoly as we describe here, but with what economists in fact call *dominance.* For example, a dominant firm may have only 40 per cent of a given market but its competitors have at most 5 per cent each. Although the press or media often refer to this situation as a monopoly, we're only interested in a firm that has 100 per cent of the market all to itself.

But forgive us for monopolising your attention (sorry!), we now get right into monopolies.

Entering the World of the Monopoly

For a producer, a monopoly is a good thing to have. The absence of competition means that you can make long run profits – which get competed away in markets that have competition. If you supply the whole market, you can raise your prices higher than a competitive firm would and not get undercut. You can also be lazy and stop innovating, because you aren't under any threat of an innovative competitor making a better product.

But consumers keenly feel the downsides of monopoly – they have to pay a higher price for goods, and society as a whole loses welfare because a monopoly doesn't have to be efficient. That's a problem, and one reason why economists are keen to recommend that markets be made competitive.

In microeconomics, a monopoly forms the opposite of the perfectly competitive market – see Chapter 10. When you understand how profits are zero and consumers get all the surplus in perfect competition, you can see where monopolies do the opposite – making things better for the producer at the expense of the consumer and society as a whole.

Contrasting monopoly and competitive markets: The case of the missing supply curve

In general, you'd use the structure of the supply and demand model in Chapter 9 to investigate the way prices, quantities and equilibrium change in a given market. When you have perfect competition, however, you change to focusing on the marginal company – as in Chapter 10 – because it helps to see how prices affect firm decisions. For a monopoly, one firm supplies the whole market, and that means that you want to look at its decisions in a slightly different way.

One of the things that changes is that you aren't looking at the aggregate of many firms' decisions: you're looking at just one firm. Therefore, you have to analyse the market the monopoly supplies in a slightly different way. We take you through that process in this section.

Here's a conundrum for you: *equilibrium* is usually identified as the point where demand and supply curves cross (as we discuss in Chapter 9). But if you look at Figure 13-1, which describes the same equilibrium features in a monopoly, you can see that the supply curve has disappeared. We deal with this situation now, as well as covering monopolies and monopolists.

Figure 13-1:
Output setting in a monopoly:
P_c = marginal cost price in a perfectly competitive industry; P_m = monopoly price; D (=AR) = demand (=average revenue); MC = marginal cost; MR = marginal revenue.

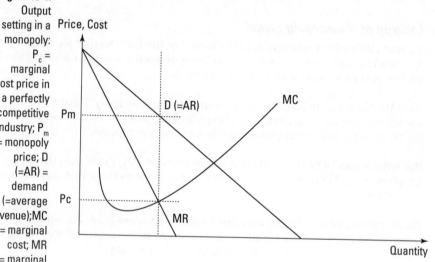

The supply curve for a 'normal' (that is, not monopolised) market comes from adding up the marginal costs of producing outputs for each of the individual firms in the market at each quantity of output.

Imagine that two firms supply a market. Now suppose that each supplies ten units of output and that the marginal cost of doing so is 10. Now the total supply to the market is 20 units, and when you add up the cost of doing so for each of the firms, the total is 20. If you then add up all the possible marginal costs of producing each firm's output, the sum is the supply curve for that market. (We look at this more closely in Chapters 9 and 10.)

But for a monopoly only one firm is supplying the market and so the supply curve for that market is the same as the marginal costs of the monopoly! Therefore, instead of looking at the equilibrium supply and demand for the market, you can just look at the cost of supplying the market for the one firm, and do away, for the moment, with considering the supply curve altogether!

Thinking like a monopolist: It's mine . . . all mine!

We now think about what the monopolist is doing and how this mindset compares to a company in a competitive market. Again, economists are focusing on decisions of the firm – what it will want to produce at what price and how much it will make for doing it. So we lead you through one now!

Looking at a monopoly model

To start, we make a restriction to the model of the firm, so that we begin with it nice and consistent: we assume that the monopolist wants to maximise profits, just as we do for all firms in this book.

With that in mind, look at the equilibrium for the monopoly. Figure 13-1 shows average and marginal cost curves looking more or less the way they do for a competitive firm (we define these curves in Chapter 7).

But what's that? The demand (or average revenue: AR) curve and the marginal revenue (MR) curve are no longer identical, something that has some important implications.

No doubt you're wondering why this happens and how it affects what a monopolist does and the results from monopoly in the marketplace. We can explain with a little bit of not too difficult maths (we hope).

This demand (or AR) curve can be expressed by the following formula:

$$AR = 10 - 2Q$$

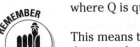

where Q is quantity.

This means that as Q goes up, AR goes down, and so the curve slopes downwards as normal demand curves do.

Now we multiply both sides of the equation by Q to turn it into total revenues (TR):

$$TR = 10Q - 2Q^2$$

Now the *marginal revenue curve,* the contribution made by each additional unit, is going to be the change in TR as quantity, Q, changes. In other words, marginal revenue (MR) is the slope of the total revenue (TR) curve.

You can find the slope in a lot of ways, the easiest being to work it out on a diagram, but we're going to use a little bit of calculus here and find the slope of TR by *differentiating it* with respect to Q:

$$MR = 10 - 4Q$$

Look at the resulting equation. The 10 (the intercept – the place where it crosses the axis) is the same on both the AR and MR equations, telling you that it crosses the vertical axis at the same place.

But the important difference is when you look at the change in MR and AR when Q changes: this is captured by the bit after the minus sign. The minus sign indicates that both curves slope downwards, but the *coefficient* in this case says that the marginal revenue curve slopes down twice as fast as the average revenue or demand curve. You may ask here, what does all this have to do with the price of beans? Well, provided the beans are supplied by a monopoly, quite a bit!

Remember the profit-maximising condition: that MC = MR. Here, the evil bean monopolies (and the evil bean counters who presumably work out how many beans they should produce) set their output to maximise profits, and then read off the demand curve the price (which, remember, equals average revenue) that the beans command in the marketplace. Looking at Figure 13-1, you can see the big difference between the marginal cost price (P_c) that you'd get in a perfectly competitive industry and the monopoly price (P_m) that you see here. So a profit-maximising monopoly supplies its relevant market at a higher price!

Using quantity over price

You may want to call shenanigans on the way we look at this issue; after all, we do everything in terms of *quantity* and only mention *price* right at the very end. Well, we do so for a very sensible reason.

Even the most evil monopolists in the world can't choose the quantity they make *and* the price the market is willing to pay for it: they have to choose one or the other, as follows:

- ✔ Set the price and allow the market to decide what quantity will be bought.
- ✔ Set the quantity and allow the market to determine the price it will pay for it.

Unless a monopolist can force price and quantity at the point of a gun, which in a marketplace they generally can't, it must choose to work with either price or quantity and not both. In this case, we prefer to model monopolists as quantity setters to make comparisons across different types of market, so that we can use the same type of maths to look at them.

Considering profits

So, the evil bean monopoly (picture a baked bean with a dismissive smirk on its face) is making the same type of decision but getting a higher price for its beans. Now, we look at its profits.

Again, remember that a firm in perfect competition makes economic profits of zero, and so the *marginal* firm is *indifferent* between being in the market and being out of it.

A monopoly, however, has *barriers to entry,* which means that if you're making profits in that industry, you no longer face the threat of a new competitor coming in and competing away those profits. So now examine the profits a monopoly makes when it behaves rationally (see Figure 13-2).

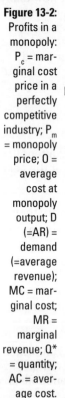

Figure 13-2:
Profits in a monopoly: P_c = marginal cost price in a perfectly competitive industry; P_m = monopoly price; 0 = average cost at monopoly output; D (=AR) = demand (=average revenue); MC = marginal cost; MR = marginal revenue; Q* = quantity; AC = average cost.

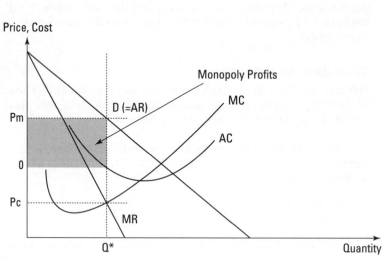

The key thing to notice is the average cost curve for the monopoly:

Profits = total revenue − total costs

and total revenue equals price multiplied by quantity. That means that we can rejig our equation a little by taking the quantity out of it. Total revenue divided by quantity is just price, and total costs divided by quantity are therefore average costs. So, to go through the stages:

Profits = (price × quantity) − total costs

Divide the terms on the right by Q to take Q out of the brackets:

Profits = Quantity (price − average cost)

If you take the *markup* on the right-hand side (price − average cost) and multiply it by quantity, you get the total level of profit, above zero, made by the monopoly.

Look at Figure 13-2 again. The area between O, Pm, Q* and the demand curve gives the profits made by the monopoly!

Refusing to stretch a point: Inelastic demand

We want to deal with one final implication of the model of a monopolist's best choices here.

Monopolists produce only where the demand curve is *inelastic* (see Chapter 9 for more on the elasticity of demand; the elasticity of demand is between 0 and 1), which means that a monopoly has an incentive to raise prices.

To see why, consider quickly the relationship between marginal revenue and demand (which we discuss in the earlier section 'Thinking like a monopolist: It's mine . . . all mine!'). The marginal revenue curve crosses the quantity axis at exactly halfway down the demand curve.

At the point where demand is exactly *unit elastic,* that is, where the marginal revenue is zero, any change in price leads to an exactly counterbalancing effect on quantity demanded. Below this point, demand is elastic, but marginal revenue is less than zero, and so at no point does marginal revenue equal marginal cost.

The fact that the monopoly only ever produces when demand is inelastic means that it faces less of a constraint in raising prices – another reason why economists dislike monopoly!

In the messy world of reality, monopoly is regulated by Competition Law (the preferred term in the UK and EU) or Antitrust Law (in the US). In general, however, the law doesn't deal with the consequences of pure monopoly as described in the textbooks, but with market dominance. The courts are treating almost no cases of a monopoly as we describe it in this chapter!

We say a little more about how this works in the later section, "Tackling Monopolies in the Real World", but, for the moment, just bear in mind that *legal monopoly* (that is, the way in which the legal system defines a monopoly) and *economic monopoly* (what we talk about in this chapter) are related but distinct concepts.

Counting the Costs of Monopolies

In any particular market, welfare is given by the sum of producer and consumer surplus – see Chapter 9 for the definitions and an example of how this works. A monopoly is no exception.

What is different is that a monopoly causes an overall welfare loss to society as a whole, because it produces a lower quantity at a higher price. It also gains more of the surplus than consumers. If a monopoly can charge different prices to each consumer, it does, which means that the monopoly gains more of the welfare, at the expense of consumers. It may, though, reduce the loss to society – the deadweight loss – by doing so. In this section, we show you the deadweight loss and three ways monopolies can get some of it back.

Carrying a deadweight

One of the costs of monopoly is the *deadweight loss* that results from monopolists producing less for more compared to competitive firms.

In Figure 13-3, we make a little comparison between the two cases.

Worrying about the deadweight loss

In a competitive market, equilibrium is achieved where demand and supply cross. Because the supply curve is the sum of marginal cost curves you can point to the market price being equivalent to marginal cost of supply. Fine!

But look at the evil bean monopoly from the earlier 'Thinking like a monopolist: It's mine . . . all mine!' section and see the difference. The bean monopoly produces where MC = MR, but less than in a competitive marketplace, which would produce up to the point where the marginal cost curve crosses the demand curve.

Figure 13-3:
Deadweight
loss: P_c =
marginal
cost price in
a perfectly
competitive
industry; P_m
= monopoly
price; 0 =
price level
equal to
average
cost; D
(=AR) =
demand
(=average
revenue);
MC = mar-
ginal cost;
MR =
marginal
revenue; Q*
= quantity;
AC = aver-
age cost.

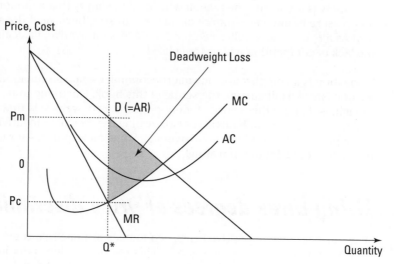

Figure 13-3:
Deadweight loss: P_c = marginal cost price in a perfectly competitive industry; P_m = monopoly price; 0 = price level equal to average cost; D (=AR) = demand (=average revenue); MC = marginal cost; MR = marginal revenue; Q* = quantity; AC = average cost.

Thus, the area bounded by P_m and P_c (on the vertical axis) and the place where the marginal cost curve crosses the demand curve represents losses in *welfare* (that is, the sum of consumer and producer surpluses – as in Chapter 9) due to the monopolist producing less and selling for more than a competitive firm. Economists call this the deadweight loss caused by monopoly: note that it consists of lost *consumer surplus* and *producer surplus*.

For economists, this deadweight loss is a troubling issue. They aim to see more produced for less overall, which requires competitive markets. Economists can accept competition not being perfect, but when the monopoly makes higher profits *and* everyone loses out as a result, they start to get a little nervous. As a result, pretty much every economist since the days of Adam Smith has tried to find ways of preventing that situation from arising.

Losing the will to innovate

Innovation – meaning putting new products to use in a marketplace – is a feature of most markets. One of the things that makes up the deadweight loss under a monopoly is the loss of new and innovative products when a monopoly is involved. The reason why is quite simply that a monopoly faces no pressure to innovate from rivals in the industry, because it doesn't have any! As a result, monopolies can tend to be less innovative, basically because the lack of competition makes them lazy!

Innovation is a complex area for microeconomics – and so the models micro-economists use fall outside the scope of this book. One thing to be aware of, though, is that another cause of monopolies' loss of welfare is that they're under less pressure to innovate. Also, turning the lack of innovative pressure into a general rule is a little controversial. Some monopolies – for instance Bell Labs – did a lot of innovating!

Using three degrees of price discrimination

When discussing competitive firms, economists assume that they can charge only one unique price for their goods. This restriction doesn't hold for a monopolist, however, which can use three cunning ruses to grab some of the welfare that would otherwise go to a consumer.

These methods are collectively known as *price discrimination* and they all have the end result of allowing a monopolist (or, in the real world, a firm with a significantly dominant position) to get hold of some of that benefit. The methods differ as to how many different prices a monopolist is able to charge for the same good, and so economists distinguish them by *degrees* just like a prosecutor distinguishes crimes by seriousness in an episode of *Law and Order*.

We start at the top with the case when a monopolist can charge every consumer a unique price for its product.

First degree (or perfect) price discrimination

In this case the evil bean (monopoly) company (from the earlier section 'Thinking like a monopolist: It's mine . . . all mine!') sells the same product (standard beans) at a different price for each consumer, such that each bean goes to the consumer who values it most (that's a whole hill of beans!).

In Figure 13-4 we look at this scenario using a greatly simplified version of the earlier diagram (Figure 13-3). Here, the monopolist charges any consumer who bids for a good at the marginal cost of production or higher, the price

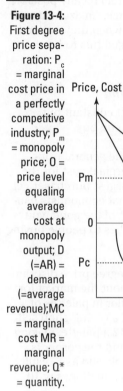

Figure 13-4:
First degree price separation: P_c = marginal cost price in a perfectly competitive industry; P_m = monopoly price; O = price level equaling average cost at monopoly output; D (=AR) = demand (=average revenue);MC = marginal cost MR = marginal revenue; Q* = quantity.

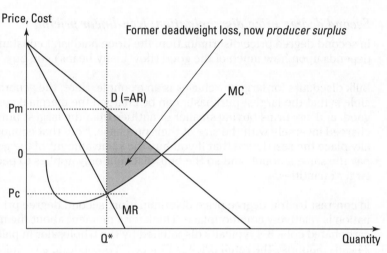

that they're willing to pay for the good. As a result, the monopolist is able to grab the welfare lost when it charges a single price, so eliminating the deadweight loss; but, and this is the real kicker, the welfare gain goes to the monopolist as producer surplus!

First degree price discrimination used to be very rare indeed, to the extent that it only existed in textbooks, largely because when you think about the practicalities of charging everybody different prices you realise how difficult keeping track of the prices or even doing simple accounting tasks must be.

But this changed a lot with the advent of widespread IT and the popularity of auction-style markets. Now doing so is a simple task, if the market is willing to pay it. Examples of first degree price discrimination include *dynamic pricing* where each customer can be quoted a unique price (and the firm may use its IT systems to optimise how it does so).

Just because charging everybody different prices is now technically possible, please don't get the idea that it's always feasible in practice. Amazon, among other companies, has fallen foul of customer complaints when they noticed different prices being quoted to different buyers and judged this to be an unfair practice.

Second degree price discrimination: Non-linear pricing

In second degree price discrimination, the price paid isn't constant but depends upon how much of the good (how many beans) you buy.

Bulk discounts for large purchases is an example. Here, the general principle is that the largest purchaser can be charged the marginal cost for the good, and any firms buying smaller quantities than the largest purchaser get charged inversely with the size of their purchase. Note that economists usually place the restriction that if you buy the same amount of the good, you pay the same amount, and so the bulk discount only applies to people buying larger quantities.

In contrast to first degree price discrimination, second degree price discrimination is relatively commonplace. Think for a moment about the market for carbonated cola. It's typically dispatched by the wholesaler in palettes of 24 cans. Suppose the retail price is £1 a can. You operate a corner shop selling, say, 5 palettes a week, and you pay the wholesaler £12 a palette, making the cost per can 50 pence. But the new supermarket around the corner is one branch of a large chain ordering 50,000 palettes a week, and as a result the wholesaler is willing to charge the marginal cost of production, say 10 pence a can.

The supermarket can now undercut you while still making more money per can; for instance, it can set a markup of 60 pence (as opposed to your 50 pence) but a market price of 70 pence a can.

Second degree price discrimination in the form of bulk discounts like this is often a reason behind such differences in the retail market.

Third degree price discrimination: The student discount

In third degree price discrimination the monopolist segments the market into different groups, and while members of a group pay the same price as each other, the individual groups pay different prices from each other group.

To dig a bit deeper, the monopolist charges the higher price to the group with the less elastic demand (who reveal themselves as willing to pay a little bit more). Our example here comes from our experience with students, who often tell us that they don't have much money (especially when it's their round!). Not having resources makes them a little more willing to shop around, which leads economists to suspect that their demand is more elastic.

A monopolist can therefore offer a lower price to students in the more elastic marketplace and a higher price to less constrained customers, as one cinema near our workplace definitely does. Similar cases exist with senior bus passes or mobile network services using the business market as the less elastic market and correspondingly charging more for its services.

Tweaking the product

The real world has many examples of firms with some degree of market power doing something that isn't exactly covered by the three cases in the preceding section but is related to them. These firms offer fundamentally the same product in different flavours or versions or with different features enabled in the higher price version – in one case a printer manufacturer offered exactly the same product but with a cable cut in the cheaper version causing the higher value features to be disabled!

This practice is common in the software industry, called *versioning,* where you often find the more expensive product labelled 'pro' even when it's not particularly sold to professional markets.

Playing with time and space

Another type of price discrimination is to release a product at different prices in different areas, capturing more of the value from the inelastic market.

A variant is very common in the film and video entertainment industry, where a film is released in different *windows.* In the first window – exhibition – the film is delivered to cinemas where those people who are most willing to pay go and see it earlier. Those who don't want to take the distributor up on the offer have the option of waiting for the DVD window, where they can view the same film at a lower cost per view. At the ultimate end of the chain is exhibition via TV where people can eventually view the same film for nothing. In this case, the distributor passes through each window, selling the product for a slightly lower price each time until the market is fully served.

This strategy is often known as *cream skimming* and also exists in the video game consoles market, where a high launch price is set and slowly allowed to fall over the lifetime of the console.

Tackling Monopolies in the Real World

In a pure monopoly, and compared to a competitive firm, the quantity a monopoly supplies is lower and the price higher (we provide the details in the preceding section). If the monopoly charges only one price, the monopoly results in a deadweight loss, because producer and consumer surplus are lost. But if the monopoly responds by charging different prices to each consumer or group of consumers, that simply makes the monopolist better off. In addition, monopolies are also likely to be less innovative, because they aren't subject to pressure from competitors.

Economists consider all these features of monopoly to be undesirable, but the question is what to do about them.

Appreciating a complex problem

Tackling monopolies is a little tricky, because the solution depends crucially on how a monopoly comes about.

Nowhere in Competition Law is having a monopoly considered to be a criminal offence! Although this seems counterintuitive, you can see why when you consider that in certain situations it may be no one's fault that one firm emerges much bigger than all its competitors (and in practice the defining point of monopoly in law is whether competitors alter your behaviour).

For instance, the marginal cost of performing an Internet search is pretty much zero, and so the more searches are performed through your company, the more profit you make. Even if you have competitors, this structure is likely to lead to a situation where a dominant firm has the bulk of the market. Another type of legal monopoly is when intellectual property, such as patents or copyrights have been granted. In this case, a person or firm is permitted to have a temporary monopoly in order to give people an incentive to do expensive research and development.

Understanding the legal response

The issues we discuss in the preceding section mean that Competition Law tends to focus instead on the behaviour of firms with a dominant position in the marketplace. So a firm simply operating more efficiently than everyone else and therefore getting bigger than all its rivals is fine, but when in a dominant position the firm can't do certain things that smaller rivals are allowed to. These actions include:

- **Full line forcing:** The firm isn't permitted to require a purchaser of one of its products to take its whole range of products.

- **Pricing below cost:** If a firm has a dominant position, most likely it can cut its prices below cost in the short run in order to drive a rival out of the market (with, naturally, the intention of raising them after it has removed the rival). This action is subject to Competition Law, where it is called *predatory pricing* (though it's very hard to prove in practice!).

- **Making restrictive agreements:** For example, favouring some purchasers over others. One principle often invoked is that if you own a port, you aren't allowed to charge your own boats less to use it than those of rivals.

The intention isn't to prevent monopoly, but to prevent monopolising markets. In other words, the monopoly can exist but it can't go around behaving like one.

Taking companies to court

Case law on monopolies tends to be reasonably rare, because very few firms exist with the type of dominant position to be able to take the kinds of actions that attract the court's attention (a principle known as *de minimis non curat lex* – the law shouldn't care about small matters). The investigations can be very long-running: for instance, the EU investigation of Microsoft for full line forcing by making its own Internet browser default for Windows users has been over a decade in the making, and the penalties can vary from behavioural undertakings and simple promises to behave better, to extremely large fines levied on global turnover, depending on the degree to which a judge can be persuaded that the case involves unfair or unjust conduct.

Famous cases (other than Microsoft) worldwide include the break-ups of AT&T in the US (where the courts agreed that competition could only be restored if the respective monopolies were broken up), *France Telecom SA v Commission* (where fines for pricing below cost totalled millions) and Laker Airways' suit against its transatlantic route rivals in 1982, which was settled out of court for $50 million.

Note that all these cases, however, involve restraints of trade in addition to monopoly power. Monopoly can quite happily exist without anyone having thought up a ruse to create one: called natural monopoly.

'You Make Me Feel Like a Natural Monopoly'

Okay, we admit that this heading's phrasing scans much better with Carole King's original words, but in this section we describe how a monopoly can come about simply because only one company can serve a market. Consider, if you will, the National Power Grid: few persuasive arguments can be made that the country would necessarily be better off if government broke it up.

The key to understanding this point is to consider the *long run average costs* (LRAC) of the monopoly and, in particular, the minimum point of LRAC, the *minimum efficient scale* (or MES). Two cases apply here, depending on whether the MES is small relative to the total size of the market or close to it; we show both scenarios in Figure 13-5.

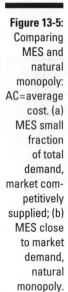

Figure 13-5: Comparing MES and natural monopoly: AC=average cost. (a) MES small fraction of total demand, market competitively supplied; (b) MES close to market demand, natural monopoly.

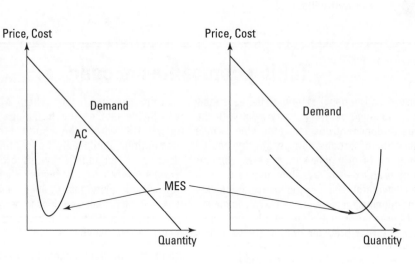

When the MES of the firm serving that market is small, firms can operate at their most efficient point when holding only a small fraction of the market. Therefore you're likely to see the market as being competitively supplied. If, however, MES is very close to or even greater than the total demand in that market, that market is only ever likely to be supplied by one firm.

The question for economists is what to do about this situation, given that they don't like monopolies very much. One option for dealing with natural monopoly where you don't expect much benefit to result from breaking the firm up, is to set up a system of regulation instead.

In practice, regulation tends to work in one of two ways:

- ✔ **Rate of return regulation:** The regulator caps the overall level of profit of a company, perhaps insisting that it can't make more than, say, 5 per cent for its activities. In practice, however, this approach has drawbacks because it requires the regulator to have a lot of knowledge about the cost and the revenue side of the company. For this reason, in the UK at least, price regulation tends to be preferred.

- ✔ **Price regulation:** This approach typically limits the amount by which a firm can raise its prices to some level below the overall rise in the Retail Prices Index (RPI) (at least usually, but not always, as in the case of water, which had suffered from so much underinvestment prior to privatisation that it was felt the formula couldn't work); hence the famous formula RPI – X used in Britain in the 1990s. The intention of this method is to get the prices charged by the monopoly close to – ideally – marginal cost; but if that isn't possible then average cost. The advantage of this approach is that the firm knows what it can charge, but has the option of becoming more efficient and getting its costs down, meaning that the regulator doesn't need to know every single thing about the firm's costs to regulate it efficiently.

Economists seldom expect the world to be perfect, no matter what some of their models are called. They do, however, prefer that monopoly is treated as a problem rather than a benefit. Where this is impossible, they look for ways to get around it, and sometimes that means interfering in markets to make them work better!

Chapter 14

Examining Market Failure: Pollution and Parks

Hot spicy sauce is a tasty way of injecting flavour into a boring dish. It's also a major public nuisance! In one case, a restaurant in central London was suspected of terrorism after passersby complained of burning sensations in their noses and throats. The police suspected chemical weapons – yes, really! – until enquiries led them to the restaurant, which made its own hot sauce on the premises. The burning fumes from this sauce had caused the disturbance! In another case, residents around a factory that produces a leading brand of hot sauce in the US banded together, complaining of similar symptoms. The result was a lawsuit against the factory.

On a seemingly different note (bear with us), a colleague of ours came back from a trip to Dundee and professed himself amazed by the quality and large number of parks clustered in one place; he was especially astounded by the fact that they were all free for the burghers of Dundee to enjoy. He was surprised because parks cost money to create and maintain, but not one charged money to enter: how could a market system possibly provide them?

To economists, these two cases are linked by the concept of *market failure*, which comes in two types:

✔ **Where a market provides something that society doesn't want:** In the case of the hot sauce makers, the market exposed people not involved in the supply or purchase of hot sauce to a cost – pollution.

✔ **When a market fails to provide something society does want:** In the case of public parks, a bias exists against producing goods for which the market has difficulty charging.

Economists spent a lot of time looking at these two types of market failure and came up with a library of ways to categorise the problems and find methods of solving them. In this chapter, we lead you through some of the simpler cases, so that you can see how economists approach the issue of market failure and what steps policy makers can take to solve it.

Coming to Grips with Externality: Too Much of a Bad Thing

Sometimes, as a result of trading, markets produce byproducts that society doesn't want or like, such as pollution from industrial processes. While looking at the specific problem of pollution, economists came up with a definition of the problem that makes sense more generally about the use of markets.

When two people make a trade and some part of the costs falls on a third party, that third person experiences an *external cost*. The general existence of external costs is called an *externality*.

Here's an illustration. In a market, two people – Molly and Nick – make a contract. In this contract, Molly decides that she wants to buy Nick's product and hands over her money, and Nick supplies the product.

On the surface, all appears fine. But suppose that Molly's and Nick's trade places a cost on a third party – Olivia – who wasn't part of that trade. The cost that falls on Olivia is the external cost.

Externalities can be one of two types:

- ✔ **Positive externalities:** Benefits conferred on a third party.
- ✔ **Negative externalities:** Costs that a third party incurs.

When economists look at externalities, they try to be careful about remedying them. For instance, Molly's and Nick's trade creates value and benefits both Molly and Nick. Only the cost that falls upon Olivia is undesirable and that's the bit economists want to remedy. As a result they don't want to impose a ban on Molly and Nick if they can avoid doing so.

Instead they want to find mechanisms that reduce the degree to which an external cost falls upon Olivia without using legal prohibitions. In this section, we discuss two of the approaches that economists advocate: one involving taxes and the other negotiation and contracts.

Both these solutions, however, depend on feasibility. For example, imagine an airline trying to negotiate with every single person affected by its landing noise! Ultimately, if you can't negotiate or work out a social-cost calculation (that is, a tax), your last resort may be legal prohibition!

Reducing externalities with taxes

Pigovian taxes, after Arthur Pigou the economist, are one method for tackling the issue of externalities. The idea is quite simple and identifies the following two sets of benefits and costs:

- ✔ **Private:** Benefits and costs gained or incurred by the two main parties in a trade.
- ✔ **Social:** Benefits and costs that fall upon everyone.

The key is to make the private cost equal to the social cost, which a government can do by taxing the private transaction.

Pigovian taxes in action

Here's how Pigou's method works. When a person is trying to get the maximum benefit from doing something, he does so up to the point where marginal benefit equals marginal cost (see Chapter 3). Thus, without a tax, the equilibrium in consumption is where marginal benefit equals marginal cost. If you measure the marginal benefit by using marginal revenue – which works for a private transaction – you can derive a simple model (see Figure 14-1).

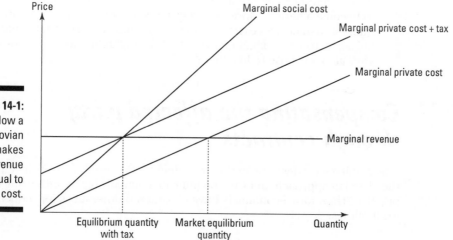

Figure 14-1:
How a
Pigovian
tax makes
revenue
equal to
social cost.

Note the presence in the figure of two types of equilibrium:

- ✔ **Market equilibrium:** Marginal private cost is equal to marginal revenue.

- ✔ **Social equilibrium:** Marginal social cost equals marginal revenue.

Assuming that the transactions themselves are costless, the government can add the Pigovian tax to each unit of a polluting good and therefore reduce the quantity of the 'bad' produced.

The difficulty of taxing

Economists often study what they call *wicked* problems, meaning that they tend to have no solutions or have solutions that themselves are subject to widespread disagreement. The case of taxing production of a 'bad' is just one of many such problems!

In particular, a number of problems exist with Pigou's approach:

- ✔ **Measurement:** Measuring and determining the social cost of something isn't easy and therefore neither is determining the right level of tax. Even Pigou found this to be a wicked problem in and of itself. For instance, some part of the cost may not be easily measurable because it's borne psychologically by the person subject to the external cost, and so doesn't readily show up in any data you can use for calculating the cost.

- ✔ **Gaming:** The level of the tax can be influenced by lobbying on behalf of the polluting industry. This gaming happened in several cases and leads to losses for society.

- ✔ **Reciprocity:** In a society all people are interconnected and one person's trade is another's external cost. To get away from this reality you'd need to become a hermit! More seriously, if you move into an area knowing that, for instance, an extremely loud nightclub is nearby that could be a nuisance, to what extent can you hold the nightclub owner responsible – after all, you chose to live there!

Compensating the affected party through contracts

The problems we describe in the preceding section don't entirely invalidate the Pigovian approach, but they do indicate some problems with using it in practice. Therefore, economists have considered other ideas for reducing externalities.

One such approach is based on people contracting with each other, instead of having the government involved via taxes. This method is a contrasting way of looking at the problem compared to Pigou's and is often used as a basis for developing policy on big, wicked problems such as climate change.

Coase theorem

Ronald Coase looked at the problem of social cost in a famous paper in 1960. His analysis became a famous result called the Coase theorem.

The *Coase theorem* features the following two related points:

- ✔ When property rights are completely assigned and parties can negotiate costlessly, the parties can always negotiate an efficient outcome; the legal framework just determines the payer of the cost.

- ✔ Negotiation is sufficient *unless* property rights are incomplete or negotiating is too costly.

The first point about property rights is a key observation. In many of the most wicked problems that economics has been asked to solve, the issue is that no one has a property right over the resource. For example, consider who owns the air: either no one, in which case the first problem exists of not being able to assign the property rights completely; or everyone, in which case negotiation between every citizen is unfeasible and costly!

Whereas Pigou's model implies that social cost can be known and measured, Coase's focus is on cases of unremedied externality as situations where property rights aren't fully assigned.

He uses a thought experiment about a doctor and a baker who work next door to each other. The doctor needs quiet to treat patients, but the baker's kneading and pounding of dough makes a noise that's essential to the baker's work. The prevailing logic was that the baker should therefore have to compensate the doctor.

Coase begins by pointing out the reciprocal problem. You can equally well frame the doctor as moving to a place where a bakery exists and then demanding that the baker bake in silence. Now suppose that a wise town councillor is fed up being harangued over the argument of who's responsible for the noise. He points out that the baker could install quieter machinery for £50 and the doctor install soundproofing for £100. The cheapest solution is therefore that the baker installs quieter machinery.

So that solves that, right? Well, not quite! In fact, two different possibilities exist depending on who has a property right over the ability to make – or be free from – noise:

✔ **If the doctor has the 'sound rights' over the building:** The baker has to pay the £50 for quieter machinery.

✔ **If the baker has the 'sound rights' over the building:** The doctor has to pay to reduce the noise. He could soundproof his own office for £100, although paying £50 to the baker for quieter machinery makes more sense as it's a far cheaper option.

Therefore, you can arrive at the best solution economically, regardless of who's responsible for the noise, as long as property rights are completely assigned and people can negotiate. Here, the cost of remedying the externality is £50, the most economically efficient outcome regardless of who has the 'sound rights' – the only difference is who ultimately pays the £50!

Coase is interested in: why parties don't negotiate when they can; and what to do when property rights aren't assigned.

One thing that the Coase theorem absolutely doesn't do is say that the market can solve all externalities: that's a completely fallacious reading of the argument. Instead, it says that if you can completely assign property rights and you can negotiate then the market *may* solve the externality. In some cases these options may be unfeasible!

Coase theorem in practice

Economists use Coase's reasoning when thinking about emissions – particularly of carbon – on a global scale; the idea spawned the approach that led to *cap and trade* policies for climate change. As regards the use of a carbon tax, no doubt you can envisage all kinds of difficulties with implementing the tax on very different nations – should a rich nation, say Norway, have the same taxes as a poorer one, say Burkina Faso?

Instead, the carbon-market approach assigns each nation a tradeable property right over its own emissions. If one country emits less than the right allows, it can sell its spare capacity to a less efficient nation; if it can't (or won't) reduce its emissions, instead of paying a tax the nation can buy 'emission certificates' from countries not using their full allocation. Thus, you hope, everyone is made as happy as possible!

Making the Market Produce What It Won't: Public Goods

The market can't produce everything that society wants, often because the good isn't something for which businesses can charge.

At the beginning of this chapter, we mention the public parks of Dundee. What's remarkable about these particular parks is that they were a gift to the city by a group of wealthy industrialists called the 'Jute Barons' who ran textiles operations. Their bequests to the city exist to this day, as do other examples of parks created by philanthropists, for instance the famous Griffith Park in Los Angeles.

Public parks are almost never provided by a market system because of the type of goods they tend to be:

- ✔ **Non-rival:** One person's consumption doesn't affect another person also enjoying the good, which means that the marginal cost (see Chapter 3) of supplying the good to one additional person is zero.

- ✔ **Non-excludable:** You can't prevent people from enjoying the good, even if they haven't paid for it.

This special set of economic circumstances means that the market doesn't provide these goods. If the marginal cost is zero and the good is non-excludable, price tends to fall to the marginal cost, which is zero. Market systems therefore have incredible difficulty pricing the good.

We discuss some suggested ways of remedying the situation in this section. As you read what follows, though, bear in mind that not everything that looks like a public good upfront turns out to be one and some things that you'd think aren't turn out to be very similar to public goods!

Defining goods by rivalry and excludability

You can categorise goods in all sorts of ways, but here we're interested in thinking through whether the good is *rival* (the marginal cost is higher than zero) or *excludable* (you can keep out someone who hasn't paid from consuming the good), or both.

Four options exist:

- ✔ **Normal good:** One that's rival and excludable, which constitutes most things the market provides.

- ✔ **Public good:** One that's non-rival and non-excludable, such as street lighting or radio broadcasts in the UK.

- ✔ **Club good:** One that's non-rival but excludable. Some pay TV services fall into this category, though you can argue that technology has eroded some of the excludability of the services by enabling people to get them by illegal means.

- ✔ **Common good:** One that's rival but non-excludable. Think about grazing rights on common land: no one owns the land and so it's non-excludable, but because grazing affects the amount of grass available to another cow or sheep, it's definitely rival. We discuss a special economic problem that affects these goods in the later section 'Considering a common (goods) tragedy'.

A few really tough cases are tricky to place in one category. One of the most difficult is the case of pure information, such as TV, software, music and other digitally transmitted material, which is non-rival – when you've written a song it doesn't matter whether one person or a billion hear it, the cost was the fixed cost of writing the song, not the transmission cost – but partially excludable and often charged for.

Viewing a screen test!

Pricing information was a wicked problem for the founders of the broadcast TV industry. TV programmes are non-rival but not easily excludable, because they're easy to pick up and view. Broadly, the industry founders came up with three different solutions for the problem:

- ✔ In the US, they decided to view the product as a way of getting people to see adverts and so got advertisers to fund programming.

- ✔ In much of Europe, they used tax funding, eventually mixed with advertising.

- ✔ In the UK, owing to suspicion about the idea of the government funding TV through taxes, they came up with a subscription model backed up by a legally mandated licence fee.

All these solutions have advantages and drawbacks, but all – more or less – worked until digital distribution made everyone rethink the economics of the industry.

Seeing spillovers, considering public benefits and providing public goods

When you get down to the simplest definitions, a market makes the cost of something equal to its benefit. A trade gets made when someone agrees to pay a cost for a given benefit. In the case of goods with public benefits, though, a difficulty exists in equating the price with the benefit. This problem is similar to the difficulty of setting Pigovian taxes – social costs and social benefits are difficult to calculate (check out the earlier section 'Reducing externalities with taxes').

A public benefit is actually another kind of externality, one that gives a benefit to a party not involved in the transaction. In this case, the person gaining the benefit is a *free rider* – which slightly unfairly compares him to a person riding a train without paying!

The wicked problem is that almost no one exactly knows what the public benefit is and, because the benefit can't be easily measured, no one really knows how to price it in to a market by negotiation. The practical result is that a market almost never provides goods that fall into the public good definition.

So how are these goods provided, and what can the public do to get more of them? Well, several mechanisms have been used over the centuries:

- **Patronage:** In the past many composers of music – which has public-good aspects – benefitted from patrons. These rich supporters of the arts decided what to give based on their estimation of how valuable a composer's work and their funding of it was to their social standing.

- **Philanthropy:** In this approach, wealthy individuals or groups bequeath items to society as a social good that fits with their view of their roles as 'good' people. Economists would be a little reluctant to rely on this method because the profession doesn't like assuming qualities such as 'goodness' as part of its basic modelling strategy.

- **Public provision:** Of course, the State can also be the patron or philanthropist from general public spending. This is one of the ways that countries get essentials such as parks or street lights. The disadvantage is that it takes provision into the political realm, and things get a little murky – too murky for some economists!

- **Crowdfunding:** This modern approach is a variant of the philanthropy or patronage models. Here, the Internet makes it cheap enough to allow a large number of people to be patrons, each contributing a small slice of revenue. The research into the effectiveness of this solution is still new (because the technologies are), but it has already brought products that the market system was unwilling to develop to the public. We both very much enjoyed the movie *Veronica Mars* that was a result of this system.

None of these systems is perfect. Crowdfunding can fail, patronage can result in too much control over the thing funded and public provision can make everything a political battle! With a little help – for instance, a tax break to induce philanthropists to part with their money – you can get more of the provision, but the systems can still fail to produce what society wants.

Considering a common (goods) tragedy

Common goods create contention wherever you go, because although they're rival, they're also non-excludable.

This specific issue is called the *Tragedy of the Commons* and it's contentious because when a good is common every user has an incentive to overuse the resource.

To see why, think about cod stocks. No one owns the sea and so it's non-excludable. But because the stocks of cod in the sea are rival, overusing the resource leads to depletion. Overuse is exactly what happened in reality, leading to the collapse of cod populations such as those on the Grand Banks in the North Atlantic (people used to say that they were so full of cod that you could walk straight over them – though you'd need to watch your step!).

Over the years, the Tragedy of the Commons has been refined, mainly in thinking about it in terms of poor management of a common resource. In particular, Elinor Ostrom did a lot of research into how indigenous people, such as the Masai in Kenya, managed common land. She found that the dimensions of the Tragedy of the Commons were overstated and relied on people not using a common framework.

Ostrom's main point is that when people can agree on a common framework for managing the commons, they can eliminate or at least lessen the tragedy. She describes four conditions that can achieve this goal:

- ✔ **Resources with definable boundaries are easier to preserve:** International waters, for example, are one of the harder cases, because the boundary definition is imprecise.

- ✔ **Communities find managing the resource easier with the threat of resource depletion and a lack of substitutes:** The fear of resource depletion is an incentive to preserve the resource.

- ✔ **The presence of a community helps manage the resource:** In particular, a strong, stable economy has a collective interest in preserving the resource.

- ✔ **The community needs a set of rules and procedures:** Such as dealing with individual overuse and agreeing common use.

In essence, when you put these four conditions together you end up with a community treating the common good *as if* it holds a property right over the resource, which means that people are willing to invest time and effort into maintaining it.

Preventing good things: Anti-commons

The flipside of the Tragedy of the Commons in the preceding section is the *anti-commons,* which reflects situations where too many private property rights prevent the development of a common benefit.

Think about the difficulties of negotiating with all the people affected by building a new road in town. At some point, because all property owners want to be compensated up to their estimation of the individual value of their property, instead of their property's value as a share of the total cost, the required buyouts can be prohibitively expensive and necessary common projects fail to take place.

The answer is a structure called the Compulsory Purchase Order (CPO) in the UK (it's called eminent domain in the US, by the way), which gets invoked and forces landowners to sell when a 'fair' price is met. That way, society gets its product and landowners get compensation – though not so much that it imperils the project. This system isn't perfect by any stretch of the imagination – court cases can still go on for years – but it does at least prevent holdouts from stopping projects going ahead.

'I can't hear you!'

One interesting case of the anti-commons effect is the issue of clearing music rights for DVDs. When broadcasts use music, a compulsory licence scheme giving standard compensation works, so that broadcasting the shows isn't prohibitively expensive. But this scheme doesn't apply to DVDs – they're not covered. So when the producers of the show want to release a DVD of the show, they have to make a separate arrangement with the music's licence holders.

In the case of the successful 1990s TV series *Northern Exposure,* many individual rights holders had to clear and all wanted full compensation. The result was that the producers abandoned the deal, and commissioned licence-free music for the bulk of the re-release. To this day – and to the dismay of fans – the show has never been released with its original music on DVD!

Another serious problem of the anti-commons effect is in the area of pharmaceuticals. Many medicines depend on prior discoveries for at least part of their formulas, and patents still cover some of them. If the patent holders demand the best possible fee, and you can't negotiate it down, investing in developing the new medicine can become uneconomic. In these cases, society loses through the excessive ability of owners of the properties to extract the highest possible price for their work.

The general remedy to this situation is compulsory or pooled licensing. In these situations, the government negotiates a standard fee with patent holders to prevent them stopping the new product.

Chapter 15

Understanding the Dangers of Asymmetric Information

. . . .

In This Chapter

▶ Spotting asymmetric information in action

▶ Encouraging people to behave 'badly'

. . . .

During the banking crisis of 2008–9, one of the key financial markets – the interbank lending market – juddered to a halt. The problem was that needing to borrow on the market had become a signal to a lender that the bank was in a poor financial state. A bank trying to engage in the perfectly normal behaviour of borrowing from another bank was telling the potential lender that it needed credit, and so inadvertently identifying itself as a risk. As a result, until more normal trading conditions returned, no one would risk lending to anyone else!

The only lenders left in the game at this point were central banks. Amid cries for bailouts, the central bankers had to ponder a difficult question: if you establish the principle that a central bank will bail out a bank in distress, aren't you saying to those banks that they can rely on you? And doesn't that mean that banks have less incentive to keep themselves honest and healthy, financially speaking? After all, if they don't, they can always come to the central bank for a bailout!

These two cases – signalling that you're risky by your need to borrow and risking giving someone a bad incentive by bailing them out – are aspects of a big economic problem called *asymmetric information:* where one side has more information than the other side in a deal. The first case is an example of *adverse selection* – the ones who want to borrow are bad risks for lenders. The second is an example of *moral hazard* – the terms of the bailout provide an incentive to behave badly. Whereas previous models (for instance, the ones in Chapters 9–14) assume that a market equilibrium exists, asymmetric information can make markets break down and 'fail', leading to no trading taking place at all.

Asymmetric information problems rear their head every time a seller knows more about the quality of her product than a buyer, which means that reading developments in many markets relies on them – asymmetric information is a regular occurrence in many markets. They're at the heart of labour market problems – when candidates know more about their abilities than hirers – and insurance problems – when buyers know their own risk levels better than insurers. They're also the bane of gambling industries, which rely on betters not knowing more about the market than bookies!

In the case of asymmetric information, what you don't know *can* hurt you – which is why you need to read this chapter!

Seeing the Effects of Asymmetric Information

The trading models that we demonstrate throughout this book (especially those in Chapters 9–14) assume either that both parties have full knowledge of all relevant information or that they're equally ignorant. When you change this core assumption, things start to look very different indeed – as you discover in this section.

Visiting the market for lemons and plums

One way in which asymmetric information can lead to market failure is when it creates a negative *externality* (a cost imposed on a third party not included in the transaction – check out Chapter 14 for more about externalities).

In 1968 George Akerlof published an extremely important article on the economics of asymmetric information. 'The Market for Lemons' shows very simply how asymmetric information affects markets – even shutting them down as bad products drive out good.

We begin by assuming that a used car market has two kinds of car:

- ✔ **Lemons:** An American term for real clunkers – products of poor quality.
- ✔ **Plums:** Products of good quality.

Suppose that 100 people are selling their cars, and that buyers know that 50 of the cars are plums and 50 lemons. The sellers know beforehand which is which, but the buyers don't know until they buy – *caveat emptor*, folks (let the buyer beware)!

Now we put in some prices. Suppose that the sellers are willing to sell a plum for £2,000 and a lemon for £1,000. That would, fairly, show that their price is related to the quality. Imagine that the buyers are willing to pay a little more than that amount: £2,400 for a plum and £1,200 for a lemon. What's the equilibrium (check out Chapter 9)?

Well, if you could immediately tell whether you're buying a plum or a lemon, you'd just have two separate equilibria where a plum went for £2,000–2,400 and a lemon for £1,000–1,200.

But buyers can't tell here! So their best strategy is to offer the expected value of the car – which you get by multiplying the buyers' offer by the probability of getting that type of car. If they know that 50 per cent of the cars are lemons then the expected value (EV) is as follows:

$$EV = (0.5 \times 2,400) + (0.5 \times 1,200) = £1,800$$

That's the maximum that a buyer would bid for a car of unknown – some may say dubious! – quality. But now suppose that the sellers know that buyers would only pay £1,800 for a car, what do they do?

Sellers of plums leave the market, because buyers are willing to pay only £1,800 for a car and plum sellers won't sell for less than £2,000! But wait, it gets worse! Now buyers know that only lemons are left in the market. They won't pay more than £1,200 for a car and so the market equilibrium drives out good cars and leaves only the market for lemons! The externality makes bad cars drive out good and the market fails.

Signalling your risk by buying cover: Adverse selection

Sometimes the externality arising from asymmetric information that we describe in the preceding section gets so bad that it can destroy an entire market. In the case of interbank lending during the financial crisis, it very nearly did. If lending banks *knew* that the only borrowers were poor risks, they couldn't very well lend at the prevailing rate!

The problem was that some banks were in real trouble, and as long as they had enough effect on the lenders' view of the average likelihood of failure in the market as a whole, the lenders couldn't lend to them.

This problem relates to hidden information – the lenders were unable to observe directly the quality of the borrowers, but they could read the need for capital as a *signal* (we talk more about signals in Chapter 19). Runaway signals eventually made lenders almost disappear from the market.

Demonstrating adverse selection with a quality-selection model

A simple way of seeing adverse selection is with a quality-selection model. Here, producers choose whether to produce a high-quality as opposed to a low-quality item. They do that with a probability q, and what you want to know is what size of q will keep the market working.

We start by loading some prices into the model so that you can see it in action. Suppose that the product is a normal good (that is, rival and excludable – see Chapter 14 for definitions), such as a standard midrange mobile phone. A better-quality one would cost you £100 and a lower-quality one £64. Manufacturers can make a midrange phone for £85. We make everything nice and easy by assuming that the industry is in perfect competition– so that the phones aren't differentiated by obvious features and the price equals marginal cost.

Starting off with that information, three things can happen:

- ✔ **If high-quality manufacturers are the only ones in the market:** The equilibrium price is somewhere between £85 and £100, but perfect competition means that it gets competed down to £85.

- ✔ **If low-quality manufacturers are the only ones in the market:** Customers are willing to pay only £64. The manufacturing cost is £85 and so no phones are produced and no market exists.

- ✔ **If high- and low-quality manufacturers are in the market:** The market clears only if q is big enough to ensure that the expected value (EV) of customers is also higher than the cost of production. So you need to know what value of q leads to EV being £85.

Finding the value of q that clears the market therefore means solving the expected value equation:

$$85 = (100q) + (64(1-q))$$

The answer is 7/12!

Graphing the equilibrium result allows you to see how this market failure manifests (check out Figure 15-1). Putting price on the vertical axis and q on the horizontal, you can show the market failure as a blank area where no items are sold. The supply is horizontal, as in perfect competition, but only above $q = 7/12$! Above that, the diagonal shows consumers' willingness to pay, that is, the expected value as q goes up (it can't be bigger than 1!). Between the two is a shaded area of consumer surplus – excess benefit the consumers get when they're willing to pay more than the £85 that producers end up charging.

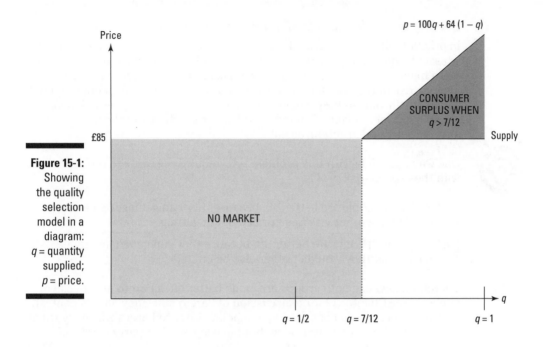

Figure 15-1:
Showing
the quality
selection
model in a
diagram:
q = quantity
supplied;
p = price.

Note that the shaded oblong – no market equilibrium – reflects the external cost of producers not producing a quality product. If enough of them exist they destroy the entire market! But if each individual producer doesn't believe that they, individually, contribute to the average quality in the marketplace, they have an incentive not to choose to produce at a high quality. Thus, poorer products tend to drive out better ones, and consumers lose out.

Seeing what happens when producers choose product quality

Adapting the model to allow producers to choose the quality of the product they'll produce shows how adverse selection can destroy both high- and low-quality markets. Suppose that the cost of making a high-quality phone is a little more, say £90, and the manufacturer can choose which to make.

Consider the position of a high-quality manufacturer. It knows that it has only a small fraction of the market, and so it too has an incentive to produce a lower-quality phone. Unfortunately the same reasoning is true of all the higher-quality manufacturers. Because a consumer will pay only £64 for a low-quality phone, no equilibrium exists and high-and low-quality markets disappear!

Dealing with adverse selection through compulsory coverage

In practice, adverse selection is generally associated with insurance markets, where two populations have two different levels of risk. When one population has a higher risk and one a lower risk, no insurance company can use the average risk of the population to price its product: lower-risk people wouldn't get a bargain, and so they wouldn't be in the market, and higher-risk people would make more claims! Therefore, the bad risks drive out the good – adverse selection in action, again!

One way of dealing with this problem is to require everyone to buy a product with the average-risk profile:

- ✔ High-risk people are better off, because they can get insurance that they'd have otherwise been priced out of getting.

- ✔ Lower-risk people are better off, because they can get an insurance policy that they wouldn't otherwise be offered.

Therefore, because both groups are made better off, a Pareto improvement applies – see Chapter 12 for a discussion of Pareto efficiency. In this context, *Pareto improvement* means getting to a point closer to Pareto efficiency when no party can be made better off without making another party worse off.

Changing Your Behaviour because of Asymmetric Information

In October 2008, recapitalising the banks by providing huge amounts of capital was part of policy makers' solution to the crisis in the financial markets. The principal aim was to prevent the financial system from descending into an even greater crisis. One side effect, however, was the need to manage something called moral hazard.

Moral hazard is a situation that gives an incentive to someone to behave 'badly'. Suppose, for instance, that you have superb all-coverage insurance. You may not have an incentive to fit a good-quality lock on your back door, because you know that if someone gets into your house, the insurer and not you is going to pay for the loss.

In the case of the bank bailouts, many commentators saw the bailouts as an invitation for banks to lend recklessly. If the banks knew that the government would pick up the bill, they had no incentive to stop lending recklessly – when things worked out well, they made large profits and when they didn't, they weren't taking the losses.

Managing moral hazard

Policy makers and companies seek to manage moral hazard in different ways, including the following:

- ✔ **Banking:** During the bailouts, the government took voting shares in the banks, essentially taking bailed-out banks into public ownership – the government still owns 22 per cent of Lloyd's, for instance. This owner-ship should give the government the ability to monitor and manage the bank although that also depends on the wisdom of the government in managing the situation. You probably have your own views on whether that's a good thing to depend on!

- ✔ **Insurance:** Loss adjusters can inspect claims, or companies can insert behavioural clauses into contracts to ensure that a person does what she says she's going to do.

- ✔ **Insurance:** Companies cover perhaps only 90 per cent of the losses to ensure that the customer bears some of the risk. This excess provides at least *some* incentive to take care!

If an insurer could observe accurately how much care a customer would take, no moral hazard problem exists and the market would work as efficiently as it should. But because the insurer doesn't know, the outcome of moral hazard is under-insurance – each consumer would like to buy more insur-ance, but the insurance companies would be less likely to provide it because rational customers who'd buy the product would have the incentive to take less care! That's why insurers insist on the type of clauses mentioned above.

Incentivising! Asymmetric information in contracts

One classic problem in which asymmetric information and moral hazard pop up is when you want to get someone to do something for you – the other person knows more about whether she's going to do it or not!

Considering the principal–agent problem

One problem of this kind is the *principal–agent problem*. It concerns a princi-pal wanting to get an agent to do something for him and an agent having her own interests that she wants to take care of first.

A good example is a Hollywood agent who gets paid a percentage of the fees of an actor she represents. The actor – the principal here – has an interest in maximising his lifetime career standing and is therefore particular about what kind of jobs he wants to take. The agent, however, just wants to maximise her percentage and tries to get the actor signed up for as many jobs as possible, regardless of quality.

More seriously, the principal–agent problem also exists in the structure of an ordinary company. Shareholders own the company and are the principals, but managers are their agents. Management may want to act in its own interests rather than the principals' interests. Thus shareholders need a scheme for making the management act in their interests. The simplest though not always most effective way is to pay managers in company stock, so that they take the same risks and gain the same benefits as do the owners. But that may not always work!

Modelling incentives for contracts

In a contract, an owner (the principal) wants a manager (the agent) to put in an effort, x^*, which is known to the manager but not the owner. The manager wants to choose her own utility-maximising level of x. What should the owner do?

Simples! The profit-maximising level of x has to be the level where the marginal product to making x amount of effort is equal to the cost of performing the effort. So the owner wants to choose x^* on that basis.

The owner needs to write this requirement into an *incentive compatible contract* – one specifying that the utility to the manager of doing anything other than x^* is less than the utility of doing x^*.

Here are three methods the owner can use to achieve this aim:

- ✔ **Rent:** The owner can charge the manager a rent, R, so that after the manager has paid R – you can think of this amount as a franchise fee if you want – any profit belongs to the manager. In that way, the manager chooses x^* in the same way as if she were the owner.

- ✔ **Wages:** Setting wages so that the marginal product of the manager's work equals the wage has the same effect as the preceding point.

- ✔ **Fixed fee:** The owner can pay the manager a fixed fee if x^* is achieved and nothing if it's not.

What won't work is a share scheme where manager and owner divvy up the output. The manager won't be trying to maximise marginal product but only the share of marginal product that she gets. Calling that share α, the manager would be trying to set α times the marginal product equal to marginal cost, and that won't give the optimal output x^*!

Now suppose that the owner is never able to determine the correct amount of effort the manager puts in – which certainly makes the model more realistic! In this case, more problems apply with the solutions:

- ✔ If the manager is more risk averse than the owner, and output is random, renting means that the manager is willing to give up some of the residual profits in favour of greater income certainty. (This problem exists with franchises.)

- ✔ Wage setting depends on owners being able to assess the amount of labour input. If the owner can't do that, using wages is necessarily inefficient.

- ✔ In a take it or leave it case, the manager is at risk of losing everything if the output can't be controlled from her desk, which places all the risk on the manager and is unlikely to be agreed to as a contract!

- ✔ If the output fluctuates, the profit-sharing solution means that both parties take on some of the risk, though not all! In turn, the manager has the incentive to produce some output but isn't carrying all the risk!

As you can see, the value of an incentive contract depends crucially on the degree to which the principal is able to monitor the efforts of the agent. If the principal can find out at some point, even if not upfront, what the agent is doing, then franchising, wages and fixed lump-sum payments are equivalent. If risk is present, so that neither the principal nor agent know how things will turn out, or the principal is never able to monitor the activity of the agent, profit-sharing becomes an efficient solution again!

Part V
Thinking Strategically: Life Is Just a Game!

	ROCK	PAPER	SCISSORS
ROCK	0,0	−1,1	1,−1
PAPER	1,−1	0,0	−1,1
SCISSORS	−1,1	1,−1	0,0

Developing strategy over the long term is an art that firms have to practise. How do they do it? By telling stories! Check out www.dummies.com/extras/microeconomics.

In this part . . .

✔ Use game theory to understand economic problems.

✔ Realise why the Nash equilibrium is such an important concept.

✔ Understand the way auction design affects strategy.

✔ Decipher people's signals that reveal their intentions.

Chapter 16

Playing Games with Economic Theory

· ·

In This Chapter

▶ Considering game design

▶ Exploring three useful game scenarios

▶ Repeating a game to affect the outcome

· ·

*G*ame theory is a powerful set of tools for probing into and modelling situations from an economist's perspective. It's a lens for looking at strategy and helping to clarify how outcomes affect behaviour and vice versa. Economists have used game theory to look at problems as diverse as nuclear deterrence, the way animals display dominance and even the best way for a striker and a goalkeeper to act in a penalty shootout in football. You can approach this range of problems using an underlying model that takes into account the behaviour of more than one party at a time and considers what people may do given a situation where the benefits – and of course the costs – depend on both sides' actions.

Game theory is one of the most popular – and more in the public conscious-ness – areas of the microeconomics course. When you know some of the models, you begin to recognise that game-theoretic situations feature in many dramas, films and TV shows, from *The Godfather* and *The Wire* to *Dr. Strangelove*. The famous Prisoners' Dilemma game (which we talk about in this chapter) is a staple of cop and detective dramas.

All these situations feature participants who want to maximise their own benefits given that another participant is trying to do exactly the same thing for himself. What emerges, generally, is an equilibrium that balances the interests of the two parties, though not necessarily so that both get exactly what they want.

In this chapter, we walk you through some basic concepts of game theory. We show you three cornerstone one-shot (played only once) models and how dealing with the situations involved has created – for good and for ill – some of the institutions people live with today. We also describe some of the ways in which you can apply game theory, sometimes all too practically, to real-world situations, and how things change when a game is repeated. We explore strategy through game theory, describe how co-operation and competition shape outcomes, and see what 'the best you can do' means when someone else is doing his best as well. Let the games commence!

Setting the Game: Mechanism Design

One of the key uses of game theory in the real world is in what theorists call *mechanism design:* setting up games so that a particular behaviour becomes the best strategy.

To show you what we mean, consider this example. You've been left with the demanding job of ensuring that two hyped-up 5 year olds cut a cake fairly between the two of them. You can set up the frame of the decision, but you can't make the decisions for the children (that has to be up to them). How do you do it?

You set up a mechanism in which one child cuts the cake and the other chooses which slice to take first. If the first child cuts the cake unfairly to try and fulfil his own self-interest, the second benefits from his unfairness by getting the first choice of the bigger slice! You've managed to design a mechanism in order to get fairness from the two children. This mechanism (often called 'I cut, you choose') is one of the simplest ways of getting a fair allocation of something between two people.

Mechanisms are very useful tools in economic policy, especially when you assume, or know, that the mechanism designer has less knowledge about the relative valuations and optimal choices of the parties who're competing or bargaining. This situation often applies in government auctions of things such as radio spectrums.

In these cases, the government knows the best maximum allocation of a resource, but not the value of the resource to all the players of the game. Therefore, the government wants to allow the players to self-select their strategies within a mechanism that forms bounds on their behaviour. By doing so, the government hopes that their individual optimal choices better matches its own objectives.

Game theory designs feature some core terms:

- ✔ **Hawk:** The party acting strictly in his own interests.

- ✔ **Dove:** The party acting in the collective interest of the group. Remember, however, that the Dove is doing so because its own individual interests lead it to do so.

- ✔ **Payoff:** The result of following any particular strategy.

Locking Horns with the Prisoners' Dilemma

The *Prisoners' Dilemma* scenario is a common starting point for exploring game theory because it's a nice simple model. It involves only two participants and an easily understood setting, which you'll recognise from many detective stories.

The set up of the Prisoners' Dilemma is an example of a mechanism designed to give the police the best chance of getting a confession. As a result, the structure of the payoffs is designed so that police have to do the least work in getting someone to play the Hawk (which we define in the preceding section). The intention is to give any given player an incentive to do as the designer of the game desires.

The Prisoners' Dilemma is a pretty dismal situation to find yourself in. After all, the police engineer the situation to extract a confession out of you. If you do find yourself being made an offer, you're already in a precarious situation!

More generally, however, the game's design allows economists to think about the behaviour that goes on in it between the participants. For instance, another way of looking at oligopoly (see Chapter 11) is as a type of Prisoners' Dilemma where firms have to decide whether to play Hawks – and produce less – or Doves –and produce more. The equilibrium found with two firms in an oligopoly is also a type of game theoretic equilibria – in this case Nash equilibria, which we talk about in the later section 'Finding the best outcome: The Nash equilibrium'.

Here we describe the Prisoners' Dilemma's set up, who it generally involves, the various ways in which it can play out and how you can avoid it – if you're ruthless enough!

Reading the plot of the Prisoners' Dilemma

The story goes like this. A bookmaker is robbed and the police apprehend two men for the crime. The detective investigating the robbery puts the two suspects into separate rooms – so that they can't communicate – and makes each one a one-time offer of a deal:

- **If neither participant confesses:** Both get six months in the slammer.

- **If one participant confesses and the other doesn't:** The participant who confesses is released, while the one who doesn't confess gets a five-year sentence.

- **If both participants confess:** They both go to jail for two years.

The question is: when the suspects are presented with the same deal, what happens?

On the face of it, you may think this is a 'no-brainer' for the suspects. Obviously, the best outcome is that neither of them confess and they end up serving six months in prison each. After all, this means that the total time served by the two suspects is the least. Obviously they'd be entirely mad to go through with any other action: so neither should confess, right?

If you do think that (and many people do before they investigate the scenario), alas you'd be wrong. Suppose that the first suspect, Mr Pink, decides that he doesn't want to confess. He doesn't know what Mr Blue (his partner in crime) has decided – so he daren't assume that Blue hasn't already taken a deal that puts Pink in prison for five years.

Similarly, locked away from Mr Pink, Mr Blue doesn't know that Pink hasn't decided to rat him out too, sending Blue to prison for five years. Because neither suspect can take the chance that the other person isn't a stool pigeon, co-operating with the police to cut himself a better deal, neither of them can take the option of relying on the other not confessing. So both confess and get a two-year sentence each – game over!

The key to understanding this result is that both participants are considered economically rational agents (as we define in Chapter 2) and therefore they want to do the best for themselves, given the actions of the other party. In this case, the two parties are thinking through what the other man may do. As a result, they both fear that the other person has a good incentive to do something that makes the first man worse off, and so neither can possibly take the offer that looks best for him!

Solving the Prisoners' Dilemma with a payoff matrix

Economists look at the Prisoners' Dilemma through some of the tools of game theory. The first and perhaps clearest way to do so is with a *payoff matrix* – a simple chart that shows what the payoffs are to both participants given their choices in the game. In this version (see Figure 16-1), we label the two participants as Mr Pink and Mr Blue, and the two actions they can perform in this setting as 'Confess' and 'Don't confess'.

		Mr Blue's moves	
Mr Pink's moves		Confess	Don't confess
	Confess	−2 −2	−5 −0
	Don't confess	−0 −5	−0.5 −0.5

Figure 16-1: Payoff matrix for the Prisoners' Dilemma.

When you read down the columns, the payoffs to Blue's actions (*moves* in game terminology) are shown against the payoffs to Pink's moves. For example, when Blue doesn't confess but Pink does, the payoffs are no loss of time in jail for Pink and a loss of five hard years for Blue. Similarly, when you read along the rows, the same pair of moves gives the payoffs: a loss of nothing for Pink and a loss of five years for Blue.

The payoffs are dependent on the actions of both participants. For instance, although confessing lets Pink out of serving jail time, it does so only *given that Blue doesn't confess*. If Blue also confesses, the advantage Pink gets from being the only one to confess is wiped out.

This sort of matrix is called the *strategic form* or *normal form* of the game, and its purpose is to clarify the payoffs so that you can see clearly which strategies wouldn't be chosen and which would be. Most importantly, it helps you to see one of the most important concepts in game theory – the Nash equilibrium.

Finding the best outcome: The Nash equilibrium

Named after the celebrated mathematician John Nash (played by Russell Crowe in the biopic *A Beautiful Mind*), the *Nash equilibrium* has a special role in game theory. It's defined as that set of strategies where no player has an incentive to change. Or less formally, the combination of strategies where players are doing the best they can given what other players are doing.

In the Prisoners' Dilemma, the Nash equilibrium is the top left corner where Blue and Pink have a pair of strategies that make them as well off as they can be given each other's options (see Figure 16-2).

		Mr Blue's moves	
Mr Pink's moves		Confess	Don't confess
	Confess	−2 −2	−5 −0
	Don't confess	−0 −5	−0.5 −0.5

Figure 16-2: Nash equilibrium in the Prisoners' Dilemma.

Nash equilibrium

The Nash equilibrium isn't the payoff where any given person is best off nor is it the one that's best for both participants collectively. Instead, it takes into account that both participants want to do the best for themselves, but are doing so given that they can't be sure whether the other party is working for their collective best or just for himself! We talk more about the Nash equilibrium's special properties in Chapter 17.

Applying the Prisoners' Dilemma: The problem of cartels

In economics, a *cartel* is a collection of organisations that act collectively to get the best deal for themselves. The most famous example is the oil and petroleum exporters' group OPEC, which attempts to restrict the supply of oil to the market in order to get as high a price as possible for its exports.

Cartels are illegal in Competition Law – where they're called a *restrictive trade practice* or a *collusive agreement* – for the good reason that they operate in their members' interests and against the public good. Therefore, the fines for being a cartel or operating one are extremely high (up to a maximum of 10 per cent of global turnover over three years, a figure that can amount to billions of pounds!). OPEC, by the way isn't an illegal cartel because it's made up of countries, rather than companies, and Competition Law doesn't make it illegal for countries to form cartels!

The fact that cartels are illegal means that its members can't rely on an enforceable contract to ensure that everyone acts in the collective best interests of the cartel. Even if all the members of the cartel do agree, for a period of time, to forego the best individual outcome in favour of the collective best, they always have an incentive to return to doing their individual best. If one does, the other members can't go to court and sue the defecting member for breach of court – because that would mean admitting being part of a criminal conspiracy! (OPEC is an interesting exception that we discuss in the nearby sidebar 'Oiling the wheels: The OPEC cartel'.)

Thus, if you think of the cartel's problem as a Prisoners' Dilemma, you can look at it using the strategic form of the game. We begin doing so by walking through the payoff matrix in Figure 16-3 for an agreement between two companies (Blue plc and Pink Ltd). Either company has a choice of playing Hawk or Dove (check out 'Setting the Game: Mechanism Design' earlier in this chapter for a definition of these terms).

		Blue plc	
Pink Ltd		Hawk	Dove
Figure 16-3: Applying the Prisoners' Dilemma to a cartel.	Hawk	5 / 5	−50 / 130
	Dove	130 / −50	100 / 100

Nash equilibrium

Looking at the payoffs in Figure 16-3 (which are all in millions of pounds), you can see that the collective best, which the cartel is formed to achieve, is in the bottom right corner, where both Blue and Pink are playing Dove.

But if one plays Hawk while the other plays Dove, the Hawk (which means cutting prices) gets a higher return (130 million in this case) by stealing market share from the other, who then takes a loss in this case (top right corner).

Neither party can trust the other to stay in line with the agreement, and so they both default to playing Hawk, and act in their own best interests. As a result, the Nash equilibrium is (Hawk, Hawk) in the top left corner and the cartel falls apart.

This is one reason why cartels don't tend to be long-lasting, irrespective of whether a regulator is able to use legal action to keep them in line. As the proverb says 'there's no honour amongst thieves', and the logic of the Prisoners' Dilemma bears that out to some extent.

Of course, regulators also help cartels to get to the Nash equilibrium – as the police do in the original Prisoners' Dilemma in the earlier 'Reading the plot of the Prisoners' Dilemma' section – by giving the parties an extra incentive to turn Queen's evidence. In the case of Competition Law, the practice is to give a free pass to the first party who talks to the authorities. That way, any party that thinks it may get caught has an incentive to come forward and tell tales on its former cartel partners!

Oiling the wheels: The OPEC cartel

Interestingly, the OPEC cartel seems to have bucked the trend about cartels not lasting. Here are two reasons why:

- **Repeated games establish possibilities for more co-operation.** The Prisoners' Dilemma model as we use it is strictly played once.

- **The role of Saudi Arabia distorts the picture.** Saudi Arabia's big oil reserves mean that it can sustain competition against a Hawk for longer than a nation playing Hawk against it. Therefore, as soon as Saudi

Arabia plays Hawk, the other members are forced to return to the negotiating table.

Yet the Prisoners' Dilemma model as we use it does explain why OPEC has seemingly always existed in a state of crisis, because member countries always have an incentive to undermine the agreement in the short run. This possibility leads to hurried oil diplomacy and rapidly convened conferences as other members try to get them to return to the original deal.

Escaping the Prisoners' Dilemma

An alternative heading for this section could be: 'How to form an organised crime syndicate without really trying!' Game theory has investigated one particularly interesting example of cartel behaviour: that of organised crime syndicates, such as the Cosa Nostra, when they operate a cartel that tends to work for the benefit of those under its influence – but not generally for society as a whole.

In Chicago during the reign of Al Capone, for instance, the local mafia had a monopoly on the supply of pasta-making machines, which were an essential piece of physical capital for any Italian restaurant in the city. The peculiar thing is that the restaurants benefitted from Capone's patronage. Sure, they had to pay him fees, but they could rely on him to take care of any competition that threatened to undercut them. Thus, the mob ended up as a way of enforcing a cartel agreement *and* guaranteeing higher profits for its favoured establishments.

An organised crime syndicate achieves this situation by changing the payoffs for its members. When you look at the syndicate as a cartel and understand its payoffs, you can see that, in essence, it changes the payoff for confessing to a crime from whatever offer the police make to the rather more simply understood 'Dead'. So if you're a member of a syndicate, and you're offered a deal that tempts you to confess, you don't choose it unless you fancy sleeping with the fishes!

In Figure 16-4, we summarise the strategic form of the Prisoners' Dilemma when a crime syndicate can change the payoffs. As you can see, the payoff to any actions involving confessing are now 'Dead' (which you can interpret as infinitely large and negative). Thus the Nash equilibrium (see the earlier section 'Finding the best outcome: The Nash equilibrium') is now *not* to confess!

Mr Pink's moves		Mr Blue's moves	
		Confess	Don't confess
	Confess	Dead / Dead	−5 / Dead
	Don't confess	Dead / −5	−0.5 / −0.5

Figure 16-4: Payoffs for an organised crime syndicate enforcing the cartel.

Nash equilibrium

This change in the Nash equilibrium provides the rationale for the formation of syndicates. If you can't get criminals to co-operate with each other, change the payoffs so that it's in their interests at least not to default. Capone, Corleone and several others took that lesson to heart!

Looking at Collective Action: The Stag Hunt

Game theorists have turned their attention to loads of different situations, ranging far and wide and covering many issues. One of these is the problem of collective action, where a bigger prize is available only to those who can co-ordinate their actions.

Collective action is a problem the world over. People can often make a gain by acting individually, but the best gains are made by co-ordinating actions so that they can get a prize bigger than they can attain individually. One way to consider these situations is by using a model known as the Stag Hunt. Don't worry, no animals are harmed in the playing of this game!

Designing the Stag Hunt

The Stag Hunt is set somewhere around the dawn of time. Littlenose and Bigfoot set out from their village one morning to go hunting. They can choose from two possible locations: one field contains a population of hares and the other stags. Any hunter on his own can capture a hare, but in order to capture a stag both hunters must work together. The model assumes that they must both make their decisions with no idea of whether the other is going to make the same choice or a different one.

We give names to the two possible strategies for Littlenose and Bigfoot:

- **Hawk:** They strike out individually looking for hares.

- **Dove:** They turn up independently at the same field as the stags, hoping to co-ordinate their actions so that they can bring home a bigger meal for the village.

Next we assign values to the potential meals:

- **Hare:** As the smaller creature, the hare gets a smaller value. Call that a value of 1.

- **Stag:** To the larger stag, we assign a larger value of 4. Any number larger than 1 will do, but we use 4 to keep things clear.

We want to compare possibilities and discover a Nash equilibrium (as in the earlier section 'Finding the best outcome: The Nash equilibrium') and so we put up the payoffs in strategic form, as in Figure 16-5.

		Littlenose	
Bigfoot		Dove	Hawk
	Dove	4 4	1 0
	Hawk	0 1	1 1

Figure 16-5: The Stag hunt payoffs.

Now look at the possible strategies and see where the Nash equilibrium lies. Can you spot it?

Sorry, that was a sly question, because two Nash equilibria exist: one that maximises payoffs (top left) and one that minimises risk (bottom right)! To see why, we think through Littlenose's decisions:

- ✔ **Littlenose plays Dove:** He goes to the field where the stags reside and hopes that Bigfoot makes the same decision. If Bigfoot doesn't, Littlenose isn't at the equilibrium. But if Bigfoot does, they successfully get a stag and the higher payoff.

- ✔ **Littlenose plays Hawk:** He goes to the hare field and whatever happens he gets something to eat. If Bigfoot also plays Hawk, they bring home a nice hare each. If not and Bigfoot plays Dove, it has no effect on Littlenose, although he could've brought home a far bigger meal if Littlenose had also played Dove and visited the stag field.

Therefore, (Dove, Dove) is the payoff-maximising equilibrium (a stag). (Hawk, Hawk) is a risk-minimising equilibrium (at minimum a hare each). But neither (Hawk, Dove) nor (Dove, Hawk) can be equilibria, because in each case one party at least could be made better off without making the other party any worse off. Plus, that party could make himself better off by changing to the same strategy as the other party (hence the game being seen as a *co-ordination game*).

Economists use the Stag Hunt game when a solution exists that makes it possible for both parties to make a gain, but also a defensive strategy that makes it less likely that they'll take a loss when trying to find a win–win solution. This case often applies in international negotiations where a treaty is the collective best, but the risk-minimising strategy is to act in your own immediate interests.

Examining the Stag Hunt in action

To our great delight, a Stag Hunt came to light in an economics faculty in an American university, where a poor choice of mechanism design led to students being able to exploit the system.

The students on a microeconomics course were to be graded to a *curve* – that is, by their position in the class instead of the results that they themselves would achieve in the exam. The students were upset about this, but they knew a bit of game theory and used it to their advantage to ensure that everyone got the top mark in the class (and that no one needed to sit an exam to get it). We immediately gave them a long-distance standing ovation for brilliant use of economic theory!

The key to this problem lies in two points:

✔ Analysing this situation, an economist would use the Stag Hunt model to see where the benefit of collective action lies.

✔ The corollary of a ranking system is that if everyone is equally terrible then everyone is equally good. Another way of looking at the problem is that if everyone gets last place, they all tie for first!

Suppose that the exact marking scheme gives the first-placed student 90 per cent, the second 89, the third 88 and so on. Call that scheme the 'teacher's offer' and denote it M:

✔ **If all students play Hawk:** They co-operate with the test scheme and their mark at the end is M_i.

✔ **If all students play Dove, don't co-operate with the test and submit blank papers:** They all receive the payoff for first place: a mark of 90.

Hawk and Dove refer to the strategies of players in co-operating with *each other* and not the teacher.

✔ **If *some* of the players play Hawk and some play Dove:** The Hawks take the test and get the teacher's offer based on their place in class, M. The Doves don't take the test and get a mark that reflects their worse performance; we call it W (for this to work the offer, W, must be worse than any given possible mark M).

Figure 16-6 shows the strategic form of the game. As in the traditional Stag Hunt in the preceding section, two Nash equilibria exist:

- ✔ **Hawk, Hawk equilibrium:** Every student goes along and takes the exam as normal and gets the teacher's offer.

- ✔ **Dove, Dove equilibrium:** Every student submits a blank paper and guarantees themselves 90 per cent.

The co-ordination problem is how to co-ordinate students' decisions so that they all end up playing Dove. This particular class solved it by waiting outside the exam room so that they were able to monitor anyone going in to the room. If they saw someone go in, they rushed after the person eager to get writing with the hope that they'd get M (rather than W) at least. In fact, no one walked into the room and all students got 90!

		Any given player	
Figure 16-6: Any given set of other players		Dove	Hawk
	Dove	90 90	M W
	Hawk	W M	M M

Figure 16-6: Strategic form of the Stag Hunt for the class economics exam.

If the tutor had wanted to get students to accept the faculty's scheme, better mechanisms would have been to spring the test on the students, or to tell them the mark scheme after the test, or even to set the test in different rooms so that no one could monitor whether anyone else was co-operating. In this one-shot game, the students would've then been unable to solve the game's co-ordination problem!

Annoying People with the Ultimatum Game

Sometimes the value of a game is in illustrating the difference between people who act according to the microeconomic model of rationality and those who don't. A classic example of a game economists use to test this aspect is the ultimatum game. Many forms exist, but we show you a simple version that characterises the problem.

In this version Polly starts with £100. She makes an offer to Quentin that she'll split the £100 between them, and if Quentin accepts the offer they'll both take home their respective shares of the £100. If, however, Quentin doesn't accept the offer, they both get zero. How much do you think Polly should offer? (To make it easy, the offer has to be in whole numbers of pounds.)

The answer is for Polly to offer Quentin £1. After all, if Quentin is economically rational, he'll realise that it was £1 he wouldn't otherwise have got and accept that he's gained utility (irrespective of how much Polly would've got; that's not relevant to his own calculation of utility!). But this is precisely not what's observed when the game is played! In fact more often, people reject any offer that doesn't give them a fair – their definition of fair, of course – share of the sum of money.

In a one-shot game, a sub-optimal strategy exists. But as behavioural economists have found, and as bounded rationality models predict, the result is surprisingly robust and places a 'fairness limit' on the type of offer a person receives! You can try this game yourself with a friend (or someone you really want to annoy) by adopting Polly's strategy and seeing what happens!

Getting out of the Dilemma by Repeating a Game

In all the models in the preceding sections, the game is *one shot* – played once only. Think of this as being tantamount to a forced deadline (often used in negotiations to get a deal, especially when one party is holding out for a better deal). The key thing is that the Nash equilibrium is affected by the fact that both parties participate only once (check out the earlier section 'Finding the best outcome: The Nash equilibrium').

But what happens if the players are in a game, such as in the Prisoners' Dilemma, where neither party can be sure whether the other's going to co-operate (see 'Locking Horns with the Prisoners' Dilemma' earlier in this chapter), which is repeated over many rounds?

Well, certainly, the players' previous histories in playing the game matter. For instance, assume that one player has a reputation for never ratting. As a result, his fellow wise guys trust him not to move towards the confession strategy, and so he has no shortage of accomplices for his nefarious deeds because they realise that they have most chance of being in the Dove,Dove Nash equilibrium.

But you may say, hang on a sec: the earlier 'Locking Horns with the Prisoners' Dilemma' section says that the Nash equilibrium for the Prisoners' Dilemma is Hawk, Hawk! Yes, but the difference between the two situations is whether the parties get to play the game again. If you play a Prisoners' Dilemma repeatedly, almost any option can be a Nash equilibrium – a result that helps inform many of the decisions about how to engineer a game situation or to play one!).

To distil this point into a bit of folk wisdom, that great economist Marx – Groucho, not Karl! – said that the key to success in life is honesty and fair play: 'If you can fake that, you got it made.' In the case of a repeated game, signalling honesty has the advantage of making it more likely that you'll move to the Dove, Dove outcome!

Investigating a repeated game using the extensive form

Unlike what theorists call the *strategic* or *normal form* of the game (a technical way of saying that the payoffs are arranged in a matrix and the Nash equilibrium found by elimination of worse and better strategies), games that go on over many rounds are often better interrogated by looking at them as if they're a set of sequential decisions. The method for doing so is called the *extensive* or *tree* form of the game.

We do this for the Prisoners' Dilemma in Figure 16-7. The important thing to notice is that the payoffs at the end of the tree are the same as the payoffs in the strategic form of the game! We do this for a one-shot game because it keeps everything simpler for now – the key point to note is that the payoffs at the end of the extensive form should be the same as the payoffs in the strategic form we use in this chapter's earlier sections.

The extensive form and the strategic form are equivalent ways of depicting a game, in the sense that the final payoffs have to be the same. The key advantage of the extensive form is that it makes the sequence of moves clearer where that's something that matters in the game. In these simple games we don't really need the extensive form all that much to tell you about the equilibrium. As games get more fiendish, however, the extensive form yields more information about the underlying structures of the game.

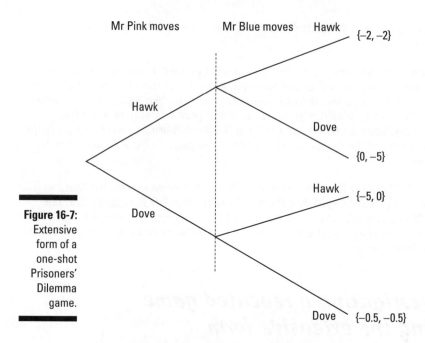

Figure 16-7:
Extensive
form of a
one-shot
Prisoners'
Dilemma
game.

Mixing signals: Looking at pure and mixed strategies

As opposed to a one-shot game, a repeated game is good at showing one of the key concepts in game theory: the difference between pure and mixed strategies:

- ✔ **Pure strategy:** Defines a specific move a player will make in any situation in the game. In the Prisoners' Dilemma, both Hawk and Dove strategies are pure strategies.

- ✔ **Mixed strategy:** The moves are made with a probability of playing one move or another. Imagine that the two players from the Prisoners' Dilemma example toss a coin to decide whether to play Hawk or Dove. In this case, each plays Hawk with 50 per cent probability and Dove with 50 per cent probability.

As a general rule, for it to be better for a player to use a mixed strategy over a pure strategy, the player has to be indifferent between using the different moves that he may play, or to be trying to hide his overarching strategy from another player.

A possible example is in the *madman strategy*. Here, a player deliberately tries to confuse the other player into making a sub-optimal move by switching between moves unpredictably. In a repeated Prisoners' Dilemma, a player using the madman strategy switches between Hawk and Dove in such a way that the other player can't extract rhyme or reason from his moves, sometimes confessing and sometimes not confessing. The effect is to create uncertainty in the other player, who's deprived of information about what the first player may do and therefore has less knowledge upon which to base his actions.

The madman strategy isn't very good for getting co-operation. A difference exists between the type of game in which one party can be said to make a gain over the other and a co-operative game where both parties gain from achieving co-operation. In a competitive game, holding an advantage over the other party can be desirable. But if co-operation is the desired goal, building trust is often the first stage, and you have difficulty trusting someone who keeps changing his moves on a seeming whim!

At the beginning of this chapter, we mention that game theory has been used to look at the best strategy for a penalty taker. The answer is to randomise the places a penalty taker aims for, so that the goalkeeper has no track record to guide him in trying to stop the striker. One problem here – the penalty taker must have the skill to be able to randomly hit the corners of the net. This skill is very rare, and only a few of the highest quality professionals manage to achieve it!

Chapter 17

Keeping Things Stable: The Nash Equilibrium

• •

In This Chapter

▶ Introducing the Nash equilibrium

▶ Discovering when a Nash equilibrium has to exist

▶ Applying the Nash equilibrium

• •

A s we explain in Chapter 16 on game theory, the Nash equilibrium is the combination of strategies whereby each player is doing the best she possibly can given the actions of other players.

The definition of a Nash equilibrium, and how you find one, are important concepts in how economists go about looking at issues of competition and co-operation. As we describe in this chapter, economists use Nash equilibria to extend economic concepts beyond exchanges in markets and into wider questions of organisation, bargaining and even international negotiations, while keeping the frame of the model related to economic rationality.

A Nash equilibrium is a point where no one has an incentive to change their behaviour. In that sense, Nash equilibria tend to be stable as long as the conditions around them stay stable. For instance, in the nearby sidebar 'A Nash equilibrium aids human survival' example, the peace between the nuclear powers was maintained for as long as nuclear weapons stayed out of the hands of rogue nations – ones that may not act 'rationally'. If, for instance, North Korea suddenly got the bomb, the stability of the arrangement would've changed, perhaps catastrophically.

You can find the same thing looking at an oligopoly – as in Chapter 11. The equilibrium between two firms – for instance, in Cournot's model – is a Nash equilibrium. Suppose, however, that a third more innovative firm enters the market? This would change the decisions of the firms in the market and probably – eventually – lead to a new Nash equilibrium.

A Nash equilibrium aids human survival

During the Cold War – approximately 1945 to 1989 – the NATO powers and the Warsaw Pact nations found themselves committed to spending astronomical sums of money on nuclear weapons, which were never (and indeed probably could never) be used. Looking at this period of history through the models of game theory, the strategy of building a nuclear arsenal and not using it is a Nash equilibrium, because no party had any incentive to move from that position. Thus, the fact that the world made it through this period is no surprise to a game theorist.

The two powers could've chosen to disarm or to use their weapons against each other, but:

✔ The party that disarmed when the other didn't would've handed an incentive to the other side to use its weapons knowing that retaliation couldn't happen.

✔ The party that used its weapons would invite instant and fatal retaliation.

So the best anyone could achieve in the contest of both parties' actions was to have the weapons, but not use them. Thus – and we know that it sounds insane to say so outside of the context of game theory – nuclear weapons have arguably been an investment in securing peace!

So finding the Nash equilibrium for any given situation is a useful tool for seeing where outcomes exist that no one has any incentive to change!

If you're not au fait with game theory, we suggest that you read Chapter 16 before proceeding with this one.

Defining the Nash Equilibrium Informally

The Nash equilibrium does have a formal definition (and proof of its existence for mixed-strategy games) but it requires some highly advanced maths. Instead, in this section we provide three *informal* definitions that amount to the same thing without having to dip into the really hard stuff:

✔ A Nash equilibrium is a set of strategies played by players such that when they're played, no one has any incentive to change strategy. Thus, for instance, the Cournot, Bertrand and Stackelberg equilibria in Chapter 11 are Nash equilibria.

✔ A Nash equilibrium exists when each player is maximising her payoff given that the other players are also making their best possible moves. Again, this applies very clearly to oligopoly models, and some other situations, for instance when one monopoly seller is negotiating with a single large buyer – as when the NHS is negotiating with a large pharmaceutical company.

✔ A Nash equilibrium is the point where adopting a strategy or making a move that makes any player better off is impossible without making other players worse off.

The last definition ties the Nash equilibrium to the concept of *Pareto efficiency,* often used when looking at how people can be made better off. Economists describe a distribution of wealth or income as Pareto efficient when no party can be made better off without making another party worse off. Thus, if those conditions hold at the Nash equilibrium, the payoffs are a Pareto efficient distribution. We discuss Pareto efficiency more deeply in Chapter 18.

Looking for Balance: Where a Nash Equilibrium Must Apply

If you like, you can think of a Nash equilibrium as being a point of balance. At a Nash equilibrium, no participants have any incentive to change their behaviour. Imagine it as being like balancing on a seesaw – both people at either end could move the seesaw down, but want to stay exactly as they are.

In order to see where a Nash equilibrium has to exist, we start by pointing out that not every game has one. A game doesn't require a Nash equilibrium in pure strategies (ones defining specific moves that players make in any situation; check out Chapter 16 for more details).

Consider, for example, the game 'rock, paper, scissors', as played by many a child in the playground. Each selection of rock, paper or scissors is defeated by exactly one opponent's move – rock blunts scissors, paper wraps rock, scissors cut paper – and also defeats exactly one opponent's move. Thus the payoff matrix or strategic form of the game (flip to Chapter 16 for a definition) is as we show in Figure 17-1. (You'll have to work out the matrix for Sheldon Cooper's far more complicated version of 'rock, paper, scissors, lizard, Spock' for yourself!)

	ROCK	PAPER	SCISSORS
ROCK	0,0	–1,1	1,–1
PAPER	1,–1	0,0	–1,1
SCISSORS	–1,1	1,–1	0,0

Figure 17-1:
Payoff matrix for pure form of 'rock, paper, scissors'.

No Nash equilibrium exists for 'rock, paper, scissors', because at any point any one player can make herself better off by changing strategy. Consider, for example, the three possible outcomes when Karen plays rock in a game against Kevin:

- ✔ If Kevin also plays rock, neither player gains (and Karen would've been better off playing paper anyway).
- ✔ If Kevin plays paper, he wins that round and Karen loses.
- ✔ If Kevin plays scissors, he'd have been better off changing his choice.

So no point exists where both players are going to stay happy with their moves. Irrespective of where you start with 'rock, paper, scissors', you always end up in a situation where at least one player can be made better off by doing something different. Hence no Nash equilibrium!

Recognising that a Nash equilibrium must exist in mixed-strategy games

The pure strategy version of 'rock, paper, scissors' has no Nash equilibrium. But if the strategies were used with a given probability – for example, Karen played rock 20 per cent of the time – then you'd see a very different outcome. With some hard maths that we don't go into, you can show that at least one Nash equilibrium must exist in any finite mixed-strategy game (we discuss this form of game in Chapter 16).

But informally and intuitively, you can consider what would happen if no Nash equilibrium applied: someone can always make herself better off by changing her strategy, no matter what her counterpart plays.

Finding a Nash equilibrium by elimination

The typical way of finding a Nash equilibrium in the strategic form of a game is by eliminating any strategies that can't be optimal. This method relies on the concept of *a dominant strategy*.

A strategy is dominant if, regardless of what any other player does, playing that strategy results in a higher payoff. A strategy can be dominant in two ways:

- ✔ **Weakly dominant:** If it's always at least as good as any other given strategy in terms of payoff.

- ✔ **Strongly dominant:** If it always gives a higher payoff than any other possible strategy.

Given this fact, you can look at the strategic form of a game and eliminate any strategies that are *dominated*. This approach involves looking at the reverse of a dominant strategy and eliminating any strategy that a rational player *won't* play, irrespective of the moves of another player.

Figure 17-2 shows an example of a strategic form of game. Player Colm has a choice of three strategies (left, middle and right) and player Rowe has two. However, for any move Rowe makes, the result for Colm is worse if Colm plays right, so Right is 'dominated' and can be eliminated. Rowe will then find that 'down' is dominated by playing any 'up' strategies. That means the 'down' row can be eliminated. That leaves Colm with a choice of 'left' or 'middle'. Middle dominates left, so the Nash equilibrium will be Rowe plays 'up' and Colm plays 'middle'.

The method used here is the *iterated elimination of dominated strategies*. It means very simply that you go through the payoffs and eliminate any strategy that wouldn't be chosen until you find a point where no player has any incentive to change strategy. Then you've 'solved' the game and found the Nash equilibrium – and can award yourself a gold star!

Suppose you come across two companies that each have 50 per cent of a market, and you suspect that they're colluding. You look through their potential strategies, however, and see that after you exclude any strategies they'd be irrational to follow – in other words, you've found a Nash equilibrium – eliminating dominated strategies means that the best each company can do, given the actions of the other, is the situation they find themselves in. Thus, you're forced to conclude that you don't simply have grounds for an inquiry.

Colm

		Left	Middle	Right
	Up	1, 0	1, 2	0, 1
Rowe				
	Down	0, 3	0, 1	2, 0

Figure 17-2:
Finding
a Nash
equilibrium
by elimi-
nation of
dominated
strategies.

This situation was what the Competition Commission found when it was looking at the stable market shares of supermarkets. It had to conclude that this
situation was one where no one had an incentive to change strategy. Thus,
it was unable to go with that line of inquiry – although it has revisited the
industry for other reasons since.

Solving a repeated game by backward induction

A *repeated game* such as the Prisoners' Dilemma (we describe both in detail
in Chapter 16) takes place over many rounds, with the payoffs computed at
the end of the game. The matrix you get by looking at the payoffs is also the
strategic form of the game (see the preceding section).

But the best way to find out which of the payoffs is a Nash equilibrium is to
perform the operation that economists and game theorists call *backward
induction*. This technique means starting at the payoffs at the end of the
game and working backwards to the beginning. As you go back through the
game, you eliminate any path that leads to an outcome that wouldn't have
been chosen.

As an example, we now describe the *trust game,* which has been applied
to the relationship between managers and workers or expanded to look at
'trust but verify' strategies in disarmament. Two participants have to decide
whether or not to trust each other. The first player, Yvonne, has to decide
between trusting the second player, Zak, and not trusting him. After Yvonne
makes her choice, Zak has to choose between honouring Yvonne's trust or
betraying it. We set up the game and see how to solve it.

Start with Yvonne:

> ✔ If Yvonne decides not to trust Zak, the relationship is over and both parties gain zero.
>
> ✔ If Yvonne does trust Zak, he makes the next choice:
>
> > • If Zak chooses to honour this trust, he gets 1 and Yvonne 1.
> >
> > • If Zak cheats, he gets 2 and Yvonne –1.
>
> ✔ If Yvonne knows this, what should she do?

To solve the game using backward induction, you start by writing the game down in *extensive form* as a tree. (Or take a look at Figure 17-3 where we do it for you.)

The payoff numbers can be equally well represented on a *strategic form* matrix, and so you can use the method in the preceding section to find the Nash equilibrium, and if you don't trust us you can verify the results by doing so!

Working backwards from the very end, Zak's round, note that Zak has a dominant strategy: being on this part of the tree means that he does better, getting 2 as opposed to 1 when he betrays Yvonne. Thus Zak will betray Yvonne.

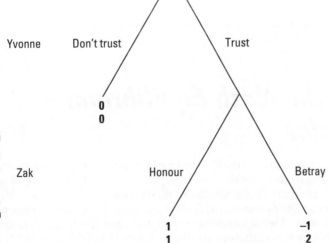

Figure 17-3:
Extensive form of the trust game.

Scoundrels don't profit in the long run

A fascinating application of the backward induction type of game reasoning is in considering the right amount of regulation for a market, a particularly relevant question at the moment for looking at the economic issues about how people regulate financial markets following the recent financial crisis. It is, you won't be surprised to discover, a huge and difficult question!

One approach is to ask about markets' inbuilt tendencies towards policing themselves. If you use a trust game set up, you arrive at the interesting result that a market that's significantly affected by distrust has fewer trades going on in it. Therefore, even though playing dishonourably may seem like a profitable strategy, it poisons the whole business environment, reducing the amount of business you do and worsening your eventual payoff!

Going back to Yvonne's move, however, if she knows what Zak's payoffs to cheating are, she knows that he's going to cheat, and so she chooses not to trust. Thus the business relationship terminates before it has a chance to be poisoned!

You can therefore say that solving this game for a Nash equilibrium finds that Yvonne and Zak do their best given each other's payoffs by staying well away from each other!

Check out the nearby sidebar 'Scoundrels don't profit in the long run' for a timely financial example.

Applying the Nash Equilibrium in Economics

Microeconomists use game theory to investigate many issues in economics – ranging from bargaining, to oligopoly equilibria, to choice of political affiliation. Here are two examples of how economists use games: first to look at what a monopoly may do to defend its dominant share of a market; and second to look at what happens to societies over the long run when members of that society have different strategies for dealing with people who'd do them wrong.

Deterring entry: A monopolist's last resort

If a company has been successful enough to gain a dominant share of a market, it's often keen to prevent a rival from coming in and stealing that market away.

Therefore, *entry deterrence* is a key concept in the economics of competition. Some pretty stern rules apply about what dominant firms are allowed to do. One of them is temporarily pricing below cost so that a competing firm can't afford to sustain competition. In that case, the would-be entrant is no longer able to afford to enter the industry.

In Figure 17-4 we set up the situation as a game between a monopolist and entrant. The entrant chooses to enter or not and the monopolist chooses to retaliate (fight the entrant) or not. The monopolist wants to make the pay-offs turn out so that the Nash equilibrium is 'don't enter'. When you analyse it, the game's a variant of the trust game in the earlier section 'Solving a repeated game by backward induction'.

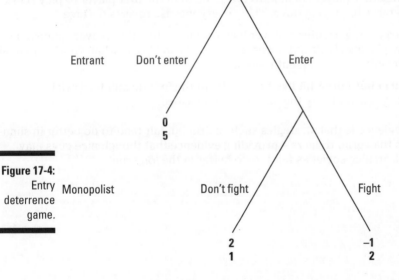

Figure 17-4: Entry deterrence game.

Analysing society with economic reasoning

Economists have strayed a long way from merely analysing markets and often look for ways of applying economic reasoning to difficult problems in other areas. One of these is the evolution of society. Here, economists like to use the insights of game theory to consider how co-operation and competition shape the strategies people use to punish those who cross them.

In society people have two ways of dealing with those who act against others: forgiving them and punishing them. If you generalise society as a set of Prisoners' Dilemma games (see Chapter 16), you can develop a model that looks at punishing and forgiving as two different strategies. If the games have Nash equilibria, you can then think about how to characterise the different ways of behaving and compare the equilibria, telling you over the long run which strategy would be preferred.

Typically, economists compare and contrast three methods (if you're unfamiliar with the roles of Hawks and Doves, check out Chapter 16):

- ✔ **Tit for tat:** Players start by playing the Dove. When one plays a Hawk, the other players default to Hawk too until the first player to play Hawk returns to playing Dove. Then, everyone else reverts to Dove.

- ✔ **Grim trigger:** After a player has defaulted, the other players punish her by playing Hawk and never return to playing Dove, whatever the original defaulter's subsequent moves.

- ✔ **Firm but fair:** A bit like tit for tat, but the first default to Hawk is forgiven, and only the second one punished.

The evidence is that strategies such as firm but fair tend to do better in simulations than grim triggers – providing evidence that though nice guys may finish last, nice societies tend to do better in the long run!

Chapter 18

Knowing How to Win at Auctions

*P*eople often associate auctions with the sale of antiques and artworks. The rarity of their exchange means that such items are usually sold in specialist auctions run by famous auction houses such as Bonhams, Christie's or Sotheby's. For example, in June 2006 Christie's in New York auctioned van Gogh's painting 'Portrait of Dr Gachet' for $82 million (which allowing for inflation over the last 10 years amounts to $152 million in today's prices – not bad for a man who sold only one painting during his lifetime!).

But all sorts of other things can be auctioned, too, and they don't need to be physical objects. For instance, in the early 2000s the UK government wanted to sell off valuable parts of the radio spectrum to mobile phone networks (that is, sell licences to the mobile network operators). Primarily the Treasury was interested in getting the largest sum of money possible and needed to design a mechanism around this goal. It settled on an auction of the licences and received a sum far in excess of its predictions, which was, of course, gratefully received by the Chancellor of the Exchequer!

In both these situations, the seller tries to maximise the value of one asset that it wants to sell. More potential buyers exist than assets, and so the seller attempts to use the ability of auctions to reveal the value that buyers ascribe to the asset in order to get the highest price possible.

Auctions can be devilishly tricky things to participate in, with sellers and bidders using all sorts of tactics and manoeuvres. In this chapter we talk you through some of the features of auctions and introduce you to the underlying theory behind auctions from the seller's, the bidder's and the auctioneer's perspective. We show you why auctions are such a useful tool for disbursing assets, and that despite their positive features they also have some limitations and downsides – even for the auction winner!

Spotting Different Kinds of Auction

The term *auction* is a category rather than a thing. Many different types of auction exist, each with their advantages and disadvantages depending on whether you take a seller's, a buyer's or even society's perspective. They all have a mechanism in which an auctioneer solicits bids for the item under the hammer, but they vary in the means they take to get to the final sale price.

Economists have explored many existing types of auction using economic theory and discovered that the results vary from auction to auction. They found that being specific pays off when describing individual types of auction!

An auction is a refinement of the conditions of a monopoly, with only one seller and several buyers. When only one buyer exists, the condition is a bilateral monopoly and the good is more likely to be disbursed by negotiation than auction. And yet, the price that buyers pay is likely to be above the marginal cost of the item, and so auctions do mean that surplus tends to go to the seller.

Knowing the type of auction you're in

Here are the most common attributes of the many types of auction. Often these categories aren't mutually exclusive and so you can talk about a sealed bid, second price, English auction (flip to the later section 'Making bidders honest with a Vickrey auction' for more on this type of auction):

- ✔ **English auction:** The most familiar type, from auction scenes in films and on TV. The auctioneer starts at a floor price – a minimum price beyond which the good won't be sold, usually selected by the auctioneer who represents the seller – and successive bids raise the price for which the item is eventually sold.

- ✔ **Dutch auction:** The price starts at a price ceiling and each successive round consists of the auctioneer dropping the price until someone takes the item.

- ✔ **Open outcry:** Each bidder reveals his bid to all other bidders by calling out the sum he wants to pay to receive the lot.

- ✔ **Sealed bid:** Bidders submit their bids in sealed envelopes, so that other bidders don't know the bids. Variants can include different degrees of disclosure required of bidders or the auctioneer.

- ✔ **First price:** The winning bid is the highest declared bid when the auctioneer finally says 'Sold!'.

✔ **Second price:** The winning bidder pays the second-highest declared bid. So, if you'd bid £100 and the winner had bid £110, the winner finally pays £100 (your second-highest bid) when he comes to take the goods home. This special refinement aims to reduce the incentives of people bidding more than they can afford.

✔ **Reservation price:** A variant with a floor price, below which the item isn't sold (check out the later section 'Setting a reservation price wisely' for more details).

✔ **Online auctions:** Sometimes these allow the seller to set a price at which the auction ends and the item goes to the first bidder to meet the 'buy it now' price.

The other major distinction that economists make between auctions concerns what's being sold:

✔ **Private-value auctions:** Every bidder may have a different valuation for the good in question, as is the case for art auctions.

✔ **Common-value auctions:** The good has the same value for every participant though their estimations of that value may differ. This case applies for some mineral-rights auctions, where the rights have the same value and bidders differ by belief.

Suppose, for example, that £10 billion barrels of oil are under Gatwick Airport and these are being allocated using an auction. Every potential bidder would get the same amount of oil if they win the auction. However, the amount that they're willing to pay depends on their belief about how much that oil would be worth to them; the amount may vary wildly among the bidders if they have different costs of extracting the oil or different beliefs about how much they'd make from selling it.

Designing an auction to get (most of) what you want

Economists are often asked to give their opinions on which particular kind of auction is best for a particular situation. They usually express their answer in terms of two criteria:

✔ **Pareto efficiency (or optimality):** The outcome of the auction should be *Pareto efficient,* meaning that making one party better off without making another party worse off isn't possible.

✔ **Profit maximisation:** The auction should yield the highest expected profit to the seller.

Given these criteria, as the economist you can examine some of the auction types and score reasons to prefer one or another in a particular context.

 An auction in this case is a type of *mechanism design,* which means designing the game that players play. When you design a mechanism, you're assuming that players have privileged information over their own strategies but that the expected payoffs are known to the designer. We discuss mechanism design more fully in Chapter 16.

Meeting an auction's two core criteria

For the mechanism to be Pareto efficient, the good must go to the bidder with the highest bid. To see why, suppose that two bidders bid for a good. Bridie bids £100 and Brian bids £80, but in this case Brian gets the good. If he now sells the good to Bridie for £90 both parties make themselves better off without making anyone worse off. So that result can't be Pareto efficient. (The seller, by the way, is part of only the original auction, not this transaction, and so you can focus on the two different bidders for Pareto efficiency.)

When you know every bidder's valuation exactly, profit maximisation is also easy. The question is what to do when the auctioneer doesn't know. Here, examining some of the auction types with economic theory helps. But the answer can only 'help' rather than 'exactly predict', for the simple reason that the behaviour of the bidders depends on their beliefs about the good, which the auctioneer can't know.

Setting a reservation price wisely

 One way to increase the likelihood of maximising profits in an auction is to set a reservation price – a minimum price lower than which the good won't be sold. Sometimes the reservation isn't met, but in all other cases the auctioneer is certain of getting a level of profit above the reservation.

This approach can be an important step in designing an auction. For example, the local TV franchises in the UK used to be very valuable (legendary industry figure Lew Grade described them as a licence to print money!). But then one franchise, for the Midlands, was contested by only one bidder, who won a valuable franchise for only £2,000 per year. The asset – the broadcast franchise – was transferred for far less than a profit-maximising outcome: setting a reservation price would've avoided that problem.

 When you set a reservation price, sometimes you'll fail to sell the item, meaning that Pareto optimality doesn't hold. But if the expected revenue from the sale is low enough, having a reservation price still maximises expected profit even though sometimes the auction fails. In this case, you're trading off between Pareto optimality and profit maximisation!

Bidding for Beginners

The most important piece of advice that economists have for bidders in an auction is to read the rules carefully! Optimal strategy varies wildly among the different auctions and because some types (check out the earlier 'Knowing the type of auction you're in' section) can be significantly more complex – especially in awarding huge procurement contracts – make sure that you have all the small print covered.

Modelling a simple auction

Despite the warning that opens this section, some of the simpler types of auction are easy to model.

Lawrence Friedman's analysis of a lowest-price, sealed-bid common-value auction provides one such framework, in which each bidder bids a sum b_i – where i is the number of the bidder. If the bid wins, the yield is $b - c$, where c is the cost of the contract over which the parties are bidding.

We now call b the winning bid, and so the probability that the ith bidder will win is:

$$F(b) = \text{Prob}(b_i \leq b)$$

F indicates the likelihood of any individual bidder bidding less than the winning bid, b. All other bidders would then have a winning probability of $1 - F_i(b)$; because probabilities must sum to 1, the probability of something not happening is $1 - F$.

We now expand the expression for winning in terms of all other participants losing. For N other bidders it must equal

$$P(b) = \left(\left(1 - F_i(b)\right) \ldots \left(1 - F_N(b)\right) \right)$$

Expected profit must be

$$P(b)(b-c)$$

where $P(b)$ indicates the probability of winning the bid. This is the expression that Friedman recommended maximising.

To do so, have as much information as possible about other bidders' past bidding behaviour!

One problem is that often the cost function is an estimate. Contractors have a best guess at what a contract will cost without ever really knowing what's going to happen to costs over that period. For instance, bidding for the franchise to operate train services between London and Uttoxeter, the Railway Company may have a plan and some guesses on how much the contract will cost, but the firm is unable to know exactly and thus may still get caught out bidding too low because costs turn out to be higher!

Providing advice on a preferential bidding strategy means that you have to make assumptions about the costs and benefits of the future value of the item.

For instance, if you know that Mondrian's reputation in the art world and therefore value at auction is about to take a tumble – art is a rough world! – the rational decision is to bid a lower price in an upcoming auction, because the value of the option to resell the item is going to be lower. Of course, as a Mondrian fan, the art value received from the item may be enough for you to contemplate bidding sub-optimally high for the item! If the auction is a private-value auction, this is all that matters to you – do you value the item at the bid price. For a common-value case, the expectation of what will happen to the value of the item is important!

Bidding late: The Internet auction phenomenon

An open-outcry, English auction allows successive rounds of bidding to reveal more information about the valuations of successive bidders, which isn't the case in – for instance – a Dutch auction (we define these different auctions earlier in 'Knowing the type of auction you're in'). It definitely happens, however, in an Internet auction, which is generally structured as a Vickrey auction (about which we say more in the later section 'Making bidders honest with a Vickrey auction').

An Internet auction goes through successive rounds of bidding up to a final deadline. What's interesting is that a high percentage of bids are made close to the deadline – around 37 per cent in the last minute.

The Internet auction house eBay calls this strategy *sniping*.

Economists have come up with two explanations for this behaviour:

> ✔ **Bidders don't want to tip their hand to other bidders:** If you're an expert on, say, rare guitars, and the auction displays your profile with your bid, you may delay bidding to prevent other people from knowing of your interest in, say, that rare Gretsch White Falcon.

> ✔ **Implicit collusion between buyers:** In this case, collusion means that they've alighted on the same strategy (of waiting until the last few moments before bidding), instead of having co-ordinated strategies to reduce the price.

In the second case, imagine a second-price auction where the prize is a White Falcon guitar worth £3,000, with a reserve price of £1,000. If the two bidders start their bids early and honestly state their true value as £3,000, they'll end up with one receiving the guitar for £3,000: great for the seller, but the buyer gets no consumer surplus. Suppose instead that they wait until the last second. Now only one of those bids may get through, and by the second-price rule of the auction, that bidder ends up paying the reservation price of £1,000!

Gaming an auction

Auctions are useful for revealing the value that a buyer is willing to pay for an item. Sometimes, though, auctions fail to work out the way the auctioneer or the buyers want. Dodgy behaviour can take place on both sides of the deal, with buyer and seller possibly having incentives to take the process away from a true and fair auction, just as they may do in a cartel (something we define in Chapter 16).

Although auction design can mitigate these 'gaming' factors, you also need to be on the lookout for 'bent' auctions. Authorities and regulators often are!

Trying to avoid an auction

In certain cases, forcing someone *not* to auction something can be a viable strategy.

When negotiating for the transfer of Gareth Bale from Tottenham Hotspur football club, the buying club Real Madrid – allegedly – tried everything to make sure that another potential buyer wasn't found. Why? Well, Tottenham could've leveraged the two potential buyers against each other to get a higher price for the player. Eventually Real Madrid paid an undisclosed sum believed to be around €90 million for Bale's services. If another bidder had emerged, the final sum may have been even higher!

Colluding

Sometimes bidders collude by not making competitive bids against each other or by pooling their bids and redistributing the returns after the auction.

Collusion was suspected in the collapse of the Italian 3G auction. The Italian mobile operators went through successive dropouts in the early rounds of bidding, and the auction was suspended when five franchises were available to four bidders. Because the franchises were no longer scarce, no one had an incentive to outbid anyone else! Collusion was alleged but never proved. The result, though, whether achieved collusively or not, was definitely the same result as would've occurred if everyone were working in cahoots!

Summoning buyers

An auctioneer can receive a higher price for a good by summoning a phantom buyer. Imagine an art auction where a phone bidder is in cahoots with the auctioneer and keeps phoning in a bid increment until the auctioneer guesses that he isn't going to get away with raising the price any higher. More potential buyers are therefore kept in the game (even if one isn't real), competing against each other to raise the price!

This situation – again, allegedly – was encountered in a football transfer where the selling club 'found' a bidder very late in the process who was willing to pay double the eventual buying club's initial bid. The buying club decided to bite the bullet and pay the fee. The selling club received double its expected compensation for the transfer.

In case you're wondering, football transfers often appear very murky because of the amount of private information involved and the relatively low requirements for disclosure compared to many other industries.

Suffering from the Winner's Curse

Oscar Wilde famously identified two tragedies in life: not getting what you want and getting what you want. The winner's curse is a problem that comes from winning an auction.

Essentially, the problem is that in an English, first-price auction (see the earlier section 'Knowing the type of auction you're in' for a definition), bidders always have an incentive to bid more than they can afford to get an item – and, of course, the auctioneer has no knowledge of what they can afford and is unable to know this until the auction concludes.

This issue is primarily a problem with common-value auctions – where the true value of the item isn't known. For examples such as bidding for train franchises, mobile phone spectrum, mineral rights or broadcast licenses, it's a perennial problem, because the true monetary value of those items is never known in advance. Microeconomics is often used to look at the allocation of goods and services, and so this makes the incentive to bid too high a real economic problem – whether you're designing the auction or bidding in one.

Making bidders honest with a Vickrey auction

Auction houses can mitigate the bidding-more-than-you-can-afford problem in a number of ways. For instance, they can require a bank guarantee before someone enters the auction, so that if a person doesn't have evidence of being able to afford the good, he can't enter the race for the Gauguin!

But consider the problem of a government auction of a valuable licence. In this case, the winner itself may not know that it has been cursed until some time into the period of the licence.

Overbidding for a train operating franchise may not be revealed until halfway through the life of the contract. In this case the government may have the ability to take the franchise back, but often at some public cost, or at least cost of political capital. This event is exactly what happened to the East Coast railway line in the UK in 2010, which had to be 're-nationalised' after the contract holder failed to pay amounts promised in its contract. Despite the state-owned, not-for-profit company earning £1 billion for the taxpayer and having high levels of passenger satisfaction, the government auctioned off the line again in 2014.

Meeting the Vickrey auction

One of the auction designs that doesn't have an incentive to overbid is the sealed-bid, second-price, English auction, better known as a *Vickrey auction* after celebrated Canadian economist William Vickrey.

In a Vickrey auction, the item under the hammer goes to the bidder who submitted the highest bid, but only at the price bid by the second-highest bidder. This design removes the incentive to bid too high, because the price that's eventually accepted is the second bid.

In a normal English auction, the good goes to the highest bidder at the price that bidder revealed itself willing to pay. The result is therefore Pareto optimal (as we explain in the earlier section 'Designing an auction to get (most of) what you want'). But in a Vickrey auction, participants make sealed bids, which makes them bid a value that honestly reflects their valuation of the bid. For a standard sealed-bid auction, this isn't necessarily the case. How does changing from a standard sealed-bid auction to a Vickrey auction change things?

Seeing the Vickrey option in action

Suppose two bidders have valuations for a good, v_1 and v_2 respectively, and bid b_1 and b_2 for it. The expected payoff for bidder 1 is:

$$\text{Prob}(b_1 \geq b_2)(v_1 - b_2)$$

You don't need to consider the case where b_2 is bigger than b_1, because in that case the bidder receives 0 and the expected payoff is zero.

Two possible bidding cases exist that get the best payoff:

- **When v_1 is bigger than b_2.** In this case bidder 1 is best off when making the probability of a winning bid as high as possible. Thus, he makes b_1 (his valuation of the item, v_1) as high as possible. So he sets $b_1 = v_1$, his true valuation of the item!

- **When $v_1 < b_2$ and bidder 1 wants to make the possibility of winning as small as possible.** How would he best do that? Well, by bidding v_1! That way, he's unlikely to win the auction and would get the best possible value by bidding less than the valuation of the person who wants it most, which would be bidder 2!

The key point here is that in either case, the incentive for the bidder is to declare his true valuation of the bid. In both the cases, the most important factor is that if the auction is set up in this way, no one has any incentive to bid other than his true valuation of the good.

Stamping approval for the Vickrey auction

Vickrey noticed how the sealed-bid, second-price auction affected bidders' behaviour while studying the market for collectable stamps. These were sold at conventions using an open-outcry, English auction and by mail order using a sealed-bid, second-price auction – now called a Vickrey auction.

Vickrey noticed that the two auctions showed the same results, although the sealed-bid,

second-price auction did so over only one round of bidding. Thus, the open-outcry, English auction's tendency to equate price with the true value of an item could be found in a sealed-bid auction, as long as the second-highest price was eventually what was paid!

Perusing the curse in public procurement

When the government auctions a licence to operate to bidders, it's trying to do the best for the public purse by maximising the value it gets for the licence under auction. The problem is that because the government and the bidder don't know what the costs or the expected revenues of the winning bid will be, public procurement contracts are often subject to winner's curse problems.

Typically, a public procurement auction tends to be a sealed-bid, lowest-price auction. Bidders bid for the lowest possible contract fee they can get from the government, the one with the lowest fee getting the franchise.

Even if the auction is completed at the second price, however, because winners don't know exactly how the revenues and costs of the franchise will work out, situations still exist in which the franchise may prove to be too expensive to operate. Typically, these issues are mitigated through the contractual system, so that the franchise may be conditional and the government or bidder can cancel the agreement (often subject to penalties).

Clearly, therefore, the ability of mechanism design to bring order to an uncertain world is limited. Often both designer and bidder are subject to significant uncertainties, and more importantly they both have a rationale for measuring the uncertainties and a technique for mitigating the penalties of getting things wrong. A bid is always an estimate, in these cases, of the value of the contract rather than a direct valuation of the contract, and so don't be too hard on parties that make errors. Being wrong about uncertain futures is easy – and people getting such things right is more surprising!

Chapter 19

Deciphering the Signals: Threats and Benefits

· ·

In This Chapter

▶ Seeking an equilibrium to remove non-credible threats

▶ Finding and using an equilibrium for positive signals

· ·

*O*ne wicked problem (in the economic sense, see Chapter 14) is that people rarely have perfect information. Sometimes this situation is asymmetric (one party knowing more than another, as we discuss in Chapter 15) and sometimes both parties are unable to know each other's best moves. In these situations, economists often turn to game theory to look at how each side behaves. In the Prisoners' Dilemma from Chapter 16, for instance, neither party *knows* what the other one will do, but *infers* it from the other's payoffs.

In reality, however, people have imperfect or limited information rather than none at all. They don't know entirely what the other party may do, but they have some information to go on, and they use that to work out the right bargain or the right move in response.

Suppose, for example, that you're deciding whether or not to employ someone. Taking a look at her CV, you notice that she worked for a prestigious employer. You see that information as a sign that the person's a good bet to take on and call her in for an interview. A candidate with a less prestigious history may not fare so well!

Economists call this type of information a *signal*. It's an imperfect piece of information, but at least it's information and can help you to figure out your next move.

In this chapter we discuss two types of signalling problem: negative ones (in other words, dealing with threats) and positive ones (dealing with benefits). In each case, game theory looks at the signal and sees what payoffs you can infer from it.

Refining the Nash Equilibrium to Deal with Threats

In general, game theory looks at threats by dividing them into two categories – credible and non-credible. Distinguishing the two types of threat is difficult in real life, because it depends on you knowing quite a bit about the other trading party and what she might do.

But using a game theoretic model allows you to work from the assumption that the person issuing the threat is economically rational and seeks the best payoff for herself. Therefore, you can eliminate any threat that leaves the person worse off if she carries it out.

In turn, this approach means using a stronger definition of the Nash equilibrium from Chapter 17 that eliminates non-credible threats: it's called a *subgame-perfect Nash equilibrium*. If, after eliminating any non-credible threats, you still have a Nash equilibrium, it's subgame perfect!

Finding a subgame-perfect Nash equilibrium by elimination

The best way to check whether a Nash equilibrium is subgame perfect is by backward induction (as we explain in Chapter 17). To do so, you need to write out the game in extensive form and work backwards from the end, eliminating any branch that relies on a non-credible threat.

If a rational person or entity wouldn't do something, that action or behaviour is non-credible from the standpoint of game theory.

The best way to eliminate non-credible threats is within the context of a game where sequential rationality is involved. *Sequential rationality* means that a rational person behaves rationally when following your move with one of hers. Therefore, subgame-perfect equilibrium is usually best approached within a game with sequential moves – if, for instance, both parties draw their moves simultaneously, the payoff depends on what each party believes the other will do and often becomes more complicated to model, so to make things more efficient, it's often best to use a sequential structure to do the hard work.

Exploring subgame perfection in an entry deterrence game

Here we explore a simple game and discuss how to eliminate non-credible actions.

The most common economic use of subgame perfection is within games of *entry deterrence* – for instance, when a competitor in a market is trying to prevent an aggressive entrant from coming into that market. This game is appropriate, because the working assumption about a business is that it's economically rational (otherwise it's unlikely to stay a business very long!) and so weeding out irrational strategies is relatively easy.

In this game, NewCo is deciding whether to enter a market currently held by the monopolist OldStuff. NewCo gets to move first, deciding whether or not to enter the market – if it does, OldStuff decides whether or not to retaliate. Given the payoffs in the tree (see Figure 19-1), what's the Nash equilibrium?

Figure 19-1:
Entry deter-
rence game
conclud-
ing no
subgame-
perfect
equilibrium.
The num-
bers give
the payoffs
to the two
companies
from fol-
lowing the
strategies in
each branch
of the tree.

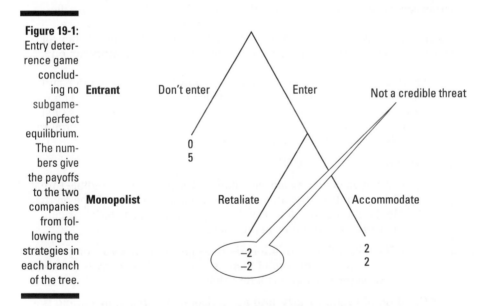

You guessed it: the Nash equilibrium is for NewCo not to enter, because if it does OldStuff can cut its prices and punish NewCo.

But is this threat credible? No, because it would leave OldStuff worse off, and so the equilibrium isn't subgame perfect; therefore NewCo can see that it's not credible. Therefore, NewCo has a dominant strategy to enter knowing that OldStuff can't punish it without hurting itself.

In Chapter 13 on monopoly, we say that a monopolist may decide to take losses in the short run to keep a competitor out. That remains true here, and the degree to which it's willing or able to do so depends on the number of rounds in the game. If final payoffs exist, however, the result of the backward induction stands.

Employing this reasoning in all real-world situations is challenging, to put it mildly. First, you may not know all the necessary information, and second, you may not be dealing with an entity that behaves rationally – think of a rogue nation or a company deploying the madman strategy we describe in Chapter 16 to confuse a potential purchaser!

Deterring entry: A guide to the dark arts

Given that we rule out strategies that involve taking a loss – because they're non-credible threats – how can a firm with a dominant position in a market signal to a would-be entrant that it should stay out?

Firms can use a number of ways in the real world, some of which are illegal for larger companies under competition or antitrust laws. All these approaches have their basis in the entry deterrence game, and so they all provide some reason to believe that they may signal a retaliatory action:

- **Limit pricing:** A monopolist can price below the monopoly price and make lower profits in the short run. This behaviour indicates to an entrant that if it tries to grab market share, it's going to be up against a dominant competitor that can support lower prices, and it's therefore unlikely to enter the market profitably.

  Two problems exist with this tactic:

  - Although economically sensible (lower profits is a credible threat), it might attract the attention of regulators – who could be on the lookout for entry deterring strategies. If you go as far as pricing below costs, you'd be acting illegally!

  - The entrant may not interpret the signal unless it's accompanied by a statement of commitment, such as making an investment in a new factory to support limit pricing.

- **Creation of brand loyalty, and advertising:** Investment in a brand is a type of sunk cost – when the money is spent, it's unrecoverable whether the investment is successful or not. The intention is to make the entrant see the cost of entry as including the cost of making a comparable effort in advertising, branding and marketing. If the effort seems sufficiently high, the entrant stays away.

✔ **Raising the cost of exit:** Again, the way to achieve this aim is by making a seemingly unproductive investment requiring a large sunk cost. This signal is intended to say that the monopolist may not be able to keep the entrant from entering the market, but it can surely create a tough operating environment!

All these strategies require some degree of *pre-commitment* to be effective: that is, committing yourself to a course of action, usually by making an investment. The value in strategic terms is that it signals to another party that you've eliminated other possibilities, so that you can be sure that you're committed to whatever action you're likely to take. If that action is costly to a rival, it acts as a deterrent signal.

The legendary Chinese strategist Sun Tzu recommended that if you want your army to win, you should burn your ships. The idea is that if you cut off your own retreat, you're signalling your determination to your opponent and therefore helping to break her morale – this is a very strong example of pre-commitment!

Signalling your good intentions

Of course, signals of pre-commitment aren't merely negative – although the main examples we use in the preceding sections are. Perhaps two players want to signal positively to each other, such as is often the case with product quality. A mark of product quality can signal to the customer that your product is of superior value, for instance.

The value of this type of mark to a consumer depends on how many people are able to fake a similar mark:

✔ **If faking is hard:** The quality guarantee helps to avoid the adverse selection problem we detail in Chapter 15.

✔ **If faking is easy:** The quality guarantee, if anything, supports the adverse selection problem and helps eliminate the market! This provides one other rationale for companies making strenuous efforts to defend the value of their brand. If the brands are fakeable, any quality signal is lost and bad competitors drive out good!

If that isn't sufficient, signalling quality by offering an expensive warranty programme does the trick. The key thing that makes it doubly effective is for the warranty to be expensive! Therefore, the signal works in the right way and less scrupulous competitors are deterred from trying to fake it! (If in doubt, pull up the Groucho Marx quote from Chapter 16 for some sage advice!)

Responding to Positive Economic Signals

One of the prominent issues of a market system is that people and firms respond to conditions without knowing for certain how things may turn out. As a result, participants in markets are often looking for information to give them a sign of how things are going to be, as much as looking for knowledge of how markets are.

Signals become most important when people and firms are looking for some guide to others' intended actions. If you don't know entirely, the best guide to deciding what to do for yourself is to look for something that gives you a sign that you may be making the right choice. In predicting markets, for instance, people look for signs of what direction prices may move in; in assessing unknowns, people look for any information that confirms their view of that unknown.

The decision whether to hire someone is a classic example of this problem. Only in retrospect do you know for sure what contribution a person makes to your firm's value. When hiring, you have some information to go on, but not a complete set by any stretch of the imagination.

Consider the level of an applicant's education. You hope that it includes all kinds of useful skills to indicate that hiring the person will enhance your company's profitability, but you don't know for certain until you hire the person! But even if you assume the worst – that education gives little or no benefit – looking at the applicant's education level and choosing the candidate with the most completed years is still worthwhile.

The reason why is that completing a certain number of years of education is a *signal* that the person has a certain amount of stickability in the job – that she won't bail when the work looks too hard – and that she's reliable – as her continued attendance in education demonstrates.

In this section we describe a model and equilibrium to show you how signalling a person's ability to stick at a job would affect wages for two different groups. This is, if you like, a use of a positive signal – a signal of employability. (We could, in fact, reverse some of the assumptions and use a similar model to show how, for instance, a criminal record signals poorer ability.) In this case, though, we use a classic model to show you how signals affect a market and how the use of positive signals may not lead to an outcome that's better for society.

Investigating signalling with a model

Economists use a framework developed in the 1970s by Michael Spence to analyse many signalling problems – the most famous of which is looking at the value of a university degree. In Spence's model, asymmetric information exists – see Chapter 15 – because one party knows more about its value than another. In this case, the applicant knows more about her potential effort or value than the hirer. The latter therefore looks for a signal – something that captures, albeit imperfectly, the ability of the applicant.

Spence's framework has two types of worker distinguished by their marginal product – the amount of value that they add to the organisation – which is denoted by a:

- ✔ **Good workers:** Have a marginal product of a_2.
- ✔ **Bad workers:** Have a product of a_1 with the constraint that $a_2 > a_1$.

This framework provides a simple way of making a clear distinction between the workers, and also leads to a first intuition: if you can clearly differentiate between the workers, working out what to pay them is easy. You set wages $w_1 = a_1$ for the poor workers and $w_2 = a_2$ for the good workers (where w = wages of any given worker). That sets a wage equal to the marginal product of labour in the two groups and is therefore efficient.

Setting up the basic model

Assuming a competitive labour market and the existence of b good workers and $(1 - b)$ poor workers, we look at what the firm would do when it *can't* distinguish the two groups of workers beforehand. It sets a wage relative to the average quality of the workers:

$$w = (1-b)\, a_1 + ba_2$$

You may recognise this expectation from Chapter 15 – where a population or a product is of two types, most of which end in market failure! Here, however, the workers find a way of telling the potential employer which group they're in: in other words, their positive signal.

The signal in this case is to do with how much education they've undergone, and it's related to a cost of doing so – you can measure that in terms of fees or make an assumption about the personal opportunity cost. Whichever way you choose to measure it, assume that type 1 workers have e_1 level of education, acquired at a cost of c_1, and that the respective figures for type 2 workers are e_2 and c_2. That makes the total cost of educating any given type 1 worker $e_1 c_1$.

Now each party needs to make a decision:

- ✔ The firm needs to decide what to pay workers with different levels of education.
- ✔ The worker needs to decide what level of education to get.

To look at these decisions in the context of signalling, assume no particular gain in productivity from any level of education. This seems ridiculous, we know, but the important part of the model at this point is the signal, not the productivity.

Supposing that the marginal cost of getting educated is lower for better workers means that $c_2 > c_1$. Also, $a_2 > a_1$ and so a unique level of education $e*$ must exist that satisfies the following:

$$(a_2 - a_1)/c_1 < e* < (a_2 - a_1)/c_2$$

Finding a signalling equilibrium

Assume that the signals hold perfectly and education is a perfect signal of the worker's marginal product. In that case, the wage must equal the marginal product and so a perfect signal is tantamount to the equilibrium where firms can observe workers directly. Now add in the constraint that a poor worker chooses zero education whereas a good worker chooses $e*$.

Is this an equilibrium? For the firm, yes! It has a clear way, based on the choice of signal, to choose between workers, and can set a wage based on their marginal product.

What about for the poorer quality workers, those with product of a_1? Is it optimal for them to buy $e*$ of education? The benefit would be $a_2 - a_1$ but the cost would be c_1e*. So a poor quality worker gets $e*$ of education only if

$$a_2 - a_1 > c_1e*$$

But you know from the choice of $e*$ that c_1e* is bigger than $a_2 - a_1$! So in this model, the benefits of getting $e*$ of education are less than the costs, and so the poorer quality workers won't invest in any education at all!

For the better quality workers, it's worth getting educated if $a_2 - a_1 > c_2e*$. The choice of $e*$ implies that this is true and so this logic works for better workers too!

Therefore, the equilibrium holds. Under these conditions neither types of workers have any reason to change their behaviour.

This equilibrium is called a *separating equilibrium,* one based on subgroups of people within a population – whether producers or consumers – behaving differently from each other. The opposite – where they make the same choice – is called a *pooling equilibrium.*

Evaluating the signalling equilibrium

The signalling equilibrium has some interesting implications for policy makers. The most important is that even if you believe that education has no effect on productivity, it's still worth getting if you're a high productivity worker and want a higher wage!

In a Yale lecture, microeconomist Ben Polak, describes the model as having a pessimistic conclusion. His points are as follows:

- ✔ For the signal to work, it has to be costly, and so $c_2 > c_1$. Within Spence's framework that means that the cost of education is its key feature. So what you studied doesn't matter, only that you paid – in money or sweat – to study it!

- ✔ If that's the point of education, spending money on teachers' salaries is socially wasteful! (We prefer that you don't believe that conclusion!)

- ✔ Given that the value of the signal is related to its cost, a separating equilibrium like this one tends to exclude any high productivity worker who starts out too poor to pay c_2. So, signalling hurts the poor and increases inequality.

Those conclusions are indeed pessimistic – for educators at least! Are they justified? Well, as long as you believe that the sole purpose of education is in signalling, you'd be entirely justified in holding those conclusions.

But education isn't only a signal. Many reasons exist for valuing education and not all are related to signalling – for instance, this framework doesn't believe that important skills exist that people can learn, or that education can improve a person's productivity.

So here's another lesson: models are garbage in – garbage out. If the thing you want to know about isn't loaded into the model, you're unlikely to be able to draw robust conclusions from it!

Evaluating the signaling equilibrium

Part VI
The Part of Tens

the part of tens

For ten ways to stretch your microeconomic knowledge into other areas, head to www.dummies.com/extras/microeconomics.

In this part . . .

- Meet ten giants of the discipline.
- Consider ten microeconomic essentials.

Chapter 20

Meeting Ten Great Microeconomists

. . . .

In This Chapter

▶ Paying tribute to some great thinkers

▶ Realising that microeconomics is the result of many hands

. . . .

*I*n this chapter we introduce you to some great names who inspired us to discover microeconomics. Microeconomics has become a broad, deep subject and although we can't possibly do justice to all their work, we want to give you a flavour of some of the great results.

Many microeconomists have also made contributions to other subjects: macroeconomics, maths, sociology, law and history being the most common. In fact, some people say that no such thing as a pure microeconomist exists! We have some agreement with that view, given the areas into which some of these greats have moved.

So what follows is a – perhaps slightly eccentric – list of inspiring and challenging thinkers. But they're just the tip of a huge iceberg, and we apologise – in some cases sadly posthumously – to all those we leave out. This job was as difficult as picking an all-time England football XI or the top ten greatest singles. We hope that given the scarcity of available places, you forgive the omissions!

Alfred Marshall (1842–1924)

The approach to microeconomics that we pursue in this book – which is the mainstream approach for the profession – is sometimes called *marginalism*, and much of it is down to Alfred Marshall. He started as a mathematician before switching to philosophy – this was before economics became a subject in its own right! That change led him to look again at the work of the utilitarian philosophers and develop a theory about how to use their work to improve the lives of the working classes.

Along the way, Marshall wrote *Principles of Economics,* which was a standard textbook for around 70 years, made economics a subject in its own right at Cambridge and invented the supply and demand graphs that economists know and love today.

Marshall's style was to try to communicate in the most understandable way, aiming much of his work outside the profession – with the meaty stuff going in technical appendices. Among the people he taught were John Maynard Keynes and Arthur Pigou, making him an important father figure to modern economics.

Joseph Alois Schumpeter (1883–1950)

Born in Triesch, in what's now the Czech Republic but was then part of Hapsburg Austria, Joseph Schumpeter made many great contributions to microeconomics, though not all were appreciated during his lifetime. He began as a law student, but moved on into economics, eventually serving on the board of two private banks – both of which eventually ran into the ground! – before moving to America to lecture at Harvard. Here Schumpeter finally began to build the reputation that he has today.

Among Schumpeter's many contributions to economics was the idea of *creative destruction.* This applies evolution to reasoning about the way firms innovate – over time, old ideas and firms are destroyed by the way newer rivals create new ideas and businesses. In his great book *Capitalism, Socialism and Democracy* (1942), he provided an account of how capitalism itself would come to an end, largely through its own successes – successful companies in capitalist societies would come to exert influence on politics leading to demands for socialist policies and a falling rate of innovation instead of the revolutionary crises foreseen by Karl Marx. He was profoundly driven to understand the mysteries of entrepreneurship, producing two complementary accounts of how it happens – one as the result of heroic visionaries with a kind of spirit or outlook driving them and one as a result of large companies having the capital to invest.

Schumpeter was a famously devoted teacher and had a keen sense of humour. He wrote that he'd only had three goals: to be the greatest economist in the world, the best horseman in Austria and the greatest lover in Vienna. He quipped that he'd only achieved two of the three, but never spelt out which two!

Gary S Becker (1930–2014)

If you've seen articles in the popular press applying economic reasoning to all kinds of things – such as marriage, discrimination or the political system – you've come across the work of Gary Becker! He grew up in the US, holding a chair at the famous Department of Economics at the University of Chicago. He applied his rigorous understanding of the utility model (which we introduce in Chapter 2) to all kinds of issues, generally things studied in sociology departments rather than economics ones.

Becker is famous, among other things, for his ground-breaking study of discrimination against minority groups. His analysis showed that the costs of discrimination tend also to fall upon people who discriminate, meaning that they tend to incur higher production costs: therefore discrimination isn't really in the economic interests of a majority group. His insights into lobby groups and the democratic process are equally startling – showing that democratic and nondemocratic societies can both have a problem with the external costs imposed on other voters (in democracies) or other citizens (in nondemocratic societies) by overly successful lobbyists.

Most startlingly, Becker points out that utility maximisation itself isn't necessarily selfish. If you place value on acting altruistically, it maximises your utility to help others, and so criticisms of the utility model are misplaced and more to do with framing than with reality.

Ronald Coase (1910–2013)

Ronald Coase was a British economist who spent much of his career as a professor at Chicago University, where he was still practising economics – he published his final book at the age of 102! – long after most people have retired! Although Coase's career covered many areas of microeconomics, he's probably most famous for his analyses of law – he edited the famous *Journal of Law and Economics*.

Two papers of Coase's are considered absolute classics in microeconomics:

- **'The Nature of the Firm':** This essay from the 1930s looks at the motivations for forming companies. Speaking in the abstract, no real reason exists for having companies do anything: probably a lot of other structures could do the job. So why do people form companies at all?

His answer is to do with the costs of using the market itself – *transactions costs* – such as the cost of finding someone to do business with, the cost of getting the deal done and the cost of enforcing the deal afterwards. A company puts those costs in one place so that they're easier to deal with. However, it does so by making them internal to the company – where they become the costs of bureaucracy.

So you can see companies as a cycle: when transactions costs are high, companies form; and when the costs are fully internalised, they choke the company leading to a breakup and the formation of new companies.

✔ **'The Problem of Social Cost':** This paper contributed to dealing with externality. Coase's insight was that without transactions costs, to whom a property right is allocated to get an efficient outcome makes no difference. But with transactions costs, it does matter: the rights should go to the person who can take the economically efficient outcome. Later, his reasoning became widely known as the basis for 'the Coase theorem' – even though he never felt that it was truly based on his work! We discuss the theorem, externality and property rights in Chapter 14.

Elinor Ostrom (1933–2012)

Any list of great microeconomists is going to be dominated by men. In fact, historically, the area of study has a male bias – don't worry, microeconomists are already studying why! But of all the recent winners of the Nobel Prize in Economics, perhaps one of the most important is Elinor Ostrom, the only woman to win the prize so far.

Ostrom was a professor at the University of Indiana, working on *public choice economics* – the area that studies how people and institutions interact. On field trips to Africa and Himalayan Asia she codified an approach to dealing with the problems of looking after things that no one owns – what microeconomists call *common pool resources,* such as the ecosystem of the plains of the Serengeti.

By looking at how indigenous peoples did things, she advanced a strong criticism of many of the approaches people used to deal with the Tragedy of the Commons (which we discuss in Chapter 14). She pointed out that as long as people can agree on certain principles, indigenous societies are perfectly capable of managing the commons without ecological collapse. This result challenges most schools of economic or political analysis!

Ostrom did a lot of her work on similar problems, which meant that she studied areas such as reciprocity or trust that aren't immediately obviously part of the economist's toolkit. Along the way, she also co-wrote one of the most important textbooks on modelling co-operation using game theory (the subject of Chapter 16)!

William Vickrey (1914–96)

Canadian economist William Vickrey was posthumously awarded the Nobel Prize in 1996, largely for his work applying game theory and incentive theory to situations with asymmetric information (see Chapter 15). He was a professor at Columbia University for much of his career, and in that role he turned out a stunning amount of work, stretching over many areas of economics – we wouldn't have even attempted Chapter 18 (on auctions) without his work! Vickrey's most famous paper was his study of stamp collector auctions in 1961, where he rediscovered and worked out the logic behind the traditional use of a second-price winner in auctions. He then showed how to use this insight to prevent winner's curse problems (again, see Chapter 18).

Vickrey's contribution to public economics, and his applied work looking at government, is also extremely important. For instance, the congestion charge zone in London, the biggest of its kind in the world, is based on some of the work that Vickrey did looking at road pricing.

A devout Quaker, Vickrey also believed that full employment in society was a moral question and devoted much of his other research time to proposing schemes to remedy idleness. In this aim, he was less successful.

George Akerlof (born 1940)

George Akerlof, currently a professor at Georgetown University, won his Nobel Prize in 2001, largely for his study on information problems – the famous 'Market for Lemons' in Chapter 15 is a classic example and a classic paper to many microeconomists.

Akerlof's work on information problems extended to his work on signalling in labour markets (see Chapter 19). He points out that paying higher wages may not be sub-optimal if the threat of losing a wage premium when going to a rival company is enough to keep worker productivity higher in the higher-paying company. He co-wrote this paper with his substantially more famous wife, Janet Yellen, who's currently Chair of the Federal Reserve, the US central bank.

More recently, Akerlof looked at how psychology is central to decision making, exploring how people's sense of identity affects their decisions. People don't just have preferences on which they act, they also have to respect certain types of social norm, which conditions how markets behave in reality.

James Buchanan (1919–2013)

One of the big names in the microeconomics of *public choice* (an area of microeconomics that looks at social choices through microeconomic thinking – we make a start on looking at it in Chapters 12 and 14), James Buchanan perhaps did most to apply economic thinking to the rules of governing a society. A socialist in his youth, he 'converted' to a market-orientated view after his service in the Second World War as a PhD student at the famously market-centred University of Chicago. For much of the rest of his career, he looked at the problems of setting rules for government.

Perhaps his most important work is *The Calculus of Consent* (written with Gordon Tullock in 1962). This book contains a serious and systematic approach to working out the costs and benefits of government action in a world where public officials are also rational and face a set of incentives. The book shows, among other things, that the 'public interest' may not be anything more than what you get when you add up the 'private' interests of lawmakers: if you could get an efficient result through a market system, you're unlikely to achieve one under any political system.

Buchanan's work is often considered divisive, with many disliking its assumptions about how public officials and government behave. However, researchers on public choice from the political left and right tend to use his work as a starting point for their analyses of all kinds of political problems!

William Baumol (born 1922)

A professor of economics at New York University, William Baumol is one of the most prolific authors in the field of microeconomics. Perhaps his most important contribution is looking at entrepreneurship, bringing Joseph Schumpeter's insights into mainstream economics and coming up with ways of dealing with one of the most important gaps in the traditional microeconomic literature.

Microeconomics' problems with innovation are many and being worked on as we write. One of the big ones is captured in a joke about how long it will take to pick up a $100 bill dropped in the middle of Wall Street. The punchline – 'if there really were a bill, someone would've picked it up by now' – expresses the way in which some forms of model have to assume that innovation and entrepreneurship happen while at the same time denying that they're possible. Baumol drew on the Schumpeterian tradition by providing an account of what entrepreneurs do to make their new companies and forms of business work. Baumol has also written about macroeconomics, the tendency of costs in service industries to rise without corresponding rises in productivity – often called Baumol's cost disease – and how the threat of entry can keep monopolies from raising their prices. He's also famous for his interest in the economics of the arts, writing a spectacular paper on the economics of composition in Mozart's Vienna!

Arthur Cecil Pigou (1877–1959)

Although we haven't gone through the enormous economic literature on the environment – yes, many economists have studied it! – we do want to pay tribute to British economist Arthur Cecil Pigou. He was Alfred Marshall's successor as Professor of Political Economy at Cambridge University, and a friend – though you wouldn't believe it from their rows! – of John Maynard Keynes.

Pigou wrote about many subjects, including a lot of the research on which modern labour economics is built. But perhaps his most enduring and best remembered work is on welfare (see Chapter 12) – his 1920 book *The Economics of Welfare* introduced the concept of externality to economics. He came up with the idea of using what's now called Pigovian taxes to remedy some of the social costs of private actions (check out Chapter 14 for details). His influence is still felt to this day in the existence of the Pigou Club, an informal and nonparty aligned group of economists who want to see carbon taxes implemented.

A conscientious objector in the First World War, he spent his vacations from Cambridge serving with the Friends Ambulance Unit on the front line – volunteering for the most dangerous rescue and recovery missions.

Chapter 21

Ten Top Tips to Take Away

In This Chapter

▶ Getting to grips with the main points of microeconomics

▶ Dealing with an imperfect world

*M*icroeconomics is a huge area of study, and no one can do the entire subject justice in one book – we're both proud owners of entire shelves full of economic textbooks! You can, however, take away many of the most important core ideas of microeconomics from this book.

So without more ado (this talk of takeaways has made us hungry!), here are ten important points to remember from this book.

Respecting Choice

All microeconomics is built on the idea that consumers and producers make choices about what to make or what to buy. As a result, economists tend to have a healthy respect for choice itself. People value things in different ways and economists want to look at the consequences of, rather than the reasons for, those values. You only get to know what value people place on something after they choose it – or as economists say, you get to know people's preferences when they've chosen (they also say that as many valuations exist as people!).

Trade is possible because people value things differently, which causes the need for a means to trade things – a market.

In a famous paper – 'The Economic Organisation of a Prisoner of War Camp' – Richard Radford, an economist interred in a POW camp, described this process in detail. Starting with Red Cross packages, prisoners traded allowances with each other to make themselves better off. For instance, Gurkhas, being strict Hindus, were only too happy to trade meat for other goods. At first, these trades were done by bartering goods directly, but eventually, through evolution and without anyone making an overall strategic decision, the camps alighted on using tobacco rations as currency – a simple form of money! At this point, very simply, the POWs had created a market!

The result of properly functioning markets is – over the long run – the betterment of everyone. This result relies on people choosing, which is why economists generally prefer solutions that allow people to choose – for instance, by designing mechanisms that let people choose within a framework – as opposed to coming in and preventing choice.

Pricing a Good: Difficult but not Impossible

In several situations a market has difficulty pricing a good. One case is when the marginal cost of the good is at or near zero – a competitive market ends up with no one pricing above zero and everyone scrabbling around for other ways to make money. Public goods – such as street lighting, public parks or even law enforcement – are another case, one made worse by the impossibility of excluding people who haven't paid from the market (check out Chapter 14).

But just because a market finding a competitively sustainable solution is difficult, doesn't make it impossible. For instance, television broadcasts can be distributed to an extra person at zero marginal cost. In this industry, firms found a way to price something else – advertising – effectively using programming as a lure to sell viewers' attention to advertisers. Another possibility is selling 'membership' to a club as a way of getting access – in essence a subscription model.

People are essentially creative in such situations. When they come up against an unfavourable economic situation, they try to find solutions to get around the problem. Economists have great respect for this creativity, which is one reason why they want to see what can be achieved without intervening, before coming up with ways to do so.

Competing on Price or Quality

In a perfectly competitive market, competition is only ever on price, which is always forced down to the marginal cost of production for the marginal firm. But in most market structures, competing on price is very hard and so firms tend to focus on their product.

If you start in monopolistic competition (see Chapter 13) – which is a common market structure – you can see why. If you compete on price, over the long run the price gets pushed down to marginal cost and the firm doesn't make profits. The alternative is to change your focus, so that you can keep making your product different from the other competitors and make nonzero profits. However, you need to invest to do that, and if you're investing in keeping the product different or better, you're using resources that you could've spent on getting costs down!

This problem is one reason why firms tend to choose either to be the lowest-cost competitor or a high-quality competitor. The alternative is generally pleasing neither people who want things cheap nor people who want good quality!

Seeking Real Markets' Unique Features

This book discusses lots of ways of structuring markets, and the literature contains many thousands more! What they all have in common is basic assumptions about what people may do – whether deciding to produce or consume – in those markets. But in reality markets tend to have unique and distinctive features – they vary from place to place and product to product.

When economists come across these features, they explore the differences between that market and a more generic one. Sometimes they propose ways to make such markets more productive. Most importantly, economists look very carefully at why a particular market exhibits those features before they rush in and call it a market failure! Instead, they ask a number of questions: is the market like that because people value things in that way; is a distortion involved, such as a tax or a subsidy; are very high sunk costs present?

Generic models form a starting point for comparison. Economists aren't trying to say a given market should be exactly like this or that!

Beating the Market in the Long Run is Very Difficult

The phrase 'you can't beat the market' is the kind of saying that drives economists to distraction. For a start, you don't always prefer to use a market, for example when transactions costs are high. Plus, it's just not realistic to suggest, for instance, that all firms should abandon management structures and replace them with internal markets – firms are market-facing on the outside, but above a certain size, many of the jobs in a given company aren't involved in handling the marketplace. Neither of ours really is, for example.

When economists say that you can't beat the market, they're pointing out that no other way exists to get to the highest level of efficiency. In a general equilibrium model (see Chapter 12), for example, the contract curve of best choices relies on people being able to trade their way to their highest level of utility. But that doesn't mean that doing so is feasible – general equilibrium rests on some strong assumptions. Nor does it mean that a market in something is practical. In the Renaissance, Italian city-states hired private armies called *condottieri*. But they had great difficulty ensuring that condottieri followed orders – in some cases the soldiers just came in and took over the city! The fact that few places would prefer a mercenary army today is no coincidence!

Having said all that, always be sceptical of people's claims that they can make long-run profits – and therefore, if you're an investor, returns – greater than those of the market they're in. Why? Well if they could, someone would come in and compete them away! If we can persuade you to take one piece of advice from us, it's watch your wallet when anyone claims to be able to beat the market in the long run!

Knowing a Tradeoff Always Exists Somewhere

The economist's model of consumers is called a *constrained optimisation* – because ultimately you're trying to do your best given that you can't have everything (see Chapter 5). As a result, at some point you have to choose between one option and another because you can't have both.

As long as things are scarce you have to make choices. To an economist this is just a fact of life, and you may as well complain about gravity as about scarcity! That means that getting your best level of utility is always about trading off one thing for another.

A similar situation happens when you try to balance efficiency and fairness. Now, in the short run a society can be so far away from peak efficiency *and* complete fairness that a gain in both is possible. But if you're at the constraint or very near it, trying to prioritise equity leads to a fall in efficiency unless you can do it by lump-sum transfers – which again may not be practical!

A good rule for looking at the world is that if you see a free lunch, ask who's paying for it: if you're not, someone else probably is! When a product seems free – as it does for some Internet services, especially in social media, check whether the product is actually you – or more accurately your personal information!

Arguing about the Next Best Thing

Throughout the book, we look at the optimal thing for people or firms (Chapters 2 to 8) or society (Chapter 12 especially) to do. Here's a little problem though: you sometimes can't get exactly what you want. Microeconomics has some advice for you though. An economic principle, the *Theory of the Second Best* reminds you that if you can't get the optimal solution, then almost anything can be a second best alternative.

Suppose, for instance, that a polluting monopoly produces your electricity – imagine that electricity can only be made using smoggy coal for the moment. Then, if you're a policy maker and you act to counteract the monopoly, you increase output and produce more smog. So your best choice under the circumstances isn't immediately clear. Should you increase production, by dealing with the market inefficiency of monopoly, or mitigate the pollution while keeping the monopoly in place?

Although getting the optimal isn't possible, you can certainly argue about what the next best thing is. Economists recommend that you look carefully at the inefficiency and the external cost in this situation, before coming up with a solution.

When you hear politicians arguing about what to do, remember that often the argument isn't about what the best thing is, but which of several 'practical' options is the second best. You can then choose, on the basis of your investigations, which party you want to support!

Using Markets Isn't Always Costless

Even though economists generally prefer free exchange – and therefore markets – as their way of achieving goals, using those markets isn't always costless. Sometimes, an accounted cost falls upon another person – an *external cost* – and sometimes costs exist associated with just finding the person to trade with – *transactions costs*.

To an economist the key question is what makes those costs as low as possible? The answer isn't as simple as just saying that a market inevitably would keep costs at the lowest possible level, because it may not be as 'free' as a market structure in a textbook implies.

If, for instance, a hundred painters of varying quality work in your town, and you don't know any of them because you've just moved there, how can you know which one to hire to paint your house? You probably spend a fair amount of time looking for one, getting recommendations as to their reliability, quality and unlikeliness of leaving your house a mess. These activities are all costs, and they all come about precisely *because* you're using a market to find the person.

Economists have two pieces of advice here:

- ✔ Think carefully about where the inevitable costs of using a market fall.
- ✔ Seek out the opportunities that always exist for entrepreneurs with good ideas for reducing a firm's transactions costs!

Believing that Competition is Good – Usually

Any time a market isn't perfectly competitive, the firms in the industry are getting the greater share of the gains to trade. As a result, they always have an interest in preventing another firm from coming in and competing away the gains. They use many 'tricks' to do so – including advertising, investing in things that involve high commitments and making their product's 'brand' different.

These tactics aim to prevent a rival from producing at a lower cost and taking the market away. Consumers lose out because the producers produce less, for higher cost, and take more of the surplus. For this reason, economists look carefully at barriers to market entry, and work to get them down as low as possible in the long run.

But that isn't the whole story. Sometimes, economists give two cheers to markets that aren't competitive. For example, a monopolist doesn't compete with itself, which can mean that you get more product diversity with a lack of competition.

Research in Australia, for instance, suggested that in order to get a different genre of programming to the prevalent soaps in a prime-time slot, the market would require five TV channels, because the first four would find that making soaps was rational. A monopolist, however, would produce a different genre for each channel, because that maximises the profit from each 'slice' of the market!

Suppose that 80 per cent of Australia liked soaps. Then the first channel would produce soaps, hoping to get 80 per cent of the market. The second would also (two channels competing for 80 per cent of the market would get 40 per cent each). So would the third and fourth (because 80 divided by 4 is 20 per cent). It's not until you get to the fifth channel that the expected share of the market from producing something different matches the expected share from producing soaps.

In some markets, competition costs too much, because it means that competitors can't produce at a big enough scale. In others, for example Internet search, competition can't happen because the market is winner takes all. But if a possibility exists of getting a result from a competitive market, many economists take it as the best option.

Getting Co-operation and Organisation in the World

Economics often gets a bad press, because the assumed behaviour of individuals in economics seems selfish, because the model of people and firms seems to make a priority of individual benefit, or even because the model of an individual doesn't try to reproduce many of the features people think of as essential. But in fact economists are the world's greatest optimists! Why? Well, economic models are built from no greater assumption than that people follow their own interests – yet the world still gets firms, organisations, production and consumption, and all the things that make the world go round!

You may disagree that this world is ideal – many people do! But what's remarkable to the economist is that even if you don't expect people to follow what Abraham Lincoln called 'the better angels' of human nature, you still get co-operation as people get together and form companies – or organisation as people following their own interests create and trade in markets!

Glossary

Adverse selection: A problem caused by *asymmetric information* where a product is selected only by the people who'll make worst returns for a supplier – for example, only people with risky lifestyles buying life insurance. The typical effect is that the market fails.

Agent: (1) Anyone who acts in an economic model. (2) In the principal–agent model, anyone who acts on behalf of the principal.

Allocative efficiency: When a firm produces up to the point where *marginal revenue* equals *marginal cost.* As a result, when firms are allocatively efficient no deadweight loss exists and price equals marginal cost.

Asymmetric information: The condition that exists when one side of a trade knows more than the other – for example, when sellers know more about their product than buyers.

Auction: A way of selling where an auctioneer calls out prices and solicits bids from potential buyers. The good being auctioned goes to one buyer – usually the highest bidder.

Average cost: Total cost divided by the number of units of output produced – in other words, total costs per unit.

Backward induction: A method of solving repeated games by starting at the end *payoffs* and working backwards, eliminating any move that would yield a lower payoff.

Barriers to entry: Anything that significantly raises the cost for a firm of entering a market and thus deters one from entering.

Bertrand oligopoly: A model of *oligopoly* where competitors react to each other's decisions on price.

Cartel: A group of firms acting together to maximise their collective *profits.* Cartels try to secure *monopoly* profits for their members and therefore impose *deadweight losses* on everyone else.

Co-ordination game: A type of *game theory* model where the best outcome depends on participants being able to co-ordinate their actions. The *stag hunt* is one such game.

Cournot oligopoly: A model of *oligopoly* where competitors react to each other's decisions on quantity.

Deadweight loss: A loss of *welfare* (producer plus consumer surpluses) that occurs because production isn't *allocative efficient.* Deadweight losses are lost to producers and consumers and therefore to society as a whole.

Demand curve: In the *supply and demand* model, relates the quantity purchased to the price of the good – holding income and tastes constant. It generally slopes downwards: as price rises, quantity demanded goes down.

Demand function: Any mathematical description of quantity purchased in terms of prices.

Deterrence: In *game theory*, deterrence strategies are those whose purpose is to deter a rival from taking an action by signalling that the rival's *payoffs* will be lower if it does act. The word is often used in terms of preventing a firm from entering a market.

Dominant strategy: A *strategy* that gives higher *payoffs* no matter what the opponent does.

Duopoly: Any market supplied by only two firms.

Dutch auction: Where the auctioneer calls out descending prices until a bidder determines that the price is low enough to buy and calls 'mine'.

English auction: Where the auctioneer starts at a low price and successive rounds of bidding raise the price until only one bidder is left.

Externality: A benefit or cost that falls on a third party not included in a transaction. Externalities can be negative – costs – or positive – benefits.

External cost: A cost that falls on a third party. If A and B trade and C, who isn't involved in the trade, gets burdened with some cost, C is experiencing an external cost.

Factor of production: The basic inputs of a firm – land, labour and capital. The firm combines them using a *technology* to produce its output.

Fixed cost: Costs that don't depend on how many units a firm produces. For example, for a football team, the cost of constructing a stadium is a fixed cost, because it costs the same to build no matter how many games are played there.

Game theory: A branch of mathematics looking at what actions participants will take given the *payoffs* to their actions and other participants' decisions. The term is used extensively in economics to examine things such as *cartels*.

General equilibrium: A concept used to define an equilibrium in all markets in an economy. In a general equilibrium, all markets are simultaneously in equilibrium; in a *partial equilibrium*, only one market is in equilibrium.

Hotelling's law: An observation that, given competition on brand or product, markets will form an equilibrium where the differences between brands are as small as they can possibly be.

Indifference curve: A utility function that has a constant level of utility along the curve.

Isocost: A cost curve where the cost is the same at all points along the curve.

Isoquant: A curve that shows all the combinations of inputs that produce the same output at all points along the curve.

Iterated elimination of dominant strategies: A method for solving games by eliminating any strategies that a rational player wouldn't choose.

Marginal cost: The cost for a firm of adding one extra unit to production.

Marginal revenue: The revenue gained from selling one extra unit of a product.

Marginal social cost: The cost to society as a whole of a firm adding one extra unit of production.

Mixed strategy: A *strategy* that assigns a probability to each of a set of pure strategies. For instance, a mixed strategy in Rock, Paper Scissors is playing each of rock, paper and scissors one-third of the time.

Monopolistic competition: A type of market structure with free entry and exit and where competitors each attempt to make their brand different. It yields some *welfare* losses, which have to be set against gains from product diversity.

Monopoly: A market served by only one firm. In competition law and policy, it means a firm is able to set higher than cost prices over the medium term.

Moral hazard: A condition in markets that have **asymmetric information** where someone takes more risks because she knows that someone else will take on the costs of those risks – for instance, leaving your door unlocked because you have generous insurance.

Nash equilibrium: In **game theory**, any outcome where each party is doing the best it can do, given that other parties are doing the same. At a Nash equilibrium, no party has an incentive to change its **strategy.**

Oligopoly: A market served by few firms, and with some barriers to entry and exit. Firms in an oligopoly interact strategically given each other's decisions.

Pareto efficiency: A distribution where making one party better off without making another party worse off is impossible.

Partial equilibrium: An equilibrium where **supply and demand** are equal in a particular market, as opposed to **general equilibrium** where they're equal in all markets.

Payoff: The benefit or loss computed at the end of a game in **game theory.**

Perfect competition: A type of market structure where a large number of producers are making the same product and have perfect information. The result is that price gets bargained down to **marginal cost** and no firm can influence price on its own.

Pooled equilibrium: Where two populations have different characteristics, a pooled equilibrium is the equilibrium you get when the two markets are taken together and summed.

Prisoners' Dilemma: A **game theory** model where two participants are unable to communicate and as a result make an individually best decision that isn't as good for the whole.

Productive efficiency: Productive efficiency happens when firms are producing for the lowest possible cost, at the minimum of the long-run average cost curve.

Profit: What's left over after all relevant costs have been taken away from a firm's revenue.

Pure strategy: A **strategy** chosen on its **payoffs** alone, and not on the probability of using it. A pure strategy is a complete specification of how a given player will play the game, as opposed to a **mixed strategy,** which needs you to know how probable it is that a player will use any given strategy.

Reaction function: A mathematical description of what one firm will do in an *oligopoly* in reaction to its competitor's decision.

Separating equilibrium: The equilibrium that you get when you look at different types in the population – for instance high and low productivity workers – as distinct groups. In a separating equilibrium, the two populations have some way of demonstrating their difference from each other, whereas in a pooled equilibrium they don't.

Signal: A *game theory* term for a move that tells other players something that they aren't able to discern directly.

Stackelberg oligopoly: A model of an *oligopoly* where one firm is the leader and able to take the reaction of other firms into account when making its decisions. A Stackelberg oligopoly produces more than a *Cournot oligopoly* at a slightly lower cost.

Stag hunt: A type of *co-ordination game* with two *Nash equilibria,* one that maximises *payoff* and one that minimises risk.

Strategy: A set of moves that a player will follow in a game, which must be complete and cover every possible outcome in the game, even if that outcome won't happen.

Sunk costs: Costs that are unrecoverable after being incurred.

Supply curve: A curve in *supply and demand* analysis that tells you how much the relevant industry will make as price changes.

Supply and demand: A model microeconomists use to look at prices and quantities in a market. The equilibrium in the model is where supply equals demand, which is where the supply and demand curves cross.

Switching cost: The cost for a firm of a consumer changing from one product to another, for example in switching from one type of word processor to another. Switching costs may come from the *sunk cost* of learning how to use a product, from having to give up complements or from loss of opportunities to trade with other consumers.

Technology: Any method for transforming inputs into outputs, most often used to describe the mix of capital and labour a firm chooses.

Tragedy of the Commons: A situation where a common resource is overexploited because no one owns it.

Transactions costs: The costs of a firm using a market, in terms of searching for people to deal with, making a bargain with others and enforcing a deal when made.

Trust game: A type of *game theory* model where player 1 has to decide whether to trust player 2, and if she does, player 2 has to decide whether or not to betray that trust.

Utility function: A mathematical description of the utility a consumer gains from performing an action. Utility functions depend on consumers' preferences.

Variable cost: A cost that depends on the number of units a firm produces.

Vickrey auction: A type of *auction* where the highest or lowest bidder gets a good for the price last bid by the second-highest or lowest bidder. Vickrey auctions are designed to avoid the incentive to overbid.

Welfare: A measure of the total utility gained across all consumers and producers. In a partial equilibrium model, it's the sum of consumer and producer surplus. In a general equilibrium model, it's the sum of all utility gained by all agents in the model.

Index

Notes

Notes

Notes

Notes

About the Authors

Peter Antonioni is a senior teaching fellow in the Department of Management Science and Innovation at University College London, where he teaches strategy. His research interests are in the economic history of music production. If not working, he can usually be found crying over Tottenham Hotspurs' most recent performance or putting his angst into playing blues guitar.

Manzur Rashid read economics at Trinity College, Cambridge, where he graduated with a double first and was elected to junior, senior and research scholarships. He completed his doctoral studies in economic theory at UCL, where he specialised in game theory, bounded rationality and industrial organisation, under the supervision of Martin Cripps.

Manzur has taught economics at UCL, Cambridge University, New College of the Humanities and Charterhouse.

Dedications

From Peter: To Tanya, Mum, Dad, Paul and Jen, who suffered most from me writing this.

From Manzur: For Ilyas.

Authors' Acknowledgements

From Peter: With many thanks to the support of my colleagues at UCL, and to the many economists who once had to explain patiently all this material to me.

From Manzur: I am grateful to all the people at Wiley – including Mike Baker, Simon Bell, Steve Edwards, Andy Finch, Annie Knight and Kate O'Leary – who have helped us to get this book into shape. I am also grateful to Ron Smith for his helpful suggestions and comments. Thanks to my friends and family for their endless support. Finally, thank you to my teachers: Martin Cripps, Hamish Low, Rupert Gatti, Steve Satchell, Gernot Doppelhofer and Kevin Sheedy.

Publisher's Acknowledgements

We're proud of this book; please send us your comments at http://dummies.custhelp.com.
For other comments, please contact our Customer Care Department within the U.S. at 877-762-2974,
outside the U.S. at (001) 317-572-3993, or fax 317-572-4002.

Some of the people who helped bring this book to market include the following:

Acquisitions, Editorial and Vertical Websites

Project Editor: Steve Edwards

Commissioning Editor: Mike Baker

Development Editor: Andy Finch

Copy Editor: Kate O'Leary

Technical Reviewer: Professor Ron B. Smith

Front Cover Image: ©iStock.com/armiblue

Production Editor: Kinson Raja

Composition Services

Layout and Graphics: SPi Technologies

Proofreaders: Erin Hartshorn

Indexer: Estalita Slivoskey

ple & Mac

d For Dummies,
Edition
-1-118-72306-7

one For Dummies,
Edition
-1-118-69083-3

cs All-in-One
Dummies, 4th Edition
-1-118-82210-4

X Mavericks
Dummies
-1-118-69188-5

gging & Social Media

ebook For Dummies,
Edition
-1-118-63312-0

ial Media Engagement
Dummies
-1-118-53019-1

rdPress For Dummies,
Edition
-1-118-79161-5

siness

ck Investing
Dummies, 4th Edition
-1-118-37678-2

esting For Dummies,
Edition
-0-470-90545-6

Personal Finance
For Dummies, 7th Edition
978-1-118-11785-9

QuickBooks 2014
For Dummies
978-1-118-72005-9

Small Business Marketing
Kit For Dummies,
3rd Edition
978-1-118-31183-7

Careers

Job Interviews
For Dummies, 4th Edition
978-1-118-11290-8

Job Searching with Social
Media For Dummies,
2nd Edition
978-1-118-67856-5

Personal Branding
For Dummies
978-1-118-11792-7

Resumes For Dummies,
6th Edition
978-0-470-87361-8

Starting an Etsy Business
For Dummies, 2nd Edition
978-1-118-59024-9

Diet & Nutrition

Belly Fat Diet For Dummies
978-1-118-34585-6

Mediterranean Diet
For Dummies
978-1-118-71525-3

Nutrition For Dummies,
5th Edition
978-0-470-93231-5

Digital Photography

Digital SLR Photography
All-in-One For Dummies,
2nd Edition
978-1-118-59082-9

Digital SLR Video &
Filmmaking For Dummies
978-1-118-36598-4

Photoshop Elements 12
For Dummies
978-1-118-72714-0

Gardening

Herb Gardening
For Dummies, 2nd Edition
978-0-470-61778-6

Gardening with Free-Range
Chickens For Dummies
978-1-118-54754-0

Health

Boosting Your Immunity
For Dummies
978-1-118-40200-9

Diabetes For Dummies,
4th Edition
978-1-118-29447-5

Living Paleo For Dummies
978-1-118-29405-5

Big Data

Big Data For Dummies
978-1-118-50422-2

Data Visualization
For Dummies
978-1-118-50289-1

Hadoop For Dummies
978-1-118-60755-8

**Language &
Foreign Language**

500 Spanish Verbs
For Dummies
978-1-118-02382-2

English Grammar
For Dummies, 2nd Edition
978-0-470-54664-2

French All-in-One
For Dummies
978-1-118-22815-9

German Essentials
For Dummies
978-1-118-18422-6

Italian For Dummies,
2nd Edition
978-1-118-00465-4

Available in print and e-book formats.

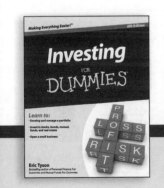
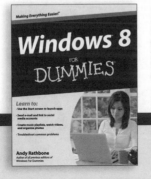

Available wherever books are sold. **For more information or to order direct visit www.dummies.com**

Math & Science

Algebra I For Dummies,
2nd Edition
978-0-470-55964-2

Anatomy and Physiology
For Dummies, 2nd Edition
978-0-470-92326-9

Astronomy For Dummies,
3rd Edition
978-1-118-37697-3

Biology For Dummies,
2nd Edition
978-0-470-59875-7

Chemistry For Dummies,
2nd Edition
978-1-118-00730-3

1001 Algebra II Practice
Problems For Dummies
978-1-118-44662-1

Microsoft Office

Excel 2013 For Dummies
978-1-118-51012-4

Office 2013 All-in-One
For Dummies
978-1-118-51636-2

PowerPoint 2013
For Dummies
978-1-118-50253-2

Word 2013 For Dummies
978-1-118-49123-2

Music

Blues Harmonica
For Dummies
978-1-118-25269-7

Guitar For Dummies,
3rd Edition
978-1-118-11554-1

iPod & iTunes
For Dummies, 10th Edition
978-1-118-50864-0

Programming

Beginning Programming
with C For Dummies
978-1-118-73763-7

Excel VBA Programming
For Dummies, 3rd Edition
978-1-118-49037-2

Java For Dummies,
6th Edition
978-1-118-40780-6

Religion & Inspiration

The Bible For Dummies
978-0-7645-5296-0

Buddhism For Dummies,
2nd Edition
978-1-118-02379-2

Catholicism For Dummies,
2nd Edition
978-1-118-07778-8

Self-Help & Relationships

Beating Sugar Addiction
For Dummies
978-1-118-54645-1

Meditation For Dummies,
3rd Edition
978-1-118-29144-3

Seniors

Laptops For Seniors
For Dummies, 3rd Edition
978-1-118-71105-7

Computers For Seniors
For Dummies, 3rd Edition
978-1-118-11553-4

iPad For Seniors
For Dummies, 6th Edition
978-1-118-72826-0

Social Security
For Dummies
978-1-118-20573-0

Smartphones & Tablets

Android Phones
For Dummies, 2nd Edition
978-1-118-72030-1

Nexus Tablets
For Dummies
978-1-118-77243-0

Samsung Galaxy S 4
For Dummies
978-1-118-64222-1

Samsung Galaxy Tabs
For Dummies
978-1-118-77294-2

Test Prep

ACT For Dummies,
5th Edition
978-1-118-01259-8

ASVAB For Dummies,
3rd Edition
978-0-470-63760-9

GRE For Dummies,
7th Edition
978-0-470-88921-3

Officer Candidate Tests
For Dummies
978-0-470-59876-4

Physician's Assistant Exam
For Dummies
978-1-118-11556-5

Series 7 Exam For Dummies
978-0-470-09932-2

Windows 8

Windows 8.1 All-in-One
For Dummies
978-1-118-82087-2

Windows 8.1 For Dummies
978-1-118-82121-3

Windows 8.1 For Dummies
Book + DVD Bundle
978-1-118-82107-7

e **Available in print and e-book formats.**

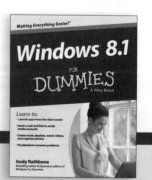

Available wherever books are sold. **For more information or to order direct visit www.dummies.com**

Take Dummies with you everywhere you go!

Whether you are excited about e-books, want more from the web, must have your mobile apps, or are swept up in social media, Dummies makes everything easier.

Visit Us

bit.ly/JE0O

Like Us

on.fb.me/1f1ThNu

Follow Us

bit.ly/ZDytkR

Watch Us

bit.ly/gbOQHn

Join Us

kd.in/1gurkMm

Pin Us

bit.ly/16caOLd

Circle Us

bit.ly/1aQTuDQ

Shop Us

bit.ly/4dEp9

For Dummies is the global leader in the reference category and one of the most trusted and highly regarded brands in the world. No longer just focused on books, customers now have access to the For Dummies content they need in the format they want. Let us help you develop a solution that will fit your brand and help you connect with your customers.

Advertising & Sponsorships

Connect with an engaged audience on a powerful multimedia site, and position your message alongside expert how-to content.

Targeted ads • Video • Email marketing • Microsites • Sweepstakes sponsorship

For Dummies is a registered trademark of John Wiley & Sons, Inc.